# INDUSTRIAL PHARMACY-1

## ESSENTIAL CONCEPTS FOR B.PHARMACY

DR. J. RAMESH | M. SUCHARITHA | P. PRIYANKA

Made with ♥ on the Notion Press Platform
www.notionpress.com

# Contents

# Preface

The field of Industrial Pharmacy encompasses a broad spectrum of activities that are crucial to the development, production, and quality assurance of pharmaceutical products. This book, "Industrial Pharmacy-1: Essential Concepts for B.Pharmacy," is meticulously crafted to provide an in-depth understanding of the foundational principles and practical aspects of industrial pharmacy, aimed at both students and professionals in the field.

Pharmaceutical sciences have always been at the forefront of improving human health by discovering, developing, and delivering safe and effective medications. The journey from a new chemical entity to a market-ready drug involves rigorous research, meticulous planning, and adherence to stringent regulatory standards. Understanding the complexities of this journey requires not only theoretical knowledge but also practical insights into the industrial processes that ensure the consistent quality and efficacy of pharmaceutical products.

This book is structured to cover the essential concepts and practices that form the backbone of industrial pharmacy. We begin with Preformulation Studies, which lay the groundwork for understanding a drug's physical and chemical properties before it is formulated into a dosage form. This section emphasizes the importance of characterizing a drug's solubility, stability, and compatibility with various excipients to develop a stable and effective pharmaceutical product.

In the Tablets section, we delve into the intricacies of one of the most commonly used dosage forms. We discuss the ideal characteristics of tablets, various types of tablets, and the critical role of excipients and formulation techniques in ensuring the quality and performance of the final product. Special attention is given to the different methods of granulation, compression, and the common processing problems encountered during tablet production.

Liquid Orals and Capsules sections further explore the formulation and manufacturing challenges associated with these dosage forms. The preparation, quality control, and stability considerations unique to each form are discussed in detail to provide a comprehensive understanding of their production.

The book also covers specialized areas such as Parenteral Products, Ophthalmic Preparations, and Cosmetics, highlighting the specific requirements and challenges in formulating these products. The chapters on Pharmaceutical Aerosols and Packaging Materials Science address the innovative approaches and materials used to ensure the safe delivery and storage of pharmaceutical products.

Throughout this book, we have incorporated real-world examples and case studies to illustrate the application of theoretical concepts in industrial settings. These examples provide practical insights and foster a deeper understanding of the complexities involved in pharmaceutical manufacturing.

We are deeply grateful to our colleagues, mentors, and students whose insights and feedback have been invaluable in the creation of this book. We hope that this book serves as a valuable resource for pharmacy students, educators, and professionals, guiding them through the essential concepts and practices of industrial pharmacy.

**Dr. J. Ramesh**
**M. Sucharitha**
**P. Priyanka**

# Industrial Pharmacy-1: Essential Concepts For B.pharmacy

***Authors***

***Dr. J. Ramesh***
*Associate Professor*
*Omega College of Pharmacy*
*Hyderabad, 501301*
*Telangana*

***M. Sucharitha***
*Assistant Professor*
*Omega College of Pharmacy*
*Hyderabad, 501301*
*Telangana*

***P. Priyanka***
*Assistant Professor*
*Omega College of Pharmacy*
*Hyderabad, 501301*
*Telangana*

***Published by Notion Press***

***Notion Press, Inc.***
*800, West El Camino Real #180,*
*California, USA 94040*

***Notion Press Media Pvt Ltd***
*#7, Red Cross Road,*

*Egmore, Chennai, Tamil Nadu 600008*

***Email ID:*** *publish@notionpress.com*
***Phone Number:*** *+91 44 46315631*

***July 2024***

# ONE

# PREFORMULATION STUDIES

## 1.1 Introduction to Preformulation

Preformulation is a crucial phase in the drug development process, involving the characterization of a drug's physical and chemical properties before the formulation of a final dosage form. This stage lays the foundation for the development of a stable, effective, and safe pharmaceutical product. It encompasses a series of investigations that help in understanding the drug's behavior under various conditions, ultimately guiding the formulation scientists in selecting the appropriate excipients, manufacturing processes, and packaging systems. Preformulation studies ensure that the drug's therapeutic efficacy is maximized, and its stability is maintained throughout its shelf life.

### 1.1.1 Goals and Objectives

The primary goals and objectives of preformulation are to gather comprehensive information about the drug's physicochemical properties, which are essential for developing a successful pharmaceutical product. These goals include determining the drug's solubility, stability, and compatibility with various excipients. Understanding these properties helps in predicting the drug's behavior in different environments, such as during storage and in the human body.

One of the key objectives is to identify potential formulation challenges early in the development process. For example, if a drug has poor solubility, preformulation studies can suggest modifications such as particle size reduction or the use of solubilizing agents. Similarly, if the drug is prone to degradation under certain conditions, stabilizers or protective coatings can be considered. By addressing these issues early, preformulation minimizes the risk of formulation failures and ensures a smoother development process.

Another objective is to establish a strong foundation for the drug's quality control and regulatory compliance. Preformulation data are critical for setting specifications for raw materials, in-process controls, and finished products. These specifications ensure that the drug product consistently meets its quality standards throughout its shelf life. Additionally, preformulation studies provide essential information for regulatory submissions, helping to justify the choice of formulation components and processes to regulatory authorities.

### 1.1.2 Importance in Drug Development

The importance of preformulation in drug development cannot be overstated. It plays a pivotal role in ensuring the success of the drug formulation process and the overall drug development program. By thoroughly characterizing the drug's properties, preformulation helps in designing a dosage form that is not only effective but also stable and safe for patient use.

Preformulation is essential for optimizing the bioavailability of the drug. Bioavailability refers to the proportion of the drug that reaches the systemic circulation and exerts its therapeutic effect. Factors such as solubility, dissolution rate, and permeability influence bioavailability. Preformulation studies help in identifying these factors and devising strategies to enhance them. For instance, if a drug has low solubility, techniques like micronization, complexation, or the use of surfactants can be explored to improve its solubility and, consequently, its bioavailability.

Moreover, preformulation is crucial for ensuring the stability of the drug product. Stability studies conducted during this phase help in identifying the conditions under which the drug remains stable and retains its potency. This information is vital for selecting appropriate storage conditions, packaging materials, and shelf life for the drug product. Stability issues identified during preformulation can be addressed through the use of stabilizers, antioxidants, or protective coatings, thereby ensuring that the drug maintains its efficacy throughout its intended shelf life.

Preformulation also aids in the selection of suitable excipients and manufacturing processes. Excipients are inactive ingredients that are used to formulate the drug into a dosage form. Their selection depends on their compatibility with the drug and their ability to enhance the drug's stability, solubility, and bioavailability. Preformulation studies provide valuable insights into excipient compatibility and guide the formulation scientist in choosing the right excipients. Additionally, preformulation data help in designing robust manufacturing processes that ensure consistent product quality and performance.

### 1.2 Physical Properties

The physical properties of a drug substance are critical in determining its behavior in both the manufacturing process and within the body. These properties influence various aspects of the drug formulation, including stability, solubility, and bioavailability. A thorough understanding of these physical properties is essential for the development of a successful pharmaceutical product.

#### 1.2.1 Physical Form (Crystal & Amorphous)

The physical form of a drug can exist as either crystalline or amorphous. Crystalline forms are characterized by a well-ordered lattice structure, which often leads to higher stability and lower solubility. In contrast, amorphous forms lack this organized structure, resulting in higher solubility but potentially lower stability. The choice between crystalline and amorphous forms depends on the desired balance between stability and solubility for the drug product. For instance, a drug with poor solubility might be formulated in its amorphous form to enhance bioavailability, while a drug requiring long-term stability might be preferred in its crystalline form.

#### 1.2.2 Particle Size and Shape

Particle size and shape significantly impact the drug's dissolution rate, bioavailability, and manufacturability. Smaller particle sizes increase the surface area available for dissolution, enhancing the drug's solubility and bioavailability. However, very fine particles can lead to poor flow properties, complicating the manufacturing process. The shape of the particles also affects these properties, with spherical particles generally exhibiting better flow characteristics compared to irregularly shaped ones. Control of particle size and shape is crucial during the formulation development to ensure consistent product performance and manufacturability.

#### 1.2.3 Flow Properties

Flow properties are essential for ensuring the uniformity and efficiency of the manufacturing process, particularly in solid dosage forms like tablets and capsules. Poor flow can lead to issues such as weight variation and segregation, affecting the quality and consistency of the final product.

Factors such as particle size, shape, and moisture content influence the flow properties of a powder. Techniques such as granulation can improve flow properties by increasing particle size and density, thereby enhancing the uniformity and efficiency of the manufacturing process.

### 1.2.4 Solubility Profile (pKa, pH, Partition Coefficient)

The solubility profile of a drug, including its pKa, pH, and partition coefficient, plays a crucial role in its bioavailability and therapeutic effectiveness. The pKa value indicates the ionization potential of the drug, which affects its solubility and absorption in different pH environments of the gastrointestinal tract. The pH of the formulation can be adjusted to enhance the drug's solubility and stability. The partition coefficient, which measures the drug's distribution between aqueous and lipid phases, provides insight into its ability to cross biological membranes. Drugs with favorable partition coefficients are more likely to permeate cell membranes and achieve effective therapeutic concentrations.

### 1.2.5 Polymorphism

Polymorphism refers to the ability of a drug to exist in more than one crystalline form. Different polymorphs of the same drug can exhibit varying physical properties, such as solubility, stability, and melting point. These differences can significantly impact the drug's bioavailability and manufacturability. Identifying and controlling the polymorphic form of a drug is crucial during the preformulation stage to ensure consistent product quality and performance. Techniques such as X-ray diffraction and differential scanning calorimetry are commonly used to characterize and monitor polymorphism in drug substances.

### 1.2 Physical Properties

The physical properties of a drug substance are critical in determining its behavior during both the manufacturing process and within the human body. These properties influence various aspects of the drug formulation, including stability, solubility, and bioavailability. A thorough understanding of these physical properties is essential for developing a successful pharmaceutical product.

| Property | Crystalline Form | Amorphous Form |
|---|---|---|
| Structure | Well-ordered lattice | Disordered, no long-range order |
| Stability | High stability | Lower stability |
| Solubility | Lower solubility | Higher solubility |
| Melting Point | Well-defined, higher melting point | Lower, less-defined melting point |
| Example | Aspirin (crystalline) | Amorphous solid dispersions |

Table 1: Comparison of Physical Forms

### 1.2.1 Physical Form (Crystal & Amorphous)

The physical form of a drug can significantly impact its performance and stability. Drugs can exist in either a crystalline form or an amorphous form, each having distinct characteristics that affect their behavior in formulations.

Crystalline forms are characterized by a well-ordered and repetitive lattice structure. This orderly arrangement provides crystalline drugs with greater stability and a well-defined melting point. Due to their structured nature, crystalline forms generally have lower solubility compared to amorphous forms. The reduced solubility can be advantageous in some cases, providing controlled release properties and enhancing the shelf life of the drug. However, this can also be a disadvantage when higher solubility is required for adequate bioavailability. Different crystalline forms, known as polymorphs, can exhibit varied physical properties like melting point, solubility, and stability, influencing the drug's effectiveness and manufacturability.

In contrast, amorphous forms lack a well-defined crystalline structure, resulting in a more disordered arrangement of molecules. This lack of order typically leads to higher solubility and faster dissolution rates, which can improve the bioavailability of poorly soluble drugs. However, the higher energy state of amorphous forms often makes them less stable than their crystalline counterparts. They may be more prone to physical and chemical degradation, posing challenges for long-term storage and stability. Techniques such as spray drying, freeze drying, and rapid precipitation are commonly used to produce amorphous forms of drugs.

The choice between crystalline and amorphous forms depends on the desired balance between stability and solubility for the drug product. For instance, if a drug has poor solubility and requires rapid onset of action, the amorphous form may be preferred to enhance bioavailability. Conversely, if the primary concern is long-term stability, the crystalline form may be chosen. Advanced analytical techniques, such as X-ray diffraction (XRD), differential scanning calorimetry (DSC), and infrared spectroscopy (IR), are employed to characterize the physical form of drug substances and ensure consistency in their production.

| Parameter | Influence on Drug |
|---|---|
| Smaller Particle Size | Increased surface area, higher solubility, faster dissolution |
| Larger Particle Size | Lower surface area, slower dissolution |
| Spherical Shape | Better flow properties, uniform packing |
| Irregular Shape | Poor flow properties, inconsistent packing |
| Analytical Techniques | Laser diffraction, dynamic light scattering, sieving, microscopy |

Table 2: Impact of Particle Size and Shape

### 1.2.2 Particle Size and Shape

**Particle Size and Shape** are fundamental physical properties that profoundly influence a drug's performance, including its solubility, dissolution rate, bioavailability, and manufacturability. The size and shape of drug particles can affect the flow properties, compaction behavior, and stability of the final dosage form.

**Particle Size** plays a critical role in the dissolution rate of a drug. According to the Noyes-Whitney equation, the dissolution rate is directly proportional to the surface area of the drug particles. Smaller particles have a larger surface area relative to their volume, leading to faster dissolution rates. This can be particularly important for drugs with poor water solubility, as increasing the dissolution rate can enhance bioavailability. However, very fine particles may pose challenges in the manufacturing process, such as poor flowability and increased tendency for agglomeration. Techniques like micronization, nano-milling, and spray drying are often employed to achieve the desired particle size.

The particle size distribution of a drug substance is typically measured using techniques such as laser diffraction, dynamic light scattering, and sieving. These methods provide information on the range and uniformity of particle sizes within a sample, which is crucial for ensuring consistent drug performance and reproducibility in manufacturing.

**Particle Shape** also affects the drug's flow properties, packing behavior, and dissolution rate. Particles can have various shapes, such as spherical, rod-like, needle-like, or irregular. Spherical particles generally exhibit better flow properties and packing density, making them preferable in many manufacturing processes. Irregular or needle-like particles, on the other hand, may have poor flowability and compaction characteristics, potentially leading to challenges in tablet formulation and uniformity.

The aspect ratio, which is the ratio of a particle's length to its width, can influence the flow and packing behavior. Particles with a high aspect ratio, such as needles or rods, tend to interlock and resist flow, while those with a low aspect ratio, such as spheres, flow more easily. Techniques such as optical microscopy, scanning electron microscopy (SEM), and image analysis are used to characterize particle shape and size.

Controlling particle size and shape is essential for achieving the desired drug performance and manufacturability. For example, in inhalation products, fine particles are required to reach the lower respiratory tract, while in oral tablets, particles need to flow well and compress into a solid form. Granulation techniques, such as wet granulation, dry granulation, and roller compaction, can modify particle size and shape to improve flow properties and compaction behavior.

### 1.2.3 Flow Properties

**Flow Properties** are crucial for the efficient processing and manufacturing of pharmaceutical products, particularly in the production of solid dosage forms like tablets and capsules. Good flow properties ensure uniform filling of dies, consistent weight, and content uniformity of tablets, and prevent segregation during mixing and storage. Poor flow properties can lead to manufacturing challenges such as sticking, bridging, and capping, which can affect the quality and consistency of the final product.

The **flowability** of a powder is influenced by various factors, including particle size, shape, surface texture, moisture content, and the presence of lubricants or flow aids. Smaller and irregularly shaped particles tend to have poor flow properties due to higher interparticle friction and cohesion. In contrast, larger and more spherical particles usually flow more easily because of lower surface area-to-volume ratios and reduced friction.

**Angle of Repose** is a common measure used to assess the flow properties of powders. It is defined as the maximum angle between the surface of a pile of powder and the horizontal plane. Powders with a lower angle of repose have better flow properties. Typically, an angle of repose less than 30 degrees indicates excellent flowability, while an angle greater than 40 degrees suggests poor flowability. This parameter provides a quick and easy method to compare the flow properties of different powder batches.

**Carr's Index** and **Hausner Ratio** are other indices used to evaluate flow properties. Carr's Index is calculated as the difference between the tapped density and bulk density of a powder, divided by the tapped density, and multiplied by 100. A lower Carr's Index (less than 15%) indicates good flowability, while a higher index (above 25%) suggests poor flowability. The Hausner Ratio is the ratio of tapped density to bulk density, with values below 1.25 indicating good flow properties and values above 1.5 indicating poor flow properties.

**Moisture Content** also significantly affects the flow properties of powders. High moisture levels can lead to particle agglomeration and increased cohesion, resulting in poor flowability. Conversely, extremely low moisture content can cause electrostatic charges to build up, which can also impede flow. Therefore, maintaining an optimal moisture level is essential for ensuring good flow properties.

To improve flow properties, various techniques can be employed. **Granulation** is a common method where fine powders are aggregated to form larger, more flowable granules. Both wet and dry granulation techniques are used depending on the drug's sensitivity to moisture and heat. The addition of **glidants** such as colloidal silicon dioxide or talc can reduce interparticle friction and enhance flowability. **Lubricants** like magnesium stearate can also be added to reduce friction between particles and equipment surfaces during processing.

**Shear Cell Testing** is an advanced technique used to measure the flow properties of powders under different stress conditions. This method provides detailed information on powder behavior, such as yield strength and cohesion, which are critical for designing and optimizing manufacturing processes.

| Factor | Effect on Flow Properties | Examples |
|---|---|---|
| Particle Size | Smaller particles = poor flow, larger particles = better flow | Micronized powders, granules |
| Particle Shape | Spherical = good flow, irregular = poor flow | Spherical granules, needle-like particles |
| Moisture Content | High moisture = poor flow, optimal moisture = good flow | Dry powders, hydrated powders |
| Improvement Techniques | Granulation, addition of glidants | Wet granulation, use of talc or colloidal silica |

Table 3: Key Points on Flow Properties

### 1.2.4 Solubility Profile (pKa, pH, Partition Coefficient)

**Solubility Profile** is a critical parameter in drug development as it directly influences the drug's bioavailability, stability, and efficacy. The solubility of a drug determines how well it can dissolve in bodily fluids, which is essential for its absorption and therapeutic action. The solubility profile includes factors such as **pKa**, **pH**, and **partition coefficient** that collectively define how a drug interacts with different environments in the body and in various formulations.

**pKa** is the acid dissociation constant and a crucial indicator of a drug's ionization state at different pH levels. It represents the pH at which half of the drug molecules are ionized and half are non-ionized. The ionization state of a drug affects its solubility and permeability. Generally, ionized drugs are more soluble in aqueous environments but less permeable through biological membranes, whereas non-ionized drugs are less soluble but more permeable. For instance, weakly acidic drugs (like aspirin) are better absorbed in the acidic environment of the stomach, while weakly basic drugs (like amphetamine) are better absorbed in the more alkaline environment of the intestines. Understanding the pKa helps in predicting the solubility and absorption of the drug in different parts of the gastrointestinal tract.

**pH** is another critical factor that affects drug solubility. The solubility of many drugs is pH-dependent, meaning their solubility can increase or decrease with changes in pH. This is particularly important for oral dosage forms, where the drug must dissolve in the varying pH environments of the gastrointestinal tract. For example, a drug with poor solubility at the pH of the stomach may dissolve better in the higher pH of the intestines. Adjusting the pH of the formulation, through the use of buffers, can enhance the solubility and stability of the drug. For example, a formulation might include buffering agents to maintain the pH at a level where the drug is most soluble.

**Partition Coefficient** (log P) is a measure of a drug's lipophilicity, indicating its distribution between an aqueous phase and a lipid phase. It provides insight into the drug's ability to cross biological membranes, which are primarily composed of lipid bilayers. The partition coefficient is defined as the ratio of the concentration of the drug in the lipid phase to its concentration in the aqueous phase. Drugs with a high partition coefficient (log P > 3) are more lipophilic and can easily permeate cell membranes, making them more likely to be absorbed through passive diffusion. However, excessively high lipophilicity can lead to poor aqueous solubility, resulting in poor dissolution and bioavailability. On the other hand, drugs with a low partition coefficient (log P < 0) are more hydrophilic and may have difficulty crossing lipid membranes. The ideal partition coefficient for optimal absorption is typically between 1 and 3, balancing sufficient solubility and membrane permeability.

| Parameter | Definition | Influence on Drug |
| --- | --- | --- |
| pKa | pH at which drug is 50% ionized | Affects solubility and absorption |
| pH | Measure of acidity/alkalinity | Affects drug solubility and stability |
| Partition Coefficient | Ratio of drug concentration in lipid vs. aqueous phase | Determines ability to cross membranes, lipophilicity |

Table 4: Solubility Profile Parameters

### 1.2.5 Polymorphism

**Polymorphism** refers to the ability of a drug substance to exist in more than one crystalline form. These different forms, known as polymorphs, can have distinct physical and chemical properties, such as melting point, solubility, dissolution rate, and stability. Polymorphism is a critical consideration in drug development because the polymorphic form of a drug can significantly impact its bioavailability, manufacturability, and overall therapeutic efficacy.

Polymorphs are formed due to variations in the arrangement of molecules in the crystal lattice. These variations can result in differences in the energy and stability of the crystal forms. Some polymorphs may be more stable and have lower free energy, while others may be metastable with higher free energy. The stable form is usually less soluble and has a higher melting point, while metastable forms are more soluble but can convert to the stable form over time, affecting the drug's performance and shelf life.

The solubility and dissolution rate of a drug are directly influenced by its polymorphic form. For instance, a more soluble polymorph will dissolve faster in bodily fluids, leading to higher bioavailability. However, if this polymorph is not stable, it may convert to a less soluble form, reducing its efficacy. Therefore, identifying and selecting the appropriate polymorph is essential during the preformulation stage to ensure consistent drug performance.

Polymorphism can also impact the drug's mechanical properties, such as flowability and compressibility, which are crucial for the manufacturing process. Different polymorphs can exhibit varying degrees of hardness and brittleness, influencing the drug's behavior during processes like milling, granulation, and tableting. For example, a polymorph with poor compressibility may result in tablets that are difficult to form or that have inconsistent hardness and disintegration times.

Analytical techniques are employed to identify and characterize polymorphs. **X-ray Powder Diffraction (XRPD)** is one of the most common methods used to determine the crystalline structure of a drug. This technique provides a unique diffraction pattern for each polymorph, allowing for their identification and quantification. **Differential Scanning Calorimetry (DSC)** is another technique used to study the thermal properties of polymorphs, such as melting point and heat of fusion. **Infrared Spectroscopy (IR)** and **Raman Spectroscopy** can also be used to identify polymorphic forms based on their vibrational spectra.

Polymorphism is not limited to simple organic molecules; it can also occur in complex molecular structures such as hydrates, solvates, and co-crystals. **Hydrates** and **solvates** are polymorphs that incorporate water or solvent molecules into their crystal lattice, respectively. These forms can have different properties from the anhydrous or non-solvated forms, influencing solubility and stability. **Co-crystals** are crystalline structures composed of the drug molecule and a co-former molecule, which can modify the drug's properties and enhance its performance.

Regulatory agencies like the FDA and EMA recognize the importance of polymorphism in drug development and require detailed characterization of polymorphic forms. This includes studies on the stability, solubility, and bioavailability of each polymorph, as well as their potential impact on the drug's safety and efficacy. Developers must demonstrate control over the polymorphic form used in the final product to ensure consistent quality and performance.

| Property | Polymorph A | Polymorph B |
|---|---|---|
| Solubility | Higher solubility | Lower solubility |
| Stability | Lower stability | Higher stability |
| Melting Point | Lower melting point | Higher melting point |
| Example | Ritonavir (amorphous vs. crystalline forms) | Carbamazepine (different polymorphs) |

Table 5: Differences between Polymorphs

### 1.3 Chemical Properties

The chemical properties of a drug are crucial in determining its stability, efficacy, and safety. These properties influence how the drug interacts with various excipients, its behavior during manufacturing, and its stability over the shelf life of the product. Understanding the chemical properties is essential for the development of a robust and reliable pharmaceutical formulation.

#### 1.3.1 Hydrolysis

**Hydrolysis** is a chemical reaction in which a compound reacts with water, resulting in the breakdown of the compound into smaller molecules. This reaction is particularly significant in the pharmaceutical field because many drug substances are susceptible to hydrolysis, which can lead to degradation and loss of efficacy. Hydrolysis can occur under various conditions, and its rate can be influenced by factors such as temperature, pH, and the presence of catalysts.

Hydrolysis can affect a wide range of chemical groups commonly found in drug molecules, including esters, amides, lactams, lactones, and carbamates. Each of these functional groups can undergo hydrolytic cleavage, resulting in the formation of different degradation products. For instance, the hydrolysis of an ester typically produces an alcohol and an acid, while the hydrolysis of an amide generates an amine and an acid.

**Esters** are particularly prone to hydrolysis. For example, aspirin (acetylsalicylic acid) can hydrolyze to salicylic acid and acetic acid, especially in the presence of moisture. This reaction not only reduces the efficacy of the drug but can also lead to the formation of potentially irritating byproducts. To mitigate hydrolysis, esters are often formulated with stabilizers or packaged in moisture-resistant containers.

**Amides** and **lactams** also undergo hydrolysis, albeit generally at a slower rate than esters. Antibiotics like penicillins and cephalosporins contain β-lactam rings, which are susceptible to hydrolysis. This reaction can be catalyzed by acidic or basic conditions, leading to the breakdown of the antibiotic and loss of antibacterial activity. To enhance stability, these drugs are often formulated with buffering agents that maintain a pH environment less conducive to hydrolysis.

**pH** plays a critical role in the rate of hydrolysis. The hydrolytic degradation of drugs can be catalyzed by acidic or basic conditions, making pH control an essential aspect of formulation development. For instance, the rate of ester hydrolysis can increase significantly in acidic or basic conditions compared to neutral pH. Therefore, the formulation might include buffering agents to maintain a stable pH environment that minimizes hydrolysis.

**Temperature** is another factor influencing hydrolysis. Higher temperatures generally increase the rate of hydrolytic reactions. This is why stability studies are often conducted under accelerated conditions (e.g., elevated temperatures and humidity) to predict the shelf life of a drug. Understanding the temperature dependence of hydrolysis helps in designing appropriate storage conditions for the drug product.

To assess the hydrolytic stability of a drug, various analytical techniques are employed. **High-Performance Liquid Chromatography (HPLC)** is commonly used to monitor the extent of hydrolysis and identify degradation products. **UV-Visible Spectroscopy** can also be used to track changes in the absorbance spectra of the drug as it undergoes hydrolysis. Additionally, **Mass Spectrometry (MS)** can provide detailed information on the molecular weight and structure of the degradation products.

Strategies to mitigate hydrolysis include the use of **protective coatings**, **stabilizers**, and **optimized packaging.** Protective coatings, such as enteric coatings, can prevent exposure of the drug to the acidic environment of the stomach, thereby reducing hydrolysis. Stabilizers, such as antioxidants or desiccants, can be incorporated into the formulation to protect the drug from moisture and other hydrolytic agents. Optimized packaging, such as blister packs or moisture-proof containers, can also play a significant role in enhancing the stability of hydrolysis-prone drugs.

\

### 1.3.2 Oxidation

**Oxidation** is a chemical reaction that involves the loss of electrons by a molecule, atom, or ion. In the context of pharmaceuticals, oxidation is a common degradation pathway that can significantly affect the stability, efficacy, and safety of a drug product. Oxidative degradation can lead to the formation of new compounds, some of which may be less active, inactive, or even toxic. Understanding and controlling oxidation is therefore essential in the development and manufacturing of stable pharmaceutical formulations.

Many drug substances are susceptible to oxidation, especially those containing functional groups such as phenols, thiols, and amines. These functional groups can react with oxygen, leading to the formation of oxidative degradation products. For instance, phenolic drugs like catecholamines and certain vitamins are prone to oxidation, resulting in a loss of potency and potential discoloration of the product. Similarly, thiol-containing drugs like captopril can oxidize to form disulfides, which can reduce the drug's therapeutic effectiveness.

**Oxidation** can be influenced by several factors, including the presence of oxygen, light, metal ions, and pH.

**Presence of Oxygen**: The presence of oxygen is a primary factor that promotes oxidation. Even small amounts of dissolved oxygen in solutions can initiate oxidative reactions. To minimize this, pharmaceutical formulations are often packaged under an inert atmosphere, such as nitrogen or argon, to displace oxygen. Additionally, oxygen scavengers like ascorbic acid can be added to the formulation to preferentially react with oxygen and protect the drug substance.

**Light**: Exposure to light, especially UV light, can accelerate oxidation by providing the energy required to initiate or propagate oxidative reactions. This is particularly relevant for light-sensitive drugs. To protect against light-induced oxidation, drug products are often packaged in light-resistant containers, such as amber glass bottles or opaque blisters. Additionally, secondary packaging, like cardboard boxes, can provide an additional layer of protection against light.

**Metal Ions**: Trace amounts of metal ions, such as iron or copper, can catalyze oxidative reactions. These metal ions can be introduced during the manufacturing process or can leach from equipment and containers. To mitigate this, chelating agents like EDTA (ethylenediaminetetraacetic acid) are commonly added to formulations to bind metal ions and prevent them from catalyzing oxidation. Additionally, using high-purity raw materials and equipment that are free from metal contaminants can reduce the risk of metal-catalyzed oxidation.

**pH**: The pH of the formulation can also influence the rate of oxidation. Some drugs are more prone to oxidation at specific pH levels. For instance, the oxidation of phenolic compounds is often accelerated in alkaline conditions. Buffering agents are used to maintain the formulation at an optimal pH that minimizes oxidative degradation. For example, ascorbic acid is often used in formulations not only as an antioxidant but also to maintain a slightly acidic pH, which helps protect the drug from oxidation.

Analytical techniques are employed to monitor oxidative stability and identify degradation products. **High-Performance Liquid Chromatography (HPLC)** coupled with **UV detection** or **Mass Spectrometry (MS)** is commonly used to quantify the extent of oxidation and characterize the degradation products. **Differential Scanning Calorimetry (DSC)** and **Thermogravimetric Analysis (TGA)** can provide information on the thermal stability and oxidative susceptibility of the drug.

To prevent oxidation, antioxidants are frequently added to pharmaceutical formulations. **Antioxidants** such as butylated hydroxytoluene (BHT), butylated hydroxyanisole (BHA), and ascorbic acid (vitamin C) act by donating electrons to free radicals, thereby neutralizing them and preventing further oxidative reactions. The choice of antioxidant depends on the drug substance and the type of formulation. Additionally, formulation strategies such as using non-reactive excipients, optimizing manufacturing processes to exclude oxygen, and selecting appropriate packaging materials can significantly enhance the oxidative stability of the drug product.

Understanding the factors that influence oxidation and implementing strategies to control oxidative degradation are crucial for ensuring the stability, efficacy, and safety of pharmaceutical products.

### 1.3.3 Reduction

**Reduction** is a chemical reaction that involves the gain of electrons by a molecule, atom, or ion. In pharmaceutical sciences, reduction is less common as a degradation pathway compared to hydrolysis and oxidation, but it can still significantly affect the stability and efficacy of certain drugs. Reduction reactions can lead to the formation of active or inactive metabolites and can alter the drug's therapeutic profile.

**Reduction** reactions can involve various functional groups, including nitro groups, carbonyl compounds, and disulfides. The susceptibility of a drug to reduction depends on its chemical structure and the environmental conditions it is exposed to during manufacturing, storage, and administration.

**Nitro Groups**: Drugs containing nitro groups can undergo reduction to form amines. This transformation can either activate or deactivate the drug's pharmacological activity. For example, the antibacterial activity of nitrofurantoin is attributed to its reduction within bacterial cells to reactive intermediates that damage bacterial DNA. However, unintended reduction of nitro groups in other drugs can lead to loss of activity or formation of toxic byproducts.

**Carbonyl Compounds**: Ketones and aldehydes can be reduced to their corresponding alcohols. This reduction can occur during metabolic processes in the body or through chemical interactions with reducing agents in the formulation. The reduction of carbonyl groups can alter the drug's pharmacokinetics and pharmacodynamics, affecting its therapeutic efficacy.

**Disulfides**: Drugs containing disulfide bonds can undergo reduction to form thiols. This reaction is particularly relevant for protein-based drugs and peptides, where the integrity of disulfide bonds is crucial for maintaining the protein's tertiary structure and biological activity. Disulfide bond reduction can lead to denaturation and loss of function in these biologics. To prevent this, formulations often include stabilizing agents that maintain the oxidized state of disulfide bonds.

Reduction reactions can be influenced by several factors, including the presence of reducing agents, pH, and temperature.

**Presence of Reducing Agents**: Reducing agents, such as ascorbic acid, sodium borohydride, and dithiothreitol (DTT), can promote reduction reactions. These agents are sometimes added deliberately to formulations to achieve specific therapeutic outcomes, such as the reduction of methemoglobin to hemoglobin by ascorbic acid in methemoglobinemia. However, unintended exposure to reducing agents can lead to unwanted degradation of susceptible drugs. Careful selection of excipients and packaging materials can minimize the risk of exposure to reducing agents.

**pH**: The pH of the formulation can influence the rate of reduction reactions. Some reduction reactions are favored under acidic conditions, while others may proceed more rapidly under alkaline conditions. Buffering agents are used to maintain the formulation at a pH that minimizes unwanted reduction. For instance, the stability of certain carbonyl-containing drugs can be enhanced by maintaining a neutral pH environment.

**Temperature**: Elevated temperatures can accelerate reduction reactions by increasing the kinetic energy of the molecules involved. This is particularly relevant during the sterilization process and long-term storage. Understanding the temperature dependence of reduction reactions helps in designing appropriate storage conditions and selecting suitable sterilization methods that do not compromise the stability of the drug.

Analytical techniques are used to monitor reduction reactions and characterize the resulting degradation products. **High-Performance Liquid Chromatography (HPLC)** and **Gas Chromatography (GC)**, often coupled with **Mass Spectrometry (MS)**, are commonly employed to detect and quantify reduced species. **Nuclear Magnetic Resonance (NMR)** spectroscopy can provide detailed structural information on the reduced forms of the drug. These techniques help in identifying potential reduction pathways and assessing the impact of reduction on drug stability.

To mitigate reduction reactions, formulation strategies such as the use of antioxidants, careful selection of excipients, and optimized manufacturing processes are employed. **Antioxidants** can sometimes act as stabilizers against reduction by scavenging free radicals that might otherwise participate in reduction reactions. Ensuring that the formulation environment is free from contaminants that could act as reducing agents is also crucial.

Understanding the reduction behavior of a drug and implementing strategies to control reduction reactions are important for ensuring the stability, efficacy, and safety of pharmaceutical products.

### 1.3.4 Racemisation

**Racemisation** is a chemical process in which an optically active compound (one that has chirality and can rotate plane-polarized light) is converted into a racemic mixture, which contains equal amounts of both enantiomers (mirror-image forms) of the compound. This process can significantly affect the pharmacological activity, efficacy, and safety of a drug because the different enantiomers of a chiral drug often have different biological activities, pharmacokinetics, and toxicity profiles.

Enantiomers are molecules that are non-superimposable mirror images of each other, much like a person's left and right hands. Many drugs are chiral and are marketed either as a single enantiomer or as a racemic mixture. The pharmacological activity of each enantiomer can vary significantly. For instance, one enantiomer might be therapeutically active while the other might be less active, inactive, or even produce adverse effects. Therefore, racemisation can lead to a change in the drug's overall therapeutic profile.

**Factors Influencing Racemisation**:

**Chemical Structure**: The likelihood of racemisation depends on the chemical structure of the drug. Compounds with a chiral center adjacent to an electron-withdrawing group (e.g., carbonyl, nitro) or a group that stabilizes the intermediate (e.g., a benzylic position) are more prone to racemisation. For example, drugs containing α-amino acids or other α-chiral centers are often susceptible to racemisation.

**pH**: The pH of the environment can significantly influence the rate of racemisation. Acidic or basic conditions can catalyze the racemisation process by facilitating the protonation or deprotonation of the chiral center. For instance, many amino acids racemise more rapidly in both strongly acidic and basic conditions. Therefore, controlling the pH of the formulation and storage environment is crucial to minimize racemisation.

**Temperature**: Higher temperatures generally increase the rate of racemisation due to the increased kinetic energy of the molecules. This is particularly relevant during the manufacturing processes that involve heat, such as drying and sterilization, as well as during storage. Understanding the temperature dependence of racemisation helps in designing appropriate storage conditions and selecting suitable manufacturing processes.

**Solvent**: The choice of solvent can affect racemisation rates. Some solvents can stabilize or destabilize the transition state of the racemisation process. For example, polar solvents can sometimes increase the rate of racemisation by stabilizing ionic intermediates. Therefore, selecting the appropriate solvent for formulations can help control the extent of racemisation.

**Light**: Exposure to light, especially UV light, can catalyze racemisation in some drugs. Photochemical energy can provide the activation energy required for racemisation. Protecting the drug from light by using light-resistant packaging and storage conditions can mitigate this effect.

**Examples of Racemisation in Pharmaceuticals**:

**Thalidomide**: Thalidomide is a notorious example where racemisation played a critical role in its effects. The drug was marketed as a racemic mixture. One enantiomer had therapeutic effects (sedative and anti-nausea), while the other caused severe teratogenic effects (birth defects). Even when one enantiomer was administered, racemisation in the body could convert it to the harmful enantiomer, leading to its tragic consequences.

**Lepirudin**: Lepirudin, an anticoagulant, also undergoes racemisation. One enantiomer is more active in inhibiting thrombin, while the other is less active. Controlling racemisation is crucial to maintain its therapeutic efficacy.

**Analytical Methods to Study Racemisation**:

Several analytical techniques are used to monitor and quantify racemisation. **Chiral High-Performance Liquid Chromatography (HPLC)** is a widely used method to separate and quantify the enantiomers of a drug. **Chiral Capillary Electrophoresis (CE)** and **Chiral Gas Chromatography (GC)** are also employed for similar purposes. **Nuclear Magnetic Resonance (NMR)** spectroscopy can provide detailed information on the chiral environment of the molecule and monitor the racemisation process.

**Strategies to Minimize Racemisation**:

Formulation strategies to minimize racemisation include optimizing the pH of the formulation, using stabilizing agents that can protect the chiral center, and selecting appropriate solvents and excipients that do not catalyze the racemisation process. Additionally, using protective packaging to prevent exposure to light and maintaining appropriate storage conditions (e.g., low temperature) can help in reducing racemisation.

Understanding racemisation and implementing strategies to control this process are crucial for ensuring the stability, efficacy, and safety of chiral pharmaceutical products.

### 1.3.5 Polymerization

**Polymerization** is a chemical process in which small molecules, known as monomers, join together to form larger molecules called polymers. In the context of pharmaceuticals, polymerization can be an unintended degradation pathway that affects the stability, efficacy, and safety of a drug product. Polymerization can lead to the formation of high molecular weight compounds that may be insoluble, inactive, or even harmful.

Polymerization can occur through various mechanisms, including addition (chain-growth) polymerization, condensation (step-growth) polymerization, and radical polymerization. The specific mechanism depends on the chemical structure of the drug and the environmental conditions to which it is exposed.

**Addition Polymerization** involves the repeated addition of monomers with unsaturated bonds, such as alkenes or alkynes, to form a polymer chain. This type of polymerization is common in drugs containing vinyl groups or other unsaturated moieties. For example, certain antifungal agents and analgesics with vinyl groups can undergo addition polymerization under suitable conditions.

**Condensation Polymerization** involves the reaction of monomers with functional groups such as hydroxyl, carboxyl, or amino groups, resulting in the formation of a polymer and a small byproduct, such as water or methanol. This type of polymerization can occur in drugs with reactive functional groups, such as antibiotics (e.g., penicillins) and peptide drugs, where condensation reactions can lead to the formation of larger, often inactive, oligomers or polymers.

**Radical Polymerization** occurs when free radicals initiate the polymerization process, leading to the formation of polymer chains. This mechanism can be catalyzed by the presence of light, heat, or radical initiators. Drugs with easily oxidizable groups, such as phenols or aromatic amines, are susceptible to radical polymerization.

**Factors Influencing Polymerization**:

**Chemical Structure**: The presence of reactive functional groups, such as vinyl, hydroxyl, carboxyl, or amino groups, increases the susceptibility of a drug to polymerization. The specific arrangement and type of these groups determine the likelihood and type of polymerization reaction.

**Environmental Conditions**: Temperature, pH, and exposure to light or oxygen can significantly influence the rate of polymerization. Elevated temperatures and extreme pH conditions can increase the kinetic energy of molecules, facilitating polymerization reactions. Similarly, exposure to light, especially UV light, can generate free radicals that initiate radical polymerization.

**Presence of Catalysts or Initiators**: Catalysts, such as acids, bases, or metal ions, can accelerate condensation polymerization by stabilizing transition states or intermediates. Radical initiators, such as peroxides or azo compounds, can generate free radicals that initiate radical polymerization.

**Examples of Polymerization in Pharmaceuticals**:

**Insulin**: Insulin can undergo polymerization, forming high molecular weight aggregates that reduce its biological activity and alter its pharmacokinetics. The polymerization of insulin can be influenced by pH, temperature, and the presence of metal ions.

**Beta-Lactam Antibiotics**: Beta-lactam antibiotics, such as penicillins and cephalosporins, can undergo polymerization through condensation reactions, leading to the formation of inactive oligomers or polymers. This process is often accelerated under acidic or basic conditions.

**Analytical Methods to Study Polymerization**:

Several analytical techniques are employed to detect and characterize polymerization. **Size Exclusion Chromatography (SEC)**, also known as Gel Permeation Chromatography (GPC), is commonly used to determine the molecular weight distribution of polymers and identify the presence of high molecular weight aggregates. **High-Performance Liquid Chromatography (HPLC)** can separate and quantify monomers, oligomers, and polymers in a sample. **Mass Spectrometry (MS)** provides detailed information on the molecular weight and structure of the polymerization products. **Nuclear Magnetic Resonance (NMR)** spectroscopy can offer insights into the chemical structure and mechanism of polymerization.

**Strategies to Minimize Polymerization**:

To minimize polymerization, formulation strategies include optimizing the pH and temperature conditions to reduce the likelihood of polymerization reactions. **Antioxidants** and **free radical scavengers** can be added to formulations to inhibit radical polymerization. For example, ascorbic acid and butylated hydroxytoluene (BHT) are commonly used antioxidants that can prevent the formation of free radicals. **Chelating agents**, such as EDTA, can bind metal ions that catalyze polymerization, reducing their availability to participate in the reaction. Additionally, selecting appropriate packaging materials that protect the drug from light and oxygen can further reduce the risk of polymerization.

### 1.4 BCS Classification of Drugs

The **Biopharmaceutics Classification System (BCS)** is a scientific framework that categorizes drugs based on their solubility and intestinal permeability. This classification system helps in predicting the drug absorption process, guiding formulation development, and supporting regulatory decisions related to drug approval. The BCS was developed to provide a standardized approach to understanding the relationship between a drug's physicochemical properties and its oral absorption, ultimately aiming to streamline the drug development process.

### 1.4.1 Definition and Categories

**Definition**: The BCS classifies drugs into four categories based on their solubility and permeability characteristics. Solubility is determined by the highest dose strength of the drug that is soluble in 250 mL or less of aqueous media over a pH range of 1 to 7.5. Permeability is assessed based on the extent of drug absorption in humans, typically using in vivo or in vitro methods. The combination of these two properties provides a basis for predicting the oral bioavailability of the drug.

**Categories**:

**Class I: High Solubility - High Permeability**

Drugs in this category exhibit high solubility and high permeability, indicating that they are likely to be well absorbed when administered orally. These drugs dissolve readily in the gastrointestinal tract, and their absorption is not limited by the dissolution process. Formulation strategies for Class I drugs focus primarily on maintaining stability and controlling release rates to achieve the desired therapeutic effect. Examples of Class I drugs include propranolol and metoprolol.

**Class II: Low Solubility - High Permeability**

Drugs in this category have low solubility but high permeability. Their absorption is often limited by the rate at which they dissolve in the gastrointestinal fluids. Formulation strategies for Class II drugs aim to enhance their solubility and dissolution rate, using techniques such as micronization, solid dispersions, and the use of surfactants or solubilizing agents. Examples of Class II drugs include ketoconazole and carbamazepine.

**Class III: High Solubility - Low Permeability**

Drugs in this category exhibit high solubility but low permeability. Their absorption is limited by their ability to permeate the intestinal mucosa. Formulation strategies for Class III drugs focus on enhancing permeability, often through the use of permeation enhancers, prodrugs, or formulation approaches that modify the intestinal environment to improve drug uptake. Examples of Class III drugs include ranitidine and atenolol.

**Class IV: Low Solubility - Low Permeability**

Drugs in this category have both low solubility and low permeability, making them the most challenging to formulate for oral administration. These drugs face significant barriers to absorption, and formulation strategies must address both solubility and permeability issues. Techniques such as nanoparticle formulations, complexation with cyclodextrins, and lipid-based delivery systems are often employed to enhance the bioavailability of Class IV drugs. Examples of Class IV drugs include paclitaxel and hydrochlorothiazide.

**Application of BCS in Drug Development**:

The BCS classification system is utilized in various stages of drug development to optimize formulation strategies and predict oral bioavailability. For regulatory purposes, the BCS can be used to justify biowaivers, which are exemptions from in vivo bioavailability and bioequivalence studies for certain drug products. Biowaivers can be granted for Class I drugs if dissolution testing shows that the drug product will dissolve rapidly under physiological conditions. This can significantly reduce the time and cost associated with drug development and approval.

Additionally, understanding the BCS classification of a drug aids in selecting appropriate formulation approaches, anticipating potential challenges in drug absorption, and designing effective drug delivery systems. By categorizing drugs based on their solubility and permeability, the BCS provides a structured approach to developing oral formulations that maximize therapeutic efficacy and patient compliance.

### 1.4.2 Significance and Applications

The **significance** and **applications** of the Biopharmaceutics Classification System (BCS) extend across various stages of drug development, regulatory processes, and formulation strategies. The BCS framework provides valuable insights into the factors influencing drug absorption and bioavailability, guiding the development of effective oral drug formulations.

**Significance**:

**Enhanced Understanding of Drug Absorption**: The BCS categorizes drugs based on their solubility and permeability, offering a clear understanding of the factors that influence oral drug absorption. This classification helps pharmaceutical scientists predict the behavior of drugs in the gastrointestinal tract, facilitating the design of formulations that maximize bioavailability.

**Streamlined Drug Development**: By identifying the solubility and permeability characteristics of a drug early in the development process, the BCS allows for the selection of appropriate formulation strategies. This targeted approach reduces the time and resources spent on trial-and-error methods, leading to more efficient drug development.

**Regulatory Compliance and Biowaivers**: The BCS framework is recognized by regulatory agencies such as the FDA and EMA. It supports the justification of biowaivers, which are exemptions from in vivo bioavailability and bioequivalence studies for certain drug products. For Class I drugs (high solubility and high permeability), regulatory agencies may grant biowaivers if in vitro dissolution testing demonstrates rapid and complete dissolution. This can significantly accelerate the approval process and reduce development costs.

**Optimization of Formulation Strategies**: The BCS guides the selection of formulation approaches based on the drug's classification. For example, Class II drugs (low solubility and high permeability) require strategies to enhance solubility, such as the use of solubilizing agents, micronization, or solid dispersions. For Class III drugs (high solubility and low permeability), formulation strategies focus on improving permeability through the use of permeation enhancers or prodrugs. Understanding the BCS classification helps in designing formulations that address the specific challenges of each drug category.

**Improved Patient Compliance and Therapeutic Outcomes**: By optimizing drug formulations based on BCS principles, pharmaceutical scientists can develop products with improved bioavailability and consistent therapeutic effects. This leads to better patient compliance and overall treatment outcomes, as patients receive the intended dose of the drug with predictable absorption and efficacy.

**Applications**:

**Formulation Development**: The BCS provides a foundation for developing oral drug formulations. For Class I drugs, the focus is on ensuring stability and controlling the release rate. For Class II drugs, enhancing solubility is critical, often achieved through techniques like nanosizing, solid dispersions, or lipid-based formulations. Class III drugs require strategies to improve permeability, such as the use of absorption enhancers or molecular modifications. Class IV drugs, which present the greatest challenge, may necessitate a combination of solubility and permeability enhancement techniques.

**Regulatory Submissions**: The BCS framework is utilized in regulatory submissions to justify biowaivers. For example, if a drug is classified as Class I, demonstrating rapid dissolution in vitro can support a biowaiver request, potentially eliminating the need for costly and time-consuming in vivo bioequivalence studies. This can expedite the approval process and bring generic versions of drugs to market more quickly.

**Quality Control and Assurance**: Understanding the BCS classification of a drug aids in setting quality control parameters. For instance, ensuring that a Class II drug meets solubility criteria is essential for maintaining its bioavailability. Quality control tests can be tailored to monitor the critical attributes defined by the BCS, ensuring consistent product performance.

**Pharmacokinetic Studies**: The BCS informs the design of pharmacokinetic studies by predicting the drug's absorption profile. For drugs with high permeability (Class I and II), studies can focus on dissolution and absorption rates. For drugs with low permeability (Class III and IV), studies may emphasize the impact of formulation modifications on enhancing absorption. This targeted approach improves the efficiency and relevance of pharmacokinetic investigations.

**Drug Delivery System Design**: The BCS influences the design of advanced drug delivery systems, such as controlled-release formulations, transdermal patches, and nanocarriers. By understanding the solubility and permeability characteristics of a drug, scientists can design delivery systems that optimize release profiles and enhance bioavailability, leading to more effective and patient-friendly therapies.

### 1.4.3 Impact on Stability of Dosage Forms

The **Biopharmaceutics Classification System (BCS)** not only aids in understanding drug absorption and bioavailability but also significantly impacts the stability of dosage forms. The solubility and permeability characteristics of a drug, as defined by the BCS, influence how the drug interacts with its environment, both during manufacturing and throughout its shelf life. Ensuring the stability of dosage forms is crucial for maintaining the drug's efficacy, safety, and quality.

#### Class I: High Solubility - High Permeability

For **Class I drugs**, which exhibit high solubility and high permeability, the primary stability concerns often relate to the chemical and physical stability of the drug substance and the formulation. These drugs dissolve readily in the gastrointestinal tract, so the formulation focus is on maintaining the drug's stability during storage and handling. Factors such as moisture, temperature, light, and oxygen exposure can lead to degradation.

**Moisture Sensitivity**: Highly soluble drugs can absorb moisture from the environment, leading to hydrolysis and other degradation reactions.

Formulations may include desiccants and moisture-barrier packaging to protect against moisture-induced degradation.

**Temperature and Light Sensitivity**: Elevated temperatures and exposure to light can accelerate degradation reactions such as oxidation. Packaging materials that provide thermal insulation and light protection (e.g., amber glass bottles) are often used to enhance stability.

**Class II: Low Solubility - High Permeability**

**Class II drugs** have low solubility but high permeability, making solubility enhancement a key formulation strategy. However, the methods used to improve solubility can impact the stability of the drug.

**Solid Dispersion Stability**: Techniques like solid dispersions can enhance the solubility of Class II drugs, but they may also affect the drug's stability. Amorphous forms used in solid dispersions can have higher energy states and be more prone to recrystallization, leading to reduced solubility and bioavailability over time. Stabilizers and appropriate storage conditions are essential to maintain the amorphous state and prevent recrystallization.

**Particle Size Reduction**: Reducing particle size (e.g., through micronization or nanosizing) increases the surface area, enhancing solubility. However, smaller particles can be more reactive and susceptible to environmental factors such as humidity and temperature. Stabilizers and protective packaging are used to maintain the stability of these finely divided drug forms.

**Class III: High Solubility - Low Permeability**

**Class III drugs** are characterized by high solubility but low permeability. The formulation focus is on improving permeability while ensuring stability.

**Permeability Enhancers**: Adding permeability enhancers to formulations can improve the absorption of Class III drugs, but these excipients can sometimes interact with the drug, affecting its stability. Compatibility studies are essential to ensure that the chosen enhancers do not degrade the drug.

**Chemical Stability**: High solubility drugs are often more susceptible to hydrolysis and other degradation reactions. Ensuring a stable pH and using antioxidants or preservatives can help maintain stability.

**Class IV: Low Solubility - Low Permeability**

**Class IV drugs** present the greatest challenge due to their low solubility and low permeability. Addressing these issues while maintaining stability requires sophisticated formulation approaches.

**Nanoparticle Formulations**: Nanoparticles can enhance the solubility and permeability of Class IV drugs, but their small size and high surface area can lead to stability issues such as aggregation or chemical degradation. Stabilizers, surfactants, and careful control of manufacturing conditions are essential to maintain the stability of nanoparticle formulations.

**Complexation**: Cyclodextrin complexes can improve the solubility of Class IV drugs, but the stability of the complex must be carefully controlled. Factors such as temperature, humidity, and pH can affect the stability of the drug-cyclodextrin complex, requiring appropriate formulation strategies and packaging.

**Lipid-Based Formulations**: Lipid-based delivery systems can enhance both solubility and permeability for Class IV drugs. However, lipids can be prone to oxidation and hydrolysis, leading to stability issues. Antioxidants and protective packaging can help maintain the stability of lipid-based formulations.

**General Stability Considerations Across BCS Classes**

Regardless of the BCS classification, several general strategies are employed to enhance the stability of dosage forms:

**Packaging**: The choice of packaging materials and technologies is critical for protecting the drug from environmental factors such as moisture, light, and oxygen. Blister packs, amber glass bottles, and airtight containers are commonly used to enhance stability.

**Storage Conditions**: Proper storage conditions, including temperature and humidity control, are essential to maintain the stability of the drug product. Refrigeration or controlled room temperature storage can prevent degradation.

**Stabilizers**: The use of stabilizers such as antioxidants, preservatives, and buffering agents can protect the drug from degradation reactions. These excipients are carefully selected based on their compatibility with the drug substance.

**Formulation Optimization**: The formulation process itself can impact stability. Techniques such as lyophilization (freeze-drying) can enhance the stability of sensitive drugs by removing water, while spray drying can produce stable amorphous forms.

| Class | Solubility | Permeability | Examples |
|---|---|---|---|
| Class I | High Solubility | High Permeability | Propranolol, Metoprolol |
| Class II | Low Solubility | High Permeability | Ketoconazole, Carbamazepine |
| Class III | High Solubility | Low Permeability | Ranitidine, Atenolol |
| Class IV | Low Solubility | Low Permeability | Paclitaxel, Hydrochlorothiazide |

Table 6: BCS Classification of Drugs

| Parameter | Definition |
|---|---|
| Solubility | Amount of drug that dissolves in 250 mL or less of aqueous media over a pH range of 1 to 7.5 |
| Permeability | Extent of drug absorption in humans, typically assessed using in vivo or in vitro methods |
| Biowaiver | Exemption from in vivo bioavailability and bioequivalence studies for certain drug products |

Table 7: Key Points on BCS Classification

| Application | Description |
|---|---|
| Formulation Strategies | Class I: Focus on stability; Class II: Enhance solubility; Class III: Enhance permeability; Class IV: Address both |
| Regulatory Submissions | Supports biowaivers for Class I drugs if rapid dissolution is demonstrated |
| Pharmacokinetic Studies | Informs design of studies based on predicted absorption profiles |
| Drug Delivery System Design | Influences design of controlled-release, transdermal, and other advanced drug delivery systems |

Table 8: Applications of BCS Classification

| BCS Class | Stability Considerations | Strategies |
|---|---|---|
| Class I | Chemical and physical stability during storage and handling | Use of desiccants, moisture-barrier packaging, light-resistant containers |
| Class II | Stability of solubility-enhancing techniques such as solid dispersions and particle size reduction | Use of stabilizers, appropriate storage conditions, protective packaging |
| Class III | Stability of permeability enhancers and maintaining solubility | Compatibility studies, use of antioxidants, and preservatives |
| Class IV | Comprehensive stability considerations due to challenges with both solubility and permeability | Combination of solubility and permeability enhancement strategies, stabilizers, and protective packaging |

Table 9: Impact on Stability of Dosage Forms

| Term | Definition |
|---|---|
| BCS Classification | System categorizing drugs based on solubility and permeability to predict oral absorption |
| High Solubility | Drug dissolves in 250 mL or less of aqueous media across a pH range of 1 to 7.5 |
| High Permeability | Drug is absorbed to an extent of 85% or more in humans |
| Biowaiver | Regulatory exemption from in vivo bioavailability and bioequivalence studies |

Table10:Summary of Key Terms

# TWO

# TABLETS

## 2.1 Introduction to Tablets

Tablets are one of the most commonly used dosage forms in the pharmaceutical industry. They are preferred for their convenience, ease of administration, accurate dosing, and stability. Tablets can be designed to deliver drugs in an immediate-release form, where the drug is quickly released after ingestion, or in a controlled-release form, where the drug is released slowly over time to provide a prolonged therapeutic effect. Tablets are manufactured by compressing the active pharmaceutical ingredient (API) along with various excipients into a solid, compact form.

### 2.1.1 Ideal Characteristics

**Uniformity of Dose**

Uniformity of dose is crucial to ensure that each tablet contains the same amount of the active ingredient. This consistency is essential for achieving the desired therapeutic effect and ensuring patient safety. For example, if a tablet contains 500 mg of an active drug, every tablet in the batch must contain close to 500 mg, with minimal variation. This uniformity is achieved through precise formulation and manufacturing processes, such as ensuring thorough mixing of the drug and excipients before compression. The United States Pharmacopeia (USP) sets specific limits for content uniformity, typically allowing a deviation of no more than 15% from the labeled amount.

**Mechanical Strength**

Mechanical strength refers to the ability of a tablet to withstand mechanical stresses during packaging, transportation, and handling without breaking or crumbling. Tablets must have sufficient hardness to resist breaking under pressure, but they should not be so hard that they resist disintegration in the gastrointestinal tract. The mechanical strength is often measured using a hardness tester, and the acceptable range of hardness varies depending on the tablet type and its intended use. For example, a typical hardness for oral tablets might range from 4 to 8 kilograms of force (kgf).

**Disintegration**

Disintegration is the process by which a tablet breaks down into smaller particles in the gastrointestinal tract, facilitating the release of the active drug. The disintegration time is a critical quality attribute, as it affects the rate at which the drug is available for absorption. The USP specifies that immediate-release tablets should disintegrate within 30 minutes. Disintegration tests are performed using a disintegration tester, where tablets are subjected to a controlled environment to measure the time required for them to disintegrate completely.

**Dissolution**

Dissolution is the process by which the drug dissolves in bodily fluids, allowing it to be absorbed into the bloodstream. The rate of dissolution can affect the onset and extent of the drug's therapeutic action. For instance, a fast-dissolving tablet will provide a quicker onset of action compared to a slow-dissolving tablet. Dissolution testing involves placing tablets in a dissolution apparatus with a specific medium and measuring the amount of drug released over time. The results are expressed as a percentage of the drug dissolved at specified time intervals.

**Stability**

Stability is the ability of a tablet to maintain its physical, chemical, and microbiological integrity over its shelf life. This includes maintaining the potency of the active ingredient, ensuring no significant degradation occurs, and preventing microbial contamination. Stability testing is conducted under various environmental conditions, such as different temperatures and humidity levels, to assess the tablet's shelf life. For example, stability studies might include storage at 25°C/60% RH (relative humidity) for long-term stability and 40°C/75% RH for accelerated stability testing.

**Appearance**

The appearance of a tablet is important for patient compliance. Tablets should be free from visible defects, such as cracks, chips, or discoloration. They should have a uniform color and shape, which helps in identifying the medication and ensuring patients are taking the correct drug. The aesthetic appeal of a tablet can be enhanced through coatings and colorants, which also protect the tablet from environmental factors.

**Palatability**

Palatability refers to the taste and odor of the tablet. While many tablets are swallowed whole and do not need to be palatable, chewable tablets, orally disintegrating tablets, and lozenges must have a pleasant taste and odor to ensure patient acceptance. Flavors and sweeteners are often added to improve palatability, especially in pediatric and geriatric formulations.

**Ease of Swallowing**

Ease of swallowing is a critical consideration for tablets, particularly for pediatric and geriatric populations who may have difficulty swallowing large tablets. The size and shape of the tablet should be designed to minimize swallowing difficulties. Tablets can be made smaller through the use of more potent drug forms or by compressing them into shapes that are easier to swallow, such as oval or capsule-shaped tablets.

**Controlled Release**

Controlled release tablets are designed to release the drug at a predetermined rate, providing a sustained therapeutic effect over a longer period. This can improve patient compliance by reducing the frequency of dosing. Controlled release is achieved through various formulation techniques, such as coating the tablet with a polymer that controls the rate of drug release or embedding the drug in a matrix that dissolves slowly. For example, a controlled release formulation might release the drug over 12 to 24 hours, maintaining a steady concentration in the bloodstream.

These ideal characteristics ensure that tablets are effective, safe, and acceptable to patients, ultimately enhancing the therapeutic outcomes and patient compliance.

| Characteristic | Description |
|---|---|
| Uniformity of Dose | Each tablet contains the same amount of active ingredient to ensure consistent therapeutic effect |
| Mechanical Strength | Sufficient hardness and resistance to withstand handling, packaging, and transport without breaking |
| Disintegration | Ability to break down into smaller particles in the gastrointestinal tract for drug absorption |
| Dissolution | The drug must dissolve in bodily fluids at a suitable rate to be absorbed into the bloodstream |
| Stability | Maintains its physical, chemical, and microbiological integrity over the shelf life |
| Appearance | Free from visible defects, with a uniform color and shape |
| Palatability | Pleasant taste and odor or absence of any undesirable taste or odor |
| Ease of Swallowing | Size and shape should be manageable for the patient to swallow without difficulty |
| Controlled Release | Ability to release the drug at a predetermined rate for sustained or targeted delivery |

Table 11: Ideal Characteristics of Tablets

### 2.1.2 Classification of Tablets

Tablets can be classified based on their formulation, method of administration, and the intended effect. This classification helps in understanding the different types of tablets available and their specific uses in treating various conditions.

**Immediate-Release Tablets**

**Immediate-release (IR) tablets** are designed to disintegrate and release the active drug immediately after administration. These tablets are typically used when a rapid onset of action is desired. For example, pain relief medications often come in immediate-release forms to provide quick relief. Immediate-release tablets are the most common type of tablets and are usually taken orally with water.

**Sustained-Release Tablets**

**Sustained-release (SR) tablets** are formulated to release the active drug slowly over a prolonged period. This allows for a longer duration of action, reducing the frequency of dosing. These tablets are beneficial for chronic conditions where maintaining a consistent drug level in the bloodstream is important. Examples include medications for hypertension or diabetes. Sustained-release tablets use various mechanisms, such as polymer coatings or matrix systems, to control the drug release rate.

**Chewable Tablets**

**Chewable tablets** are designed to be chewed and then swallowed. They are formulated to disintegrate rapidly in the mouth and provide a pleasant taste, making them suitable for children or individuals who have difficulty swallowing conventional tablets. Chewable tablets often contain flavoring agents and sweeteners. Common examples include vitamins and antacid tablets.

**Effervescent Tablets**

**Effervescent tablets** dissolve in water to form a solution or suspension that can be easily ingested. They contain ingredients that react with water to release carbon dioxide, creating effervescence. This type of tablet is beneficial for patients who have difficulty swallowing tablets and for those requiring a fast onset of action. Examples include vitamin C tablets and certain pain relievers.

**Sublingual and Buccal Tablets**

**Sublingual tablets** are placed under the tongue, while **buccal tablets** are placed between the cheek and gum. These tablets dissolve quickly and are absorbed directly into the bloodstream through the mucous membranes in the mouth, bypassing the digestive system. This route provides a rapid onset of action and avoids first-pass metabolism by the liver. Examples include nitroglycerin tablets for angina and certain hormone therapies.

**Orally Disintegrating Tablets (ODTs)**

**Orally disintegrating tablets (ODTs)** dissolve rapidly in the mouth without the need for water. They are particularly useful for patients who have difficulty swallowing or lack access to water. ODTs are often formulated with taste-masking agents to enhance palatability. Examples include anti-nausea medications and psychiatric drugs.

**Enteric-Coated Tablets**

**Enteric-coated tablets** are coated with a material that prevents their disintegration in the acidic environment of the stomach. Instead, they dissolve in the more neutral or alkaline environment of the intestines. This coating protects the drug from stomach acid, prevents stomach irritation, and ensures that the drug is released where it can be best absorbed. Examples include certain pain relievers and aspirin tablets designed to reduce gastrointestinal side effects.

**Film-Coated Tablets**

**Film-coated tablets** are covered with a thin layer of a polymeric material. This coating can improve the tablet's appearance, make it easier to swallow, and provide some protection against moisture and environmental factors. Film coatings can also be used to control the release of the drug. An example is ibuprofen, which is often film-coated to make the tablet smoother and easier to swallow.

**Layered Tablets**

**Layered tablets** consist of multiple layers, each containing different drugs or different release profiles. These tablets can deliver a combination of drugs in a single dosage form or provide a sequential release of drugs. This is useful for medications that require a complex dosing regimen. Examples include some combination cardiovascular drugs.

**Sugar-Coated Tablets**

**Sugar-coated tablets** are coated with a layer of sugar to improve their taste and appearance. The coating also provides some protection against moisture and environmental factors. However, sugar-coating increases the size and weight of the tablet. Examples include some multivitamins and certain cough and cold medications.

**Molded Tablets**

**Molded tablets**, also known as tablet triturates, are made by molding rather than compressing. They are generally softer than compressed tablets and are designed to dissolve rapidly. Molded tablets are often used for sublingual or buccal administration. Examples include certain fast-acting vasodilators.

**Vaginal Tablets**

**Vaginal tablets** are designed for insertion into the vagina, where they dissolve and exert a local effect. These tablets are used to treat infections, hormonal imbalances, or other conditions affecting the vaginal area. Examples include antifungal tablets for treating yeast infections and hormone replacement therapy tablets.

**Implantable Tablets**

**Implantable tablets** are designed for insertion into the body tissues, where they release the drug over an extended period. These tablets are used for long-term treatments, such as hormone replacement therapy or certain types of cancer treatment. Examples include testosterone implants and certain chemotherapeutic agents.

**2.2 Excipients and Formulation**

**Excipients** are inactive substances formulated alongside the active ingredient of a medication, serving various roles in the manufacturing process and the final product. They are crucial in ensuring the stability, bioavailability, and acceptability of the drug product. While the active ingredient provides therapeutic effects, excipients ensure that the drug product is safe, effective, and easy to administer.

### 2.2.1 Types of Excipients

#### Binders

**Binders** are excipients that help hold the ingredients of a tablet together, ensuring that the tablet remains intact after compression and during handling. They provide mechanical strength to the tablet. Common binders include starch, gelatin, and polyvinylpyrrolidone (PVP). For example, PVP is often used due to its strong binding properties and solubility in water.

#### Fillers (Diluents)

**Fillers**, also known as **diluents**, are used to increase the volume of the tablet, making it easier to handle and produce. They are particularly important when the dose of the active ingredient is very small. Common fillers include lactose, microcrystalline cellulose, and calcium phosphate. For instance, microcrystalline cellulose is widely used due to its excellent compressibility and flow properties.

#### Disintegrants

**Disintegrants** are added to tablets to ensure that they break down into smaller fragments in the gastrointestinal tract, facilitating the release of the active ingredient. Common disintegrants include sodium starch glycolate, croscarmellose sodium, and crospovidone. Sodium starch glycolate is often used because of its high efficiency in promoting rapid disintegration.

#### Lubricants

**Lubricants** reduce friction between the tablet ingredients and the machinery used in tablet production. This prevents sticking to the equipment and ensures smooth ejection of tablets from the press. Common lubricants include magnesium stearate, stearic acid, and talc. Magnesium stearate is the most commonly used lubricant due to its effectiveness at low concentrations.

#### Glidants

**Glidants** are added to improve the flow properties of the powder mixture before compression into tablets. They reduce interparticle friction and enhance the flowability of the granules. Common glidants include colloidal silicon dioxide and talc. Colloidal silicon dioxide is often preferred for its high surface area and ability to improve flow.

**Sweeteners**

**Sweeteners** are used to improve the taste of oral formulations, especially chewable tablets and orally disintegrating tablets. Common sweeteners include sucrose, aspartame, and saccharin. Aspartame is widely used due to its high sweetness potency and low caloric value.

**Flavoring Agents**

**Flavoring agents** mask the unpleasant taste of certain active ingredients, making the medication more palatable, especially for pediatric and geriatric patients. Common flavoring agents include natural and artificial flavors like orange, cherry, and mint. For example, cherry flavor is commonly used in pediatric formulations to improve taste.

**Coloring Agents**

**Coloring agents** enhance the appearance of tablets and help in identifying and differentiating between different medications. They also improve patient compliance. Common coloring agents include FD&C dyes and natural colors like beet powder and turmeric. FD&C Blue No. 1 is often used to color tablets blue for easy identification.

**Preservatives**

**Preservatives** are added to prevent microbial growth and prolong the shelf life of the formulation. They are particularly important in multi-dose containers and liquid formulations. Common preservatives include parabens, benzalkonium chloride, and sodium benzoate. Parabens are widely used due to their broad-spectrum antimicrobial activity.

**Antioxidants**

**Antioxidants** protect the active ingredient from oxidative degradation, thereby enhancing the stability and shelf life of the formulation. Common antioxidants include ascorbic acid, butylated hydroxyanisole (BHA), and butylated hydroxytoluene (BHT). Ascorbic acid (vitamin C) is frequently used because it is effective and safe.

**Solubilizing Agents**

**Solubilizing agents** enhance the solubility of poorly soluble drugs, improving their bioavailability. Common solubilizing agents include cyclodextrins, surfactants like sodium lauryl sulfate, and co-solvents like ethanol. Cyclodextrins are often used to form inclusion complexes with drugs, increasing their solubility.

**Coating Agents**

**Coating agents** are applied to the surface of tablets to protect the active ingredient, mask unpleasant tastes, and control the release of the drug. Common coating agents include hydroxypropyl methylcellulose (HPMC), ethylcellulose, and enteric coatings like cellulose acetate phthalate. HPMC is widely used due to its film-forming properties and safety profile.

| Excipients | Function | Examples |
|---|---|---|
| Binders | Hold ingredients together, provide mechanical strength | Starch, gelatin, PVP |
| Fillers (Diluents) | Increase volume, ease of handling | Lactose, microcrystalline cellulose, calcium phosphate |
| Disintegrants | Facilitate tablet breakup in GI tract | Sodium starch glycolate, croscarmellose sodium |
| Lubricants | Reduce friction during tablet production | Magnesium stearate, stearic acid |
| Glidants | Improve powder flow properties | Colloidal silicon dioxide, talc |
| Sweeteners | Improve taste | Sucrose, aspartame |
| Flavoring Agents | Mask unpleasant taste | Orange, cherry, mint flavors |
| Coloring Agents | Enhance appearance, aid identification | FD&C dyes, beet powder |
| Preservatives | Prevent microbial growth | Parabens, sodium benzoate |
| Antioxidants | Prevent oxidative degradation | Ascorbic acid, BHA, BHT |
| Solubilizing Agents | Enhance solubility of drugs | Cyclodextrins, sodium lauryl sulfate |
| Coating Agents | Protect active ingredient, mask taste, control release | HPMC, ethylcellulose, cellulose acetate phthalate |

Table 12: Summary of Key Types of Excipients

### 2.2.2 Granulation Methods

**Granulation** is a key process in the production of tablets that involves the aggregation of powder particles to form larger, multi-particle entities called granules. Granulation enhances the flow and compressibility of the powder mixture, ensuring uniformity and consistency in the final tablet product. There are several granulation methods, each with specific applications and advantages.

#### Wet Granulation

**Wet granulation** is the most common method of granulation and involves the addition of a liquid binder to the powder mixture to form granules. The liquid binder helps to agglomerate the powder particles. This method can be performed using different techniques such as high-shear granulation, fluid bed granulation, and low-shear granulation.

**High-Shear Granulation**

**High-shear granulation** involves the use of high-shear mixers or granulators, where the powder and binder solution are mixed under high shear forces to form granules. This method provides dense and uniform granules with good flow properties and compressibility. It is suitable for formulations requiring a high degree of granulation and can handle a wide range of binder viscosities. For example, high-shear granulation is often used in the production of tablets containing poorly compressible drugs.

**Fluid Bed Granulation**

**Fluid bed granulation** involves suspending the powder particles in an air stream and spraying the binder solution onto the fluidized particles. This method allows for efficient drying and uniform granule formation. Fluid bed granulation is ideal for heat-sensitive materials as the drying process is gentle and controlled. It also provides excellent control over granule size and moisture content. An example of its application is in the granulation of vitamins and nutraceuticals.

**Low-Shear Granulation**

**Low-shear granulation** uses low-shear mixers, where the powder and binder solution are mixed under gentle agitation to form granules. This method is less intensive compared to high-shear granulation and is suitable for heat-sensitive or shear-sensitive materials. It produces granules with lower density and hardness. Low-shear granulation is often used for formulations where a mild granulation process is required, such as in the granulation of some herbal extracts.

**Dry Granulation**

**Dry granulation** involves the formation of granules without the use of a liquid binder. This method is suitable for moisture-sensitive materials and heat-sensitive drugs. It is performed using two main techniques: slugging and roller compaction.

**Slugging**

**Slugging** involves compressing the powder mixture into large tablets or slugs, which are then broken down into granules. This method is simple and cost-effective but may result in less uniform granules with variable size distribution. It is suitable for small-scale production and for formulations where other methods are not feasible. Slugging is often used in the granulation of ingredients for chewable tablets.

**Roller Compaction**

**Roller compaction** involves passing the powder mixture between two counter-rotating rollers to form a compacted ribbon or sheet, which is then broken down into granules. This method provides more uniform granules compared to slugging and is suitable for large-scale production. Roller compaction is ideal for drugs that are sensitive to moisture and heat. It is commonly used in the granulation of drugs like ibuprofen and paracetamol.

**Spray Drying**

**Spray drying** is a granulation method where the solution or suspension of the drug and excipients is sprayed into a hot drying chamber. The solvent evaporates quickly, leaving behind fine, uniform granules. This method is suitable for heat-sensitive materials and provides excellent control over granule size and moisture content. Spray drying is often used for drugs that require rapid dissolution, such as instant-release formulations.

**Extrusion-Spheronization**

**Extrusion-spheronization** is a specialized granulation method used to produce spherical granules or pellets. The process involves extruding a wet mass through a die to form cylindrical extrudates, which are then broken into smaller segments and rounded in a spheronizer. This method is ideal for controlled-release formulations and multi-particulate systems. An example is the production of sustained-release pellets for oral dosage forms.

| Granulation Method | Process | Advantages | Applications |
|---|---|---|---|
| Wet Granulation | Addition of liquid binder to form granules | Good flow and compressibility | Immediate-release, controlled-release tablets |
| High-Shear Granulation | Mixing powder and binder under high shear forces | Dense, uniform granules | Poorly compressible drugs |
| Fluid Bed Granulation | Suspending powder in air stream, spraying binder solution | Efficient drying, uniform granules | Heat-sensitive materials |
| Low-Shear Granulation | Mixing powder and binder under gentle agitation | Suitable for sensitive materials | Herbal extracts |
| Dry Granulation | Formation of granules without liquid binder | No heat or moisture | Moisture-sensitive, heat-sensitive drugs |
| Slugging | Compressing powder into large tablets, breaking into granules | Simple, cost-effective | Small-scale production |
| Roller Compaction | Passing powder between rollers to form ribbons, breaking into granules | Uniform granules, large-scale production | Ibuprofen, paracetamol |
| Spray Drying | Spraying solution/suspension into hot chamber to form granules | Rapid drying, uniform granules | Instant-release formulations |
| Extrusion-Spheronization | Extruding wet mass through die, rounding in spheronizer | Spherical granules, controlled release | Sustained-release pellets |

Table 13: Summary of Granulation Methods

### 2.2.3 Compression and Processing Problems

**Compression and processing problems** are common challenges encountered during the manufacturing of tablets. These issues can affect the quality, efficacy, and safety of the final product. Understanding these problems and their potential causes is essential for ensuring consistent production and maintaining the integrity of the tablets.

**Capping and Lamination**

**Capping** refers to the partial or complete separation of the top or bottom part of the tablet from the main body. **Lamination** is the separation of the tablet into two or more layers. These defects occur during the ejection of the tablet from the die cavity.

**Causes**:

- **Air entrapment** during compression.

- **Insufficient binder** in the formulation.
- **Improper tablet design** with sharp edges.
- **High compression force** leading to excessive stress.

**Solutions**:

- **Adjusting compression parameters** to reduce air entrapment.
- **Increasing binder concentration** to enhance cohesion.
- **Modifying tablet design** to eliminate sharp edges.
- **Optimizing compression force** to balance mechanical strength.

**Sticking and Picking**

**Sticking** occurs when the tablet material adheres to the punch faces, while **picking** refers to the removal of material from the tablet surface by the punch, leading to an uneven surface.

**Causes**:

- **Inadequate lubrication** in the formulation.
- **High moisture content** in the granules.
- **Worn or damaged punches.**

**Solutions**:

- **Increasing the amount of lubricant** in the formulation.
- **Drying the granules properly** to reduce moisture content.
- **Regular maintenance and replacement** of punches to ensure smooth surfaces.

**Chipping**

**Chipping** is the breaking of tablet edges during handling or packaging. This defect compromises the tablet's appearance and can lead to dose variation.

**Causes**:

- **Low moisture content** making the tablets too brittle.
- **Insufficient binder** resulting in weak tablets.
- **High compression speed** leading to mechanical stress.

**Solutions**:

- **Optimizing moisture content** in the granules to prevent brittleness.
- **Increasing binder concentration** to enhance tablet strength.
- **Adjusting compression speed** to reduce mechanical stress.

**Cracking**

**Cracking** refers to the formation of fine cracks on the tablet surface, often due to expansion of the tablet core after compression.

**Causes**:

- **Rapid expansion** of the tablet core after compression.
- **Improper granule size distribution.**
- **High compression force.**

**Solutions**:

- **Using pre-compression** to reduce air entrapment and expansion.
- **Ensuring uniform granule size distribution.**
- **Optimizing compression force** to prevent excessive stress.

**Mottling**

**Mottling** is the uneven distribution of color on the tablet surface, resulting in a marbled appearance.

**Causes**:

- **Uneven dye distribution** in the formulation.
- **Migration of soluble dyes** during drying.
- **Incompatibility between dye and excipients.**

**Solutions**:

- **Ensuring uniform mixing** of dye with the granules.
- **Using insoluble colorants** to prevent migration.
- **Testing compatibility** of dye with other formulation components.

**Weight Variation**

**Weight variation** refers to the inconsistency in the weight of individual tablets within a batch, which can lead to dose variation.

**Causes:**

- **Poor flow properties** of the granules.
- **Irregular die fill** due to equipment malfunction.
- **Inconsistent granule size.**

**Solutions:**

- **Improving flow properties** with glidants.
- **Regular calibration and maintenance** of compression equipment.
- **Ensuring uniform granule size distribution.**

**Hardness Variation**

**Hardness variation** affects the mechanical strength of tablets, influencing their disintegration and dissolution profiles.

**Causes:**

- **Inconsistent compression force.**
- **Variable granule size.**
- **Inadequate binder concentration.**

**Solutions:**

- **Standardizing compression force** during production.
- **Ensuring uniform granule size distribution.**
- **Optimizing binder concentration** to achieve desired hardness.

**Double Impression**

**Double impression** occurs when a free-rotating punch causes a second, lighter imprint on the tablet surface.

**Causes:**

- **Free rotation** of punches with engraved designs.
- **Loose punch holders.**

**Solutions:**

- **Using anti-turn devices** to prevent punch rotation.
- **Tightening punch holders** to secure punches in place.

**Friability**

**Friability** refers to the tendency of tablets to crumble or break during handling and transportation.

**Causes**:

- **Low tablet hardness.**
- **Insufficient binder** in the formulation.
- **High friability of granules.**

**Solutions**:

- **Increasing tablet hardness** by optimizing compression force.
- **Enhancing binder concentration** to improve cohesion.
- **Using friability testers** to assess and improve tablet durability.

| Problem | Cause | Solution |
|---|---|---|
| Capping and Lamination | Air entrapment, insufficient binder, improper design, high force | Adjust compression, increase binder, modify design |
| Sticking and Picking | Inadequate lubrication, high moisture, worn punches | Increase lubricant, dry granules, maintain punches |
| Chipping | Low moisture, insufficient binder, high speed | Optimize moisture, increase binder, adjust speed |
| Cracking | Rapid expansion, improper granule size, high force | Use pre-compression, uniform granule size, optimize force |
| Mottling | Uneven dye, dye migration, incompatibility | Uniform mixing, use insoluble colorants, test compatibility |
| Weight Variation | Poor flow, irregular die fill, inconsistent granules | Improve flow, calibrate equipment, uniform granules |
| Hardness Variation | Inconsistent force, variable granule size, inadequate binder | Standardize force, uniform granules, optimize binder |
| Double Impression | Free-rotating punch, loose holders | Use anti-turn devices, tighten holders |
| Friability | Low hardness, insufficient binder, high granule friability | Increase hardness, enhance binder, use friability testers |

Table 14: Summary of Compression and Processing Problems

## 2.3 Equipment and Tablet Tooling

In tablet manufacturing, various types of equipment are used to ensure the efficient production of high-quality tablets. These pieces of equipment are designed to handle different stages of the tablet production process, from powder blending to granulation, compression, and coating.

### 2.3.1 Types of Equipment

**Powder Blending Equipment**

**Powder blending** is a critical step in tablet production, ensuring uniform distribution of the active pharmaceutical ingredient (API) and excipients. Various types of blenders are used depending on the properties of the materials and the scale of production.

**V-Blender**

**V-Blenders** consist of two cylindrical sections joined at an angle to form a "V" shape. They are used for dry blending of free-flowing powders and granules. The tumbling action provides thorough mixing, making them ideal for producing homogeneous blends in pharmaceutical formulations.

**Ribbon Blender**

**Ribbon blenders** have a horizontal trough containing a central shaft with helical ribbons that move the powder in opposite directions, ensuring uniform mixing. They are suitable for blending powders and granules with varying densities and particle sizes.

**Double Cone Blender**

**Double cone blenders** consist of a rotating cylindrical shell that forms a double cone shape. The tumbling action ensures uniform mixing of powders and granules. They are used for blending free-flowing materials and are known for their gentle mixing action, minimizing material degradation.

**Granulation Equipment**

**Granulation** converts powders into granules, improving flow and compressibility. There are two main types of granulation equipment: wet granulation and dry granulation equipment.

**High-Shear Granulator**

**High-shear granulators** use a combination of impellers and choppers to mix powders and binders, forming dense granules. They are suitable for producing uniform granules with good flow properties and compressibility.

**Fluid Bed Granulator**

**Fluid bed granulators** fluidize the powder particles in an air stream while spraying a binder solution. This method provides uniform granulation and efficient drying, making it ideal for heat-sensitive materials.

**Roller Compactor**

**Roller compactors** are used in dry granulation. They compress powder between two rollers to form ribbons, which are then milled into granules. This equipment is suitable for moisture-sensitive and heat-sensitive drugs.

**Tablet Compression Equipment**

**Tablet compression** is the process of compressing granules into tablets. The equipment used in this process must ensure uniform tablet weight, hardness, and thickness.

**Single-Station Press**

**Single-station presses**, also known as eccentric presses, have one set of punches and dies. They are used for small-scale production and laboratory applications. These presses are simple to operate and provide precise control over tablet properties.

**Rotary Tablet Press**

**Rotary tablet presses** are used for high-speed, large-scale production. They consist of multiple sets of punches and dies mounted on a rotating turret. As the turret rotates, the punches compress the granules into tablets. These presses are capable of producing thousands of tablets per hour, ensuring high efficiency and consistent quality.

Rotary Tablet Press

**Tablet Coating Equipment**

**Tablet coating** enhances the appearance, taste, and stability of tablets. It can also control the release of the active ingredient.

**Pan Coater**

**Pan coaters** are used for film and sugar coating. Tablets are placed in a rotating pan while the coating solution is sprayed onto them. The rotation ensures even distribution of the coating. Pan coaters are versatile and widely used in pharmaceutical manufacturing.

**Fluid Bed Coater**

**Fluid bed coaters** suspend tablets in an air stream while spraying the coating solution. This method provides uniform coating and efficient drying. Fluid bed coaters are suitable for enteric and sustained-release coatings.

**Tablet Tooling**

**Tablet tooling** refers to the punches and dies used in tablet compression equipment. Proper tooling ensures the production of tablets with the desired shape, size, and imprint.

**Punches**

**Punches** are metal rods that compress the granules into tablets. They come in various shapes and sizes to produce different tablet forms. Punches are typically made of hardened steel or other durable materials to withstand high compression forces.

**Dies**

**Dies** are hollow metal cylinders that hold the granules during compression. The punches fit into the dies to form the tablets. Dies must be precisely machined to ensure uniform tablet dimensions and prevent defects.

**2.3.2 Tablet Tooling Details**

Tablet tooling is a critical component in the tablet manufacturing process, involving the punches and dies used in tablet compression machines. Proper tooling ensures the production of tablets with the desired shape, size, and imprint. The quality and precision of tablet tooling directly affect the uniformity, appearance, and functionality of the final product.

**Punches**

**Punches** are metal rods that play a crucial role in the tablet compression process. They come in various shapes and sizes, depending on the desired form and characteristics of the tablet. Punches consist of two main parts: the upper punch and the lower punch.

**Upper Punch**

**Upper punches** compress the granules into the die cavity from the top. They are responsible for shaping the top surface of the tablet. The design of the upper punch impacts the tablet's appearance and functionality, including aspects like debossing or engraving for identification.

**Lower Punch**

**Lower punches** provide the bottom compression force and shape the bottom surface of the tablet. They rise to eject the tablet from the die after compression. The alignment and condition of lower punches are crucial to prevent defects like capping or lamination.

**Punch Shapes and Designs**

Punches can have various shapes and designs, including:

- **Flat-faced punches**: Produce tablets with flat surfaces, commonly used for simple tablets.
- **Beveled-edge punches**: Create tablets with beveled edges to prevent chipping.
- **Concave punches**: Form tablets with concave surfaces, often used for chewable tablets.
- **Embossed punches**: Include specific designs or logos, which are embossed on the tablet surface for branding or identification purposes.

**Materials Used for Punches**

Punches are typically made from high-quality materials to withstand the high pressures involved in tablet compression:

- **Stainless steel**: Offers excellent corrosion resistance and durability.
- **Tool steel**: Provides high strength and wear resistance, suitable for high-volume production.
- **Tungsten carbide**: Extremely hard and durable, used for abrasive or hard-to-compress materials.

**Dies**

**Dies** are hollow cylindrical components that hold the powder or granules during compression. The lower punch fits into the die to form the base of the tablet, while the upper punch compresses the material from above. The precision and quality of dies are crucial for producing tablets with uniform dimensions and preventing defects.

**Die Shapes and Sizes**

Dies come in various shapes and sizes to accommodate different tablet designs:

- **Round dies**: The most common shape, used for standard tablets.
- **Oval and oblong dies**: Used for tablets that are easier to swallow.
- **Multilayer dies**: Designed for producing layered tablets with different drugs or release profiles.
- **Shaped dies**: Customized shapes like hearts or stars for specific branding or patient compliance.

**Materials Used for Dies**

Dies are made from materials that offer durability and precision:

- **Stainless steel**: Commonly used for its resistance to corrosion and wear.
- **Tool steel**: Provides strength and durability for high-pressure applications.
- **Ceramic dies**: Used for specialized applications requiring high wear resistance and low friction.

**Tooling Maintenance and Care**

Proper maintenance and care of tablet tooling are essential to ensure the production of high-quality tablets and prolong the life of the equipment.

**Cleaning and Polishing**

Regular cleaning and polishing of punches and dies are necessary to remove any residues and prevent contamination. This process involves:

- **Ultrasonic cleaning**: Using ultrasonic waves to remove fine particles and residues.
- **Polishing**: Using specialized tools and compounds to maintain a smooth surface and prevent sticking.

**Inspection and Replacement**

Routine inspection of punches and dies for wear and damage is crucial to prevent defects in tablets. Key inspection points include:

- **Surface integrity**: Checking for scratches, dents, or other surface damage.

- **Dimensional accuracy**: Ensuring punches and dies meet precise dimensional specifications.
- **Alignment**: Verifying that punches and dies are correctly aligned to prevent capping, lamination, and other defects.

**Lubrication**

Proper lubrication of punches and dies reduces friction, prevents sticking, and extends the life of the tooling. Lubricants used must be compatible with the pharmaceutical formulation and should not interfere with the tablet's properties.

**Types of Tablet Tooling**

Tablet tooling involves various types of punches and dies used in tablet compression machines. The selection of appropriate tooling is crucial for ensuring the quality, consistency, and functionality of the tablets produced. Here are the different types of tablet tooling:

**B-Type Tooling**

**B-Type tooling** is one of the most commonly used standards in tablet manufacturing. It is characterized by its versatility and ability to produce a wide range of tablet sizes and shapes. B-Type tooling is typically used in rotary tablet presses and includes both punches and dies.

**Standard B-Type**

**Standard B-Type tooling** has a punch barrel diameter of 19.00 mm and a die outer diameter of 30.16 mm. It is suitable for producing tablets with diameters up to 16 mm. This tooling is commonly used for various tablet forms, including round, oval, and oblong shapes.

**Special B-Type**

**Special B-Type tooling** includes modifications to the standard B-Type dimensions to accommodate specific tablet designs or production requirements. This may involve changes in the punch length, head shape, or die dimensions.

**D-Type Tooling**

**D-Type tooling** is another common standard used in tablet manufacturing, particularly for larger tablets. It is designed to produce tablets with diameters greater than those made with B-Type tooling.

**Standard D-Type**

**Standard D-Type tooling** has a punch barrel diameter of 25.35 mm and a die outer diameter of 38.10 mm. It is suitable for producing tablets with diameters up to 25 mm. This tooling is ideal for applications requiring larger tablets, such as vitamins and nutritional supplements.

**Special D-Type**

**Special D-Type tooling** includes variations of the standard dimensions to meet specific production needs. These modifications can involve different punch lengths, head shapes, or die sizes to accommodate unique tablet designs.

**BB-Type Tooling**

**BB-Type tooling** is a variation of B-Type tooling with smaller dimensions, allowing for the production of smaller tablets. It is often used for producing tablets with diameters less than 10 mm.

**Standard BB-Type**

**Standard BB-Type tooling** has a punch barrel diameter of 19.00 mm and a die outer diameter of 24.00 mm. It is suitable for producing small, precise tablets, commonly used in pharmaceuticals requiring low-dose medications.

**Special BB-Type**

**Special BB-Type tooling** includes modifications to standard dimensions to meet specific requirements for small tablets. This may involve changes in punch and die dimensions to achieve the desired tablet size and shape.

**Multi-Tip Tooling**

**Multi-tip tooling** involves punches with multiple tips, allowing the production of multiple tablets with each compression cycle. This increases production efficiency and is used for high-volume manufacturing.

**Multi-Tip Punches**

**Multi-tip punches** can have two, three, or more tips, depending on the desired number of tablets produced per cycle. This tooling is ideal for large-scale production, significantly increasing output without compromising quality.

**Custom Tooling**

**Custom tooling** is designed to meet specific requirements that standard tooling cannot fulfill. This includes specialized shapes, sizes, and imprinting needs. Custom tooling is tailored to the unique specifications of the tablet design and production process.

**Special Shapes**

**Special shapes** include non-standard tablet shapes such as stars, hearts, or other custom designs. These shapes are often used for branding purposes or to enhance patient compliance.

**Embossing and Engraving**

**Embossing and engraving** involve custom designs or logos on the punch faces to create specific imprints on the tablet surface. This is commonly used for branding, identification, or dosage information.

| Tooling Type | Description | Dimensions/Examples |
|---|---|---|
| B-Type Tooling | Versatile standard for a wide range of tablet sizes and shapes | Standard: 19.00 mm punch barrel, 30.16 mm die |
| D-Type Tooling | Standard for larger tablets, such as vitamins and supplements | Standard: 25.35 mm punch barrel, 38.10 mm die |
| BB-Type Tooling | Variation of B-Type for smaller tablets | Standard: 19.00 mm punch barrel, 24.00 mm die |
| Multi-Tip Tooling | Punches with multiple tips for high-volume production | Two, three, or more tips per punch |
| Custom Tooling | Specialized shapes, sizes, and imprinting to meet unique requirements | Custom shapes like stars, hearts, embossed logos |
| Special B-Type | Modifications to standard B-Type dimensions for specific needs | Varies based on requirements |
| Special D-Type | Modifications to standard D-Type dimensions for specific needs | Varies based on requirements |
| Special BB-Type | Modifications to standard BB-Type dimensions for specific needs | Varies based on requirements |

Table 15 : Summary of Types of Tablet Tooling

## 2.4 Tablet Coating

### 2.4.1 Types of Coating

Tablet coating is an essential process in pharmaceutical manufacturing that enhances the functionality and aesthetics of tablets. There are several types of tablet coatings, each serving specific purposes, such as protecting the tablet's core, controlling the release of the active ingredient, or simply improving the tablet's appearance.

**Sugar Coating**: This traditional method involves multiple steps, including sealing, sub-coating, syruping, smoothing, coloring, and polishing. The process begins with the application of a **sealant** to protect the core from moisture. A **sub-coating** layer is then applied to increase the tablet's weight and size. **Syruping** follows, where sugar syrup is applied in layers to build up the coating. This is followed by **smoothing**, which involves the use of diluted syrup to even out the surface. **Coloring** is achieved by adding pigments to the syrup. Finally, **polishing** is done to give the tablet a shiny finish. This type of coating is thick and can significantly increase the tablet's size, which might be a disadvantage for patients who have difficulty swallowing large tablets. The entire process can take several days, making it labor-intensive and time-consuming.

**Film Coating**: This modern method uses a thin polymer-based coating, which is applied in a single step, making it more efficient and faster than sugar coating. The **film-forming polymers** used, such as hydroxypropyl methylcellulose (HPMC), ethylcellulose, and polymethacrylates, dissolve or disperse in water or organic solvents. The **coating solution** is sprayed onto the tablets in a rotating drum while heated air dries the solution, forming a thin, uniform layer. Film coatings can be designed to be **immediate-release**, **sustained-release**, or **enteric-release** depending on the choice of polymers and plasticizers used. Immediate-release coatings dissolve quickly in the stomach, while sustained-release coatings control the release of the active ingredient over an extended period. Enteric coatings remain intact in the stomach but dissolve in the alkaline environment of the intestines, protecting the active ingredient from stomach acid or protecting the stomach lining from irritating drugs.

**Enteric Coating**: This specific type of film coating is designed to withstand the acidic environment of the stomach and dissolve in the more alkaline pH of the small intestine. Commonly used **enteric polymers** include cellulose acetate phthalate (CAP), hydroxypropyl methylcellulose phthalate (HPMCP), and polyvinyl acetate phthalate (PVAP). Enteric coatings are crucial for drugs that can be destroyed by stomach acid, irritate the gastric mucosa, or need to be absorbed in the intestine. For instance, **aspirin** and certain **antibiotics** benefit from enteric coatings to prevent stomach irritation and ensure proper absorption.

**Compression Coating**: Unlike traditional coatings applied as liquids, compression coating involves compressing a coating layer around a pre-formed tablet core. This method is particularly useful for **layered tablets** where different active ingredients need to be separated. Compression coating can protect **moisture-sensitive** drugs, mask unpleasant tastes, and create **controlled-release** profiles. The outer layer is compressed around the core, which can contain an active ingredient that needs to be released at a different rate or location within the gastrointestinal tract.

**Hot Melt Coating**: In this innovative method, the coating material is applied in a molten state and solidifies upon cooling. Materials such as **waxes** (e.g., carnauba wax, beeswax) and **polymers** with low melting points are commonly used. Hot melt coatings are beneficial for creating **sustained-release** tablets as they form a dense, uniform barrier that controls the drug's release rate. This method eliminates the need for organic solvents, making it an environmentally friendly option.

Each type of tablet coating offers unique advantages and is chosen based on the specific needs of the drug formulation. Factors such as the desired release profile, protection of the active ingredient, patient compliance, and manufacturing efficiency play crucial roles in determining the appropriate coating technique. As technology advances, new coating materials and methods continue to enhance the effectiveness and versatility of tablet coatings in the pharmaceutical industry.

### 2.4.2 Coating Materials

Tablet coating materials play a critical role in the pharmaceutical industry by providing protection, controlled release, and improved patient compliance. Various materials are used for different coating purposes, each with unique properties and applications. These materials can be broadly classified into **polymers**, **plasticizers**, **colorants**, and **solvents**.

**Polymers**: Polymers are the backbone of most tablet coatings, providing structural integrity and specific functional properties. Commonly used polymers include:

- **Hydroxypropyl Methylcellulose (HPMC)**: This water-soluble polymer is widely used for film coatings due to its excellent film-forming properties, stability, and ease of application. HPMC coatings can be designed for immediate or sustained release depending on the formulation.
- **Ethylcellulose**: Insoluble in water, ethylcellulose is used for sustained-release coatings. It forms a barrier that controls the drug's release rate over time. Ethylcellulose coatings are often combined with other materials to modify their permeability.
- **Polyvinyl Alcohol (PVA)**: Known for its excellent film-forming capabilities and low viscosity, PVA is used in both immediate and controlled-release formulations. Its water solubility can be adjusted by modifying its chemical structure.
- **Methacrylic Acid Copolymers**: These enteric polymers, such as Eudragit, dissolve at specific pH levels, making them ideal for enteric coatings. They protect the drug from stomach acid and ensure release in the intestines.

**Plasticizers**: Plasticizers are added to polymer coatings to enhance their flexibility and reduce brittleness. Common plasticizers include:

- **Triethyl Citrate**: Used with polymers like HPMC and Eudragit, triethyl citrate improves the film's flexibility and reduces the risk of cracking.
- **Polyethylene Glycol (PEG)**: Available in various molecular weights, PEG is used to modify the film's properties, such as flexibility and solubility. Higher molecular weight PEGs provide more flexibility, while lower molecular weights enhance solubility.
- **Glycerin**: A common plasticizer, glycerin is used to improve the elasticity and smoothness of the coating film.

**Colorants**: Colorants are added to coatings for identification, branding, and patient compliance. They include:

- **Synthetic Dyes**: These water-soluble dyes provide vibrant colors and are commonly used in film coatings. Examples include FD&C Red No. 40 and FD&C Blue No. 1.
- **Lakes**: Insoluble pigments made by adsorbing dyes onto substrates like aluminum hydroxide. Lakes provide consistent coloring and are used in both aqueous and non-aqueous coatings.
- **Iron Oxides**: Natural pigments used for coloring, providing a range of colors from yellow to red to black. Iron oxides are stable and non-toxic, making them suitable for pharmaceutical applications.
- **Titanium Dioxide**: A white pigment used to provide opacity and whiteness to coatings. It also offers protection from light, which can degrade certain drugs.

**Solvents**: Solvents are used to dissolve or disperse coating materials, facilitating their application. They can be classified into aqueous and organic solvents:

- **Water**: The most common solvent, water is used for dissolving water-soluble polymers like HPMC. It is safe, environmentally friendly, and cost effective. However, it is not suitable for moisture-sensitive drugs.
- **Ethanol**: An organic solvent used for dissolving polymers like ethylcellulose. Ethanol evaporates quickly, reducing drying times and improving manufacturing efficiency.

- **Isopropanol**: Another organic solvent, isopropanol is used in combination with other solvents to dissolve coating materials. It is particularly useful for moisture-sensitive formulations.
- **Methylene Chloride**: A powerful solvent used for dissolving polymers like cellulose acetate phthalate. It is effective but poses health and environmental risks, requiring careful handling and disposal.

**Additional Excipients**: Various excipients are added to coating formulations to improve their performance and stability. These include:

- **Surfactants**: Used to enhance the wettability and spreadability of the coating solution. Common surfactants include polysorbates and sodium lauryl sulfate.
- **Anti-tacking Agents**: Added to prevent the coated tablets from sticking to each other. Talc and magnesium stearate are commonly used anti-tacking agents.
- **Opacifiers**: These materials, like titanium dioxide, are used to make the coating opaque, protecting light-sensitive drugs from degradation.

The selection of coating materials is a critical aspect of tablet formulation, impacting the drug's stability, release profile, and patient acceptability. Advances in coating technology continue to enhance the functionality and versatility of these materials, driving innovation in pharmaceutical manufacturing.

### 2.4.3 Formulation of Coating Composition

The formulation of tablet coating composition is a crucial step in the pharmaceutical manufacturing process. It involves selecting the appropriate materials and their proportions to achieve the desired coating characteristics, such as protection, controlled release, and patient compliance. The formulation must be carefully designed to ensure the stability, efficacy, and quality of the final product. The main components of a coating formulation include **polymers**, **plasticizers**, **colorants**, **solvents**, and **additional excipients**.

**Polymers**: The choice of polymer significantly impacts the properties of the coating. For instance, **Hydroxypropyl Methylcellulose (HPMC)** is widely used for film coatings due to its excellent film-forming properties and stability. The concentration of HPMC typically ranges from 2% to 20% of the coating solution, depending on the desired thickness and release profile.

For enteric coatings, **Methacrylic Acid Copolymers**, such as Eudragit, are used at concentrations of 5% to 30%, ensuring the coating dissolves at specific pH levels.

**Plasticizers**: Plasticizers are added to improve the flexibility and elasticity of the coating film, preventing cracks and ensuring smooth application. Common plasticizers like **Triethyl Citrate** and **Polyethylene Glycol (PEG)** are used at concentrations of 10% to 30% of the polymer weight. For example, PEG 400, with its low molecular weight, enhances the solubility and flexibility of the coating film.

**Colorants**: Colorants are incorporated to improve the appearance and identification of the tablets. **Synthetic Dyes** such as FD&C Red No. 40 and FD&C Blue No. 1 are used in small quantities, typically less than 1% of the coating composition. **Iron Oxides** and **Titanium Dioxide** are added at concentrations up to 5% to provide opacity and light protection. The choice of colorant must consider stability, safety, and regulatory compliance.

**Solvents**: Solvents dissolve or disperse the coating materials, facilitating their application. The most common solvent is **Water**, used for water-soluble polymers like HPMC. Water-based coatings are preferred for their safety and environmental benefits. However, for moisture-sensitive drugs, **Ethanol** or **Isopropanol** is used. Solvent concentration usually ranges from 30% to 70% of the coating solution. **Methylene Chloride** may be used for specific polymers but requires careful handling due to its toxicity.

**Additional Excipients**: Various excipients are added to enhance the performance and stability of the coating. **Surfactants**, such as polysorbates, are included at 0.1% to 1% to improve wettability and dispersion of the coating solution. **Anti-tacking Agents** like talc and magnesium stearate, added at 1% to 5%, prevent the coated tablets from sticking to each other during the drying process. **Opacifiers** such as titanium dioxide are used to make the coating opaque, protecting light-sensitive drugs and enhancing the tablet's appearance.

The formulation process begins with dissolving or dispersing the polymer in the chosen solvent. The plasticizer is then added to the solution to ensure the coating film's flexibility. Colorants are incorporated to achieve the desired hue and opacity. Surfactants and anti-tacking agents are added to improve the coating's application properties. The final coating solution is mixed thoroughly to ensure uniformity and consistency.

The coating process involves spraying the formulated coating solution onto the tablets in a coating pan or fluidized bed coater. The tablets are rotated or fluidized while the solution is applied, ensuring even distribution. Heated air is used to evaporate the solvent, leaving behind a uniform coating layer. The process parameters, such as spray rate, air temperature, and rotation speed, are carefully controlled to achieve the desired coating quality.

The formulation of coating composition is a complex and precise process that requires careful selection and optimization of various components. The goal is to produce a coating that meets the desired functional and aesthetic requirements while ensuring the stability and efficacy of the final pharmaceutical product. Advances in coating technology continue to improve the formulation process, offering new opportunities for innovation and improvement in drug delivery systems.

### 2.4.4 Methods of Coating

The methods of tablet coating are diverse and have evolved significantly to enhance the efficiency and quality of the coating process. The choice of coating method depends on the specific requirements of the tablet formulation, including the desired release profile, protection, and aesthetic appeal. The primary methods of tablet coating include **sugar coating**, **film coating**, **enteric coating**, **compression coating**, and **electrostatic coating**. Each method has its unique process, advantages, and applications.

**Sugar Coating**: This traditional method involves multiple steps and is used to mask the taste of bitter drugs, improve appearance, and protect the tablet core. The process includes **sealing**, **sub-coating**, **syruping**, **smoothing**, **coloring**, and **polishing**. Initially, a sealant such as shellac or cellulose acetate phthalate is applied to protect the tablet core from moisture. The sub-coating process involves applying a sugar-based solution to increase the tablet's size and weight. Syruping further builds up the coating with layers of concentrated sugar syrup. Smoothing is achieved by applying diluted syrup to create a uniform surface. Coloring involves adding dyes or pigments to the syrup, and polishing provides a shiny finish using waxes. Although sugar coating results in an attractive product, it is labor-intensive, time-consuming, and increases the tablet size significantly.

**Film Coating**: Film coating is a modern and efficient method that involves the application of a thin polymer-based film onto the tablet surface. This method is quicker and requires fewer steps than sugar coating. The coating solution typically contains polymers such as **hydroxypropyl methylcellulose (HPMC)**, **ethylcellulose**, or **polyvinyl alcohol**, along with plasticizers, colorants, and solvents. The tablets are placed in a rotating drum or fluidized bed, where the coating solution is sprayed onto them while hot air is circulated to evaporate the solvent, leaving a thin, uniform film. Film coatings can be designed for immediate-release, sustained-release, or enteric-release purposes. The process parameters, such as spray rate, air temperature, and tablet rotation speed, are carefully controlled to ensure a consistent and high-quality coating.

**Enteric Coating**: This specialized type of film coating protects the drug from the acidic environment of the stomach and ensures its release in the intestines. Enteric coatings are made using polymers such as **cellulose acetate phthalate (CAP)**, **hydroxypropyl methylcellulose phthalate (HPMCP)**, or **methacrylic acid copolymers**. The coating solution is similar to that used in film coating but includes enteric polymers that dissolve at a higher pH, typically above 5.5. The application process involves spraying the enteric coating solution onto the tablets in a coating pan or fluidized bed, followed by drying with hot air. Enteric coatings are essential for drugs that can be destroyed by stomach acid or irritate the gastric mucosa, such as aspirin and certain antibiotics.

**Compression Coating**: Unlike other methods that apply coatings in liquid form, compression coating involves compressing a coating layer around a pre-formed tablet core. This method is particularly useful for creating **layered tablets** where different active ingredients need to be separated. The process involves placing the core tablet in a die and compressing a coating material, such as a mixture of excipients, around it. Compression coating can protect moisture-sensitive drugs, mask unpleasant tastes, and create controlled-release profiles. It also allows for the incorporation of different drugs in separate layers, which can be beneficial for combination therapies.

**Electrostatic Coating**: This innovative method utilizes electrostatic charges to apply the coating material. The tablets are given an electrical charge opposite to that of the coating particles. The coating particles are sprayed onto the tablets, and the electrostatic attraction ensures a uniform coating. This method is particularly useful for coating fine powders and achieving a high degree of uniformity with minimal coating material. Electrostatic coating is less common but offers advantages such as reduced solvent usage and improved coating efficiency.

**Fluidized Bed Coating**: In this method, tablets are suspended in an upward flow of air within a coating chamber. The coating solution is sprayed from the bottom or top of the chamber while the tablets are kept in a fluidized state by the air flow. This ensures an even distribution of the coating material on the tablets. Fluidized bed coating is highly efficient and suitable for both aqueous and solvent-based coatings. It provides excellent uniformity and can be used for immediate-release, sustained-release, and enteric coatings.

Each coating method has its advantages and specific applications, making the selection of the appropriate method crucial for achieving the desired tablet characteristics. Advances in coating technology continue to enhance these methods, improving efficiency, quality, and the ability to meet diverse pharmaceutical needs.

### 2.4.5 Equipment Employed

The equipment used in tablet coating processes is designed to ensure efficient, uniform, and high-quality application of the coating materials. Each type of coating method requires specific equipment tailored to its unique requirements. The primary types of equipment employed in tablet coating include **traditional coating pans**, **perforated coating pans**, **fluidized bed coaters**, **electrostatic coating machines**, and **compression coating machines.**

**Traditional Coating Pans**: Traditional coating pans, also known as standard coating pans, are among the earliest types of coating equipment used in the pharmaceutical industry. These pans are typically made of stainless steel and have a circular, rotating drum where the tablets are placed. The coating solution is manually or mechanically poured over the tablets as they tumble in the rotating pan. Heated air is directed into the pan to dry the coating. While traditional coating pans are simple and cost-effective, they are labor-intensive and can lead to inconsistent coatings due to manual application.

**Perforated Coating Pans**: Perforated coating pans are an advancement over traditional coating pans, offering better control and efficiency. These pans have perforated walls that allow hot air to flow through the pan, improving drying efficiency and coating uniformity. The tablets are loaded into the pan, which rotates to ensure even distribution of the coating solution. The solution is sprayed onto the tablets through spray guns mounted inside the pan. The perforated design allows for continuous air circulation, enhancing the drying process and reducing coating time. Examples of perforated coating pans include the Accela-Cota and Glatt coating systems.

**Fluidized Bed Coaters**: Fluidized bed coaters, also known as air suspension coaters, are widely used for applying both aqueous and solvent-based coatings. In this equipment, tablets are suspended in an upward flow of air within a coating chamber. The coating solution is sprayed from the bottom or top of the chamber while the tablets are kept in a fluidized state by the air flow. This ensures an even distribution of the coating material on the tablets. Fluidized bed coaters provide excellent uniformity and are suitable for immediate-release, sustained-release, and enteric coatings. They are highly efficient and can handle large batches of tablets. The Wurster coater and Glatt fluidized bed systems are popular examples.

**Electrostatic Coating Machines**: Electrostatic coating machines utilize electrostatic charges to apply the coating material. The tablets are given an electrical charge opposite to that of the coating particles. The coating particles are sprayed onto the tablets, and the electrostatic attraction ensures a uniform coating. This method is particularly useful for coating fine powders and achieving a high degree of uniformity with minimal coating material. Electrostatic coating is less common but offers advantages such as reduced solvent usage and improved coating efficiency.

**Compression Coating Machines**: Compression coating machines are used for applying coatings by compressing a coating layer around a pre-formed tablet core. The core tablet is placed in a die, and a mixture of excipients is compressed around it to form the coating layer. This method is particularly useful for creating layered tablets where different active ingredients need to be separated. Compression coating machines are capable of producing tablets with complex release profiles and protecting moisture-sensitive drugs. Examples of compression coating machines include the Manesty DryCota and the Kilian Coater.

**Spray Guns and Nozzles**: Spray guns and nozzles are critical components in many coating systems, including perforated pans and fluidized bed coaters. These devices atomize the coating solution and spray it onto the tablets in fine droplets, ensuring an even application. The design and configuration of spray guns and nozzles can significantly impact the quality of the coating. Factors such as spray pattern, droplet size, and spray rate are carefully controlled to achieve the desired coating properties.

**Drying Systems**: Efficient drying is essential in the tablet coating process to ensure the stability and quality of the coating. Drying systems, including heated air blowers and dehumidifiers, are integrated into coating equipment to provide consistent and controlled drying conditions. The choice of drying system depends on the type of coating and the specific requirements of the formulation.

**Automated Coating Systems**: Modern coating processes often employ automated systems that integrate various components, such as spray guns, drying systems, and control units. These systems offer precise control over process parameters, including spray rate, air temperature, and tablet rotation speed. Automation enhances the efficiency, consistency, and reproducibility of the coating process, reducing the need for manual intervention and minimizing the risk of errors.

### 2.4.6 Defects in Coating

Coating defects in tablets can compromise the quality, efficacy, and appearance of the final product. These defects arise from various factors such as improper formulation, equipment malfunction, or process parameter deviations. Understanding and identifying these defects is crucial for maintaining high standards in pharmaceutical manufacturing. The most common coating defects include **picking and sticking**, **orange peel effect**, **roughness**, **blistering**, **color variation**, **cracking**, **peeling and flaking**, and **mottling**.

**Picking and Sticking**: Picking occurs when parts of the coating stick to the equipment or other tablets, resulting in a patchy appearance. Sticking happens when tablets adhere to each other during the coating process. These issues are often caused by inadequate drying, excessive application of the coating solution, or high humidity levels. Adjusting the spray rate, air temperature, and humidity can help prevent picking and sticking.

**Orange Peel Effect**: The orange peel effect is characterized by a rough, textured surface on the tablet, resembling the skin of an orange. This defect usually results from improper atomization of the coating solution, leading to uneven droplet sizes. Factors such as incorrect spray nozzle settings, high solution viscosity, and low spray pressure can contribute to this defect. Ensuring proper atomization and optimizing process parameters can mitigate the orange peel effect.

**Roughness**: Roughness on the tablet surface is often due to the presence of undissolved particles in the coating solution or an uneven application. It can also occur if the coating solution dries too quickly, causing particles to aggregate. Proper filtration of the coating solution, maintaining appropriate spray rates, and ensuring uniform drying conditions can help achieve a smooth coating.

**Blistering**: Blistering appears as bubbles or blisters on the tablet surface, caused by trapped air or solvent within the coating layer. Rapid drying or excessive heat can lead to solvent evaporation, resulting in blisters. Controlling the drying rate, using appropriate solvents, and adjusting the air temperature can reduce the risk of blistering.

**Color Variation**: Inconsistent color across the tablet batch is a common defect resulting from uneven distribution of colorants in the coating solution or fluctuations in process parameters. Variations in spray rate, tablet movement, and drying conditions can all affect color uniformity. To achieve consistent color, it is essential to ensure thorough mixing of the coating solution and maintain stable process conditions.

**Cracking**: Cracking occurs when the coating film breaks or cracks, typically due to insufficient flexibility of the coating material. This can happen if the plasticizer concentration is too low or if the tablets are exposed to extreme environmental conditions. Adjusting the formulation to include adequate plasticizers and controlling the environmental conditions during storage can help prevent cracking.

**Peeling and Flaking**: Peeling and flaking involve the detachment of the coating layer from the tablet surface. This defect can result from poor adhesion between the coating and the tablet core, often due to inadequate surface preparation or incompatible coating materials. Ensuring proper cleaning of the tablet surface and selecting compatible coating materials can enhance adhesion and prevent peeling and flaking.

**Mottling**: Mottling is the uneven distribution of color, resulting in a speckled or blotchy appearance. This defect can occur due to variations in the concentration of colorants, improper mixing, or differences in drying rates. Using consistent and thoroughly mixed coating solutions, along with controlled drying processes, can help achieve a uniform appearance and minimize mottling.

To minimize coating defects, it is crucial to carefully control and monitor the coating process parameters, including **spray rate**, **air temperature**, **humidity**, and **tablet rotation speed**. Regular maintenance and calibration of coating equipment, as well as rigorous quality control measures, are essential to ensure consistent and high-quality coatings. Advances in coating technology and process optimization continue to improve the ability to prevent and address these defects, contributing to the production of high-quality pharmaceutical tablets.

## 2.5 Quality Control Tests

### 2.5.1 In-Process Tests

In-process quality control (IPQC) tests are critical in ensuring the quality, consistency, and safety of pharmaceutical products during the manufacturing process. These tests are conducted at various stages of production to monitor and control the manufacturing environment, materials, and processes. By identifying and addressing potential issues early, IPQC tests help maintain high standards and prevent costly post-production corrections. The primary in-process tests for tablet coating include **appearance, weight variation, thickness, hardness, disintegration**, and **dissolution**.

**Appearance**: Monitoring the appearance of tablets during the coating process is essential to ensure uniformity and aesthetics. Inspecting tablets for defects such as **color variation, mottling, cracking**, and **peeling** helps identify potential issues with the coating formulation or application parameters. Visual inspections are conducted at regular intervals, and any deviations from the expected appearance are promptly addressed.

**Weight Variation**: Weight variation tests ensure that each tablet receives the correct amount of coating material. Consistent weight is crucial for maintaining dosage accuracy and uniformity. Tablets are randomly sampled from the batch and weighed individually. The average weight is calculated, and individual weights are compared to the average. Acceptable limits for weight variation are defined, and any tablets outside these limits indicate potential issues with the coating process, such as uneven spraying or inadequate drying.

**Thickness**: The thickness of the coating layer affects the tablet's release profile, appearance, and mechanical properties. Measuring the coating thickness ensures uniform application and helps maintain the desired release characteristics. Thickness is measured using micrometers or other specialized equipment. Tablets are sampled at various stages of the coating process to monitor thickness and ensure it meets the specified range.

**Hardness**: The hardness of coated tablets is a critical parameter that affects their mechanical stability and handling. Hardness tests are conducted to ensure that the coating does not compromise the tablet's structural integrity. A hardness tester applies force to the tablet until it breaks, and the force required is recorded. Tablets should exhibit consistent hardness within defined limits, indicating proper coating application and adequate tablet core strength.

**Disintegration**: Disintegration tests measure the time it takes for coated tablets to break down into smaller particles when exposed to a specific medium, such as water or simulated gastric fluid. This test ensures that the coating does not excessively delay the release of the active ingredient unless designed for extended release. Tablets are placed in a disintegration apparatus, and the time taken for them to disintegrate completely is recorded. The results are compared to specified limits to ensure compliance.

**Dissolution**: Dissolution tests evaluate the rate and extent of the active ingredient's release from the coated tablet into a dissolution medium. This test is crucial for determining the bioavailability and therapeutic effectiveness of the drug. Tablets are placed in a dissolution apparatus, and samples of the dissolution medium are taken at specified intervals. The concentration of the active ingredient in the samples is measured using analytical techniques such as UV spectroscopy or high-performance liquid chromatography (HPLC). The dissolution profile is compared to the specified requirements to ensure the coating performs as intended.

**Uniformity of Dosage Units**: This test ensures that each tablet contains the correct amount of active ingredient, providing consistent therapeutic effects. Uniformity of dosage units is assessed by measuring the content of the active ingredient in individual tablets and comparing it to the average content. The results should fall within acceptable limits, indicating uniform distribution of the active ingredient and consistent coating application.

**Adhesion Testing**: Adhesion tests evaluate the strength of the bond between the coating layer and the tablet core. Poor adhesion can lead to peeling or flaking, compromising the tablet's quality and efficacy. Adhesion is tested by applying force to the coating layer and measuring the resistance to detachment. Consistent and strong adhesion indicates proper surface preparation and compatible coating materials.

**Friability**: Friability tests measure the tendency of coated tablets to break or crumble under mechanical stress. Tablets are subjected to a rotating drum or other mechanical devices that simulate handling and transportation conditions. The weight loss of the tablets is measured before and after the test. Acceptable friability limits ensure that the tablets can withstand mechanical stress without significant degradation.

By implementing these in-process tests, pharmaceutical manufacturers can ensure that coated tablets meet the required quality standards and specifications. Regular monitoring and control of the coating process help identify and address potential issues early, ensuring the production of high-quality, safe, and effective pharmaceutical products. Advances in analytical techniques and process control continue to enhance the precision and reliability of in-process quality control tests in tablet coating.

**2.5.2 Finished Product Tests**

Finished product tests are essential for ensuring that coated tablets meet the required quality standards and regulatory specifications before they are released into the market. These tests evaluate the final product's physical, chemical, and performance characteristics to ensure consistency, safety, and efficacy. The main finished product tests for coated tablets include **appearance and physical integrity**, **uniformity of dosage units**, **dissolution testing**, **disintegration testing**, **moisture content**, **assay of active ingredients**, **stability testing**, and **microbial contamination testing.**

**Appearance and Physical Integrity**: The appearance of the finished product is critically examined to ensure it meets the aesthetic standards and does not exhibit any defects such as **color variation**, **mottling**, **cracking**, **peeling**, or **roughness.** Tablets are visually inspected and compared against reference standards. Any deviations from the expected appearance are documented and investigated to determine their cause and prevent recurrence.

**Uniformity of Dosage Units**: This test ensures that each tablet contains the correct amount of active ingredient within specified limits, providing consistent therapeutic effects. The test involves sampling a number of tablets from the batch and measuring the content of the active ingredient in each tablet. The results are compared to the average content, and the variation should fall within acceptable limits, indicating uniform distribution of the active ingredient.

**Dissolution Testing**: Dissolution testing is crucial for evaluating the rate and extent of the active ingredient's release from the coated tablet into a dissolution medium. This test determines the bioavailability and therapeutic effectiveness of the drug. Tablets are placed in a dissolution apparatus, and samples of the dissolution medium are taken at specified intervals. The concentration of the active ingredient in the samples is measured using analytical techniques such as **UV spectroscopy** or **high-performance liquid chromatography (HPLC)**. The dissolution profile is compared to the specified requirements to ensure the coating performs as intended.

**Disintegration Testing**: Disintegration testing measures the time it takes for coated tablets to break down into smaller particles when exposed to a specific medium, such as water or simulated gastric fluid. This test ensures that the coating does not excessively delay the release of the active ingredient unless designed for extended release. Tablets are placed in a disintegration apparatus, and the time taken for them to disintegrate completely is recorded. The results are compared to specified limits to ensure compliance.

**Moisture Content**: The moisture content of coated tablets is measured to ensure they are within acceptable limits. Excess moisture can affect the stability and performance of the tablets, while insufficient moisture can lead to brittleness and cracking. Moisture content is typically measured using techniques such as **Karl Fischer titration** or **loss on drying (LOD)**. Maintaining optimal moisture levels is crucial for ensuring the quality and longevity of the tablets.

**Assay of Active Ingredients**: The assay test measures the exact amount of active ingredient present in the finished product. This test ensures that the tablets contain the correct dosage as specified on the label. Analytical techniques such as **HPLC**, **gas chromatography (GC)**, or **UV spectroscopy** are used to quantify the active ingredient. The results are compared to the specified limits to ensure the tablets meet the required potency standards.

**Stability Testing**: Stability testing evaluates the ability of the coated tablets to maintain their quality, safety, and efficacy over time under various environmental conditions, such as temperature, humidity, and light. Tablets are stored under controlled conditions and sampled at predetermined intervals to assess their physical, chemical, and microbiological stability. Stability testing helps establish the shelf life and storage conditions for the product. This includes **accelerated stability testing**, where tablets are stored at elevated temperatures and humidity levels to predict their long-term stability.

**Microbial Contamination Testing**: Microbial contamination testing ensures that the finished product is free from harmful microorganisms that could compromise patient safety. This test involves sampling the tablets and testing for the presence of bacteria, fungi, and other microorganisms. Techniques such as **plate counting**, **membrane filtration**, and **rapid microbiological methods (RMM)** are used to detect and quantify microbial contamination. Ensuring microbial purity is critical for the safety and efficacy of the tablets.

By conducting these comprehensive finished product tests, pharmaceutical manufacturers can ensure that coated tablets meet the highest quality standards and regulatory requirements. These tests help verify the consistency, safety, and efficacy of the final product, ensuring that patients receive effective and reliable medications. Advances in analytical techniques and quality control processes continue to enhance the precision and reliability of finished product testing in the pharmaceutical industry.

# THREE

# LIQUID ORALS

## 3.1 Formulation and Manufacturing Considerations

### 3.1.1 Syrups

**Introduction to Syrups**

Syrups are one of the most common forms of liquid oral dosage forms in pharmaceuticals. They are concentrated aqueous preparations containing sugar or sugar substitutes, designed to improve the taste and palatability of medicinal substances. Syrups can be classified into medicated syrups, which contain therapeutic agents, and non-medicated syrups, used as vehicles in compounding.

**Formulation Considerations**

The formulation of syrups involves careful consideration of several factors to ensure stability, efficacy, and patient acceptability. The primary components of a syrup include the active ingredient, sweeteners, viscosity agents, preservatives, flavoring agents, and sometimes colorants.

**Active Ingredient**: The active ingredient in a syrup is the therapeutic agent intended to exert the desired medicinal effect. The concentration of the active ingredient must be precisely controlled to ensure accurate dosing. The solubility of the active ingredient in water is a critical consideration, as it affects the stability and homogeneity of the syrup. If the active ingredient is not sufficiently soluble in water, solubilizing agents or cosolvents may be required.

**Sweeteners**: Sweeteners are essential in syrups to mask the bitter or unpleasant taste of the active ingredients. Common sweeteners include sucrose, glucose, fructose, and artificial sweeteners like saccharin and aspartame. Sucrose is the most widely used sweetener due to its pleasant taste and ability to increase the viscosity of the syrup, which can help in masking the taste of the active ingredient. The concentration of sucrose in syrups typically ranges from 60% to 85% (w/v) to ensure proper sweetness and viscosity.

**Viscosity Agents**: Viscosity agents are added to syrups to enhance their consistency and mouthfeel, making them more palatable and easier to administer. These agents also help to stabilize the syrup by preventing the sedimentation of suspended particles. Common viscosity agents include glycerin, sorbitol, and propylene glycol. The concentration of these agents varies depending on the desired viscosity and stability of the syrup.

**Preservatives**: Preservatives are critical in syrups to prevent microbial growth and extend the shelf life of the product. The high sugar content in syrups can support microbial growth, making preservatives essential. Common preservatives include benzoic acid, sodium benzoate, methylparaben, and propylparaben. The concentration of preservatives must be carefully controlled to ensure efficacy without compromising the safety of the syrup.

**Flavoring Agents**: Flavoring agents are added to syrups to improve their taste and enhance patient compliance. These agents can be natural or synthetic and are selected based on the target patient population. For example, fruit flavors like cherry, orange, and grape are commonly used in pediatric syrups. The concentration of flavoring agents should be optimized to ensure a pleasant taste without overpowering the other components.

**Colorants**: Colorants are used in syrups to improve their appearance and make them more appealing to patients. They also help in product identification and differentiation. Common colorants include synthetic dyes and natural pigments. The use of colorants must comply with regulatory guidelines to ensure safety.

**Manufacturing Considerations**

The manufacturing process of syrups involves several critical steps to ensure the quality and consistency of the final product. These steps include the preparation of the syrup base, incorporation of the active ingredient, and quality control testing.

**Preparation of the Syrup Base**: The syrup base is typically prepared by dissolving the sweeteners and viscosity agents in water with the application of heat. The solution is heated to facilitate the dissolution of the components and to achieve the desired concentration. Once dissolved, the solution is cooled to room temperature.

**Incorporation of the Active Ingredient**: The active ingredient is then incorporated into the syrup base. This step requires careful mixing to ensure uniform distribution of the active ingredient. If the active ingredient is not soluble in water, it may be pre-dissolved in a suitable solvent or dispersed using a suspending agent.

**Addition of Other Components**: After the active ingredient is incorporated, preservatives, flavoring agents, and colorants are added to the syrup. Each component must be added in the correct order and quantity to ensure the stability and efficacy of the final product.

**Quality Control Testing**: Quality control tests are conducted at various stages of the manufacturing process to ensure the consistency, stability, and safety of the syrup. These tests include pH measurement, viscosity testing, microbial testing, and assay of the active ingredient. The final product is also tested for appearance, taste, and odor to ensure it meets the desired specifications.

**Packaging and Storage**: Once the syrup is prepared and tested, it is filled into suitable containers, such as glass or plastic bottles, and sealed. The containers are labeled with the necessary information, including the name of the product, active ingredient concentration, dosage instructions, and expiration date. Proper storage conditions, such as temperature and humidity control, are essential to maintain the stability and shelf life of the syrup.

In conclusion, the formulation and manufacturing of syrups require careful consideration of various factors to ensure the quality, efficacy, and patient acceptability of the final product. Advances in pharmaceutical technology continue to enhance the formulation and production processes, providing improved therapeutic options for patients.

### 3.1.2 Elixirs

#### Introduction to Elixirs

Elixirs are clear, sweetened, hydroalcoholic liquids intended for oral use, containing active ingredients dissolved in a suitable solvent system. They are popular in pharmaceutical formulations due to their ability to solubilize both water-soluble and alcohol-soluble drugs, making them versatile and effective in delivering various therapeutic agents. Elixirs are typically used when the drug's solubility or stability is an issue in purely aqueous systems.

#### Formulation Considerations

The formulation of elixirs involves several key components: the active ingredient, solvent system, sweeteners, flavoring agents, colorants, and preservatives. Each component plays a crucial role in ensuring the stability, efficacy, and palatability of the final product.

**Active Ingredient**: The active ingredient in an elixir is the therapeutic agent intended to provide the desired medicinal effect. The concentration of the active ingredient must be carefully controlled to ensure accurate dosing. The solubility of the active ingredient in the chosen solvent system is a critical factor in formulation development. Elixirs are particularly useful for drugs that require a hydroalcoholic medium for optimal solubility.

**Solvent System**: The solvent system in an elixir typically consists of a combination of water and alcohol. The alcohol content can vary widely, usually ranging from 5% to 40%, depending on the solubility requirements of the active ingredient and other formulation considerations. Alcohol acts as a solvent, preservative, and taste enhancer. However, the alcohol concentration must be balanced to avoid adverse effects, especially in pediatric formulations.

**Sweeteners**: Sweeteners are added to elixirs to improve their taste and make them more palatable. Common sweeteners include sucrose, sorbitol, glycerin, and artificial sweeteners like saccharin and aspartame. Sucrose is often preferred for its pleasant taste and ability to increase viscosity. The concentration of sweeteners must be optimized to ensure the elixir is sufficiently sweet without becoming too viscous or sticky.

**Flavoring Agents**: Flavoring agents are incorporated into elixirs to enhance their taste and patient acceptability. Natural and synthetic flavors are used based on the target patient population and the nature of the active ingredient. Common flavors include fruit flavors such as orange, lemon, cherry, and mint. The concentration of flavoring agents is adjusted to mask any unpleasant taste of the active ingredient without overpowering the overall flavor profile.

**Colorants**: Colorants are used to improve the appearance of elixirs, making them more visually appealing to patients. They also help in product identification and differentiation. Both synthetic dyes and natural pigments can be used, provided they comply with regulatory guidelines. The choice of colorant must consider stability, safety, and compatibility with other components of the elixir.

**Preservatives**: Preservatives are essential in elixirs to prevent microbial growth and extend shelf life. The combination of water and alcohol provides some antimicrobial activity, but additional preservatives may be necessary to ensure complete protection. Common preservatives include benzoic acid, sodium benzoate, methylparaben, and propylparaben. The concentration of preservatives is carefully controlled to ensure efficacy without compromising safety.

**Manufacturing Considerations**

The manufacturing process of elixirs involves several critical steps to ensure the quality and consistency of the final product. These steps include preparation of the solvent system, dissolution of the active ingredient, incorporation of other components, and quality control testing.

**Preparation of the Solvent System**: The solvent system, typically a mixture of water and alcohol, is prepared first. The required amount of alcohol is measured and mixed with water. The mixture is stirred to ensure homogeneity. If necessary, the solvent system is heated gently to facilitate the dissolution of subsequent components.

**Dissolution of the Active Ingredient**: The active ingredient is then dissolved in the prepared solvent system. This step requires thorough mixing to ensure complete dissolution and uniform distribution of the active ingredient. Depending on the solubility characteristics, the active ingredient may be dissolved in alcohol first before mixing with water to ensure complete solubilization.

**Addition of Other Components**: After the active ingredient is dissolved, sweeteners, flavoring agents, colorants, and preservatives are added to the solution. Each component must be added in the correct order and quantity to ensure the stability and efficacy of the final product. The mixture is stirred continuously to ensure even distribution and homogeneity.

**Quality Control Testing**: Quality control tests are conducted at various stages of the manufacturing process to ensure the consistency, stability, and safety of the elixir. These tests include pH measurement, viscosity testing, specific gravity determination, microbial testing, and assay of the active ingredient. The final product is also tested for appearance, taste, and odor to ensure it meets the desired specifications.

**Packaging and Storage**: Once the elixir is prepared and tested, it is filled into suitable containers, such as glass or plastic bottles, and sealed. The containers are labeled with the necessary information, including the name of the product, active ingredient concentration, dosage instructions, and expiration date. Proper storage conditions, such as temperature control, are essential to maintain the stability and shelf life of the elixir.

**3.1.3 Suspensions**

**Introduction to Suspensions**

Suspensions are a type of liquid dosage form where solid particles are dispersed throughout a liquid medium. Unlike solutions, the active ingredient in a suspension is not dissolved but suspended in the liquid, providing a means to deliver poorly soluble drugs in a palatable and stable form. Suspensions are particularly useful for pediatric and geriatric patients who may have difficulty swallowing tablets or capsules.

**Formulation Considerations**

Formulating a suspension involves several key components: the active ingredient, suspending agents, wetting agents, preservatives, flavoring agents, sweeteners, and colorants. Each component plays a critical role in ensuring the stability, efficacy, and acceptability of the final product.

**Active Ingredient**: The active ingredient in a suspension is the therapeutic agent intended to provide the desired medicinal effect. The particle size of the active ingredient is a crucial factor, as smaller particles tend to remain suspended longer and provide a more uniform dose. Micronization or milling techniques are often used to achieve the desired particle size.

**Suspending Agents**: Suspending agents are essential to maintain the uniform distribution of solid particles in the liquid medium. They increase the viscosity of the suspension, preventing the particles from settling too quickly. Common suspending agents include **methylcellulose**, **carboxymethylcellulose (CMC)**, **xanthan gum**, **tragacanth**, and **bentonite**. The concentration of suspending agents typically ranges from 0.5% to 5% (w/v) depending on the required viscosity.

**Wetting Agents**: Wetting agents are used to reduce the surface tension between the solid particles and the liquid medium, facilitating the dispersion of particles. Wetting agents such as **polysorbates (e.g., Tween 80)** and **sodium lauryl sulfate** are commonly used. They help prevent the formation of clumps and ensure a homogeneous suspension.

**Preservatives**: Preservatives are critical in suspensions to prevent microbial growth and extend the shelf life of the product. The aqueous nature of suspensions makes them susceptible to contamination. Common preservatives include **benzoic acid**, **sodium benzoate**, **methylparaben**, and **propylparaben**. The concentration of preservatives must be carefully controlled to ensure efficacy without compromising safety.

**Flavoring Agents**: Flavoring agents are added to suspensions to improve their taste and enhance patient compliance. Natural and synthetic flavors are used based on the target patient population and the nature of the active ingredient. Common flavors include fruit flavors such as **orange**, **lemon**, **cherry**, and **grape**. The concentration of flavoring agents is adjusted to mask any unpleasant taste of the active ingredient.

**Sweeteners**: Sweeteners are incorporated into suspensions to improve their palatability. Common sweeteners include **sucrose**, **sorbitol**, **glycerin**, and artificial sweeteners like **saccharin** and **aspartame**. Sucrose is often preferred for its pleasant taste and ability to increase viscosity. The concentration of sweeteners must be optimized to ensure the suspension is sufficiently sweet without becoming too viscous or sticky.

**Colorants**: Colorants are used to improve the appearance of suspensions, making them more visually appealing to patients. They also help in product identification and differentiation. Both synthetic dyes and natural pigments can be used, provided they comply with regulatory guidelines. The choice of colorant must consider stability, safety, and compatibility with other components of the suspension.

**Manufacturing Considerations**

The manufacturing process of suspensions involves several critical steps to ensure the quality and consistency of the final product. These steps include the preparation of the dispersion medium, incorporation of the active ingredient, homogenization, and quality control testing.

**Preparation of the Dispersion Medium**: The dispersion medium, typically an aqueous solution, is prepared by dissolving the suspending agents, wetting agents, sweeteners, preservatives, and flavoring agents in water. The solution is heated gently, if necessary, to facilitate the dissolution of these components. Once dissolved, the solution is cooled to room temperature.

**Incorporation of the Active Ingredient**: The active ingredient is then dispersed in the prepared dispersion medium. This step requires thorough mixing to ensure uniform distribution of the solid particles. The active ingredient may be pre-wetted with a small amount of wetting agent to ensure proper dispersion. High-shear mixers or homogenizers are often used to achieve a fine and uniform suspension.

**Homogenization**: Homogenization is a crucial step in the manufacturing of suspensions. It involves the application of mechanical force to break down agglomerates and ensure uniform particle size distribution. Homogenizers apply high pressure to the suspension, reducing particle size and improving stability. This process helps achieve a smooth and consistent suspension with improved bioavailability.

**Quality Control Testing**: Quality control tests are conducted at various stages of the manufacturing process to ensure the consistency, stability, and safety of the suspension. These tests include **particle size analysis, sedimentation rate, viscosity measurement, pH testing, microbial testing**, and **assay of the active ingredient**. The final product is also tested for appearance, taste, and odor to ensure it meets the desired specifications.

**Packaging and Storage**: Once the suspension is prepared and tested, it is filled into suitable containers, such as glass or plastic bottles, and sealed. The containers are labeled with the necessary information, including the name of the product, active ingredient concentration, dosage instructions, and expiration date. Proper storage conditions, such as temperature control, are essential to maintain the stability and shelf life of the suspension. Suspensions should be stored in a cool, dry place, and shaking the bottle before use is usually recommended to ensure uniform distribution of the active ingredient.

### 3.1.4 Emulsions

#### Introduction to Emulsions

Emulsions are biphasic liquid dosage forms consisting of two immiscible liquids, typically oil and water, with one liquid dispersed in the other in the form of small droplets. Emulsions are stabilized by emulsifying agents that prevent the separation of the two phases. They are commonly used in pharmaceutical formulations to deliver drugs that are poorly soluble in water, improve bioavailability, and enhance the palatability of the medication.

#### Formulation Considerations

The formulation of emulsions involves several key components: the dispersed phase, the continuous phase, emulsifying agents, stabilizers, preservatives, flavoring agents, and colorants. Each component plays a crucial role in ensuring the stability, efficacy, and acceptability of the final product.

**Dispersed Phase**: The dispersed phase (internal phase) is the liquid that is present in the form of small droplets. It can be either oil-in-water (O/W) where oil droplets are dispersed in water, or water-in-oil (W/O) where water droplets are dispersed in oil. The choice of the dispersed phase depends on the solubility of the drug and the desired therapeutic effect.

**Continuous Phase**: The continuous phase (external phase) is the liquid in which the dispersed phase is distributed. For O/W emulsions, water acts as the continuous phase, while for W/O emulsions, oil acts as the continuous phase. The continuous phase affects the texture, stability, and application of the emulsion.

**Emulsifying Agents**: Emulsifying agents are critical to the stability of emulsions. They reduce the surface tension between the oil and water phases, preventing the coalescence of droplets. Emulsifying agents can be classified into natural, synthetic, and finely divided solids. Common emulsifiers include **lecithin, polysorbates (e.g., Tween 80), spans (e.g., Span 80), sodium lauryl sulfate**, and **acacia**. The concentration of emulsifying agents typically ranges from 0.5% to 5% (w/v) depending on the required stability.

**Stabilizers**: Stabilizers are added to emulsions to enhance their physical stability by preventing phase separation and improving viscosity. Common stabilizers include **gums (e.g., xanthan gum, acacia gum)**, **cellulose derivatives (e.g., carboxymethylcellulose)**, and **polymers (e.g., polyvinyl alcohol)**. The concentration of stabilizers varies depending on the desired viscosity and stability of the emulsion.

**Preservatives**: Preservatives are essential in emulsions to prevent microbial growth and extend shelf life. The presence of water in emulsions makes them susceptible to contamination. Common preservatives include **methylparaben**, **propylparaben**, **benzoic acid**, and **sodium benzoate**. The concentration of preservatives must be carefully controlled to ensure efficacy without compromising safety.

**Flavoring Agents**: Flavoring agents are added to emulsions to improve their taste and enhance patient compliance. Natural and synthetic flavors are used based on the target patient population and the nature of the active ingredient. Common flavors include fruit flavors such as **orange**, **lemon**, **cherry**, and **mint**. The concentration of flavoring agents is adjusted to mask any unpleasant taste of the active ingredient without overpowering the overall flavor profile.

**Colorants**: Colorants are used to improve the appearance of emulsions, making them more visually appealing to patients. They also help in product identification and differentiation. Both synthetic dyes and natural pigments can be used, provided they comply with regulatory guidelines. The choice of colorant must consider stability, safety, and compatibility with other components of the emulsion.

**Manufacturing Considerations**

The manufacturing process of emulsions involves several critical steps to ensure the quality and consistency of the final product. These steps include the preparation of the oil and water phases, emulsification, homogenization, and quality control testing.

**Preparation of the Oil and Water Phases**: The oil and water phases are prepared separately by dissolving or dispersing the respective components, such as the active ingredient, emulsifying agents, stabilizers, and preservatives, in the appropriate phase. The phases are typically heated gently to facilitate dissolution and mixing.

**Emulsification**: The emulsification process involves mixing the oil and water phases together to form the emulsion. This is typically done by slowly adding the dispersed phase to the continuous phase with constant stirring. The mixing process can be carried out using high-shear mixers, blenders, or colloid mills to ensure the formation of small, uniform droplets.

**Homogenization**: Homogenization is a crucial step in the manufacturing of emulsions. It involves applying mechanical force to break down large droplets into smaller, uniform droplets, enhancing the stability and bioavailability of the emulsion. High-pressure homogenizers or ultrasonic homogenizers are commonly used for this purpose. The homogenization process helps achieve a smooth and consistent emulsion with improved stability.

**Quality Control Testing**: Quality control tests are conducted at various stages of the manufacturing process to ensure the consistency, stability, and safety of the emulsion. These tests include **particle size analysis**, **zeta potential measurement**, **viscosity testing**, **pH testing**, **microbial testing**, and **assay of the active ingredient**. The final product is also tested for appearance, taste, and odor to ensure it meets the desired specifications.

**Packaging and Storage**: Once the emulsion is prepared and tested, it is filled into suitable containers, such as glass or plastic bottles, and sealed. The containers are labeled with the necessary information, including the name of the product, active ingredient concentration, dosage instructions, and expiration date. Proper storage conditions, such as temperature control, are essential to maintain the stability and shelf life of the emulsion. Emulsions should be stored in a cool, dry place, and shaking the bottle before use is usually recommended to ensure uniform distribution of the active ingredient.

### 3.1.5 Filling and Packaging

#### Introduction to Filling and Packaging

Filling and packaging are crucial steps in the production of liquid oral formulations such as syrups, elixirs, suspensions, and emulsions. These processes ensure that the final product is accurately measured, securely contained, and appropriately labeled for safe and effective use by patients. Proper filling and packaging techniques help maintain the stability, efficacy, and quality of the pharmaceutical products throughout their shelf life.

**Filling Process**

The filling process involves transferring the prepared liquid formulation into suitable containers. This step must be carried out with precision to ensure consistent dosing and to prevent contamination or degradation of the product. The filling process can be broadly categorized into **manual filling, semi-automatic filling**, and **automatic filling**.

**Manual Filling**: Manual filling is typically used for small-scale production or in situations where the volume of production is low. This method involves using manual pumps, syringes, or pipettes to transfer the liquid formulation into containers. While this process is simple and cost-effective, it is labor-intensive and may lead to variability in fill volumes.

**Semi-Automatic Filling**: Semi-automatic filling machines combine manual and automated processes. Operators manually place the containers on the filling line, and the machine dispenses the liquid formulation into the containers with high accuracy. Semi-automatic machines are suitable for medium-scale production, offering improved efficiency and consistency compared to manual filling.

**Automatic Filling**: Automatic filling machines are used for large-scale production, providing high-speed, precision filling of liquid formulations. These machines are equipped with multiple filling heads, conveyors, and automated systems to handle large batches of products. Automatic filling ensures consistent fill volumes, minimizes the risk of contamination, and enhances overall production efficiency. Common types of automatic filling machines include **piston fillers, peristaltic fillers**, and **overflow fillers.**

**Filling Equipment**

The choice of filling equipment depends on the type of liquid formulation, the required fill volume, and the production scale. Key factors to consider include the viscosity of the liquid, the desired filling speed, and the accuracy of fill volumes. Some commonly used filling equipment includes:

- **Piston Fillers**: Ideal for viscous liquids such as syrups and suspensions. Piston fillers use a piston mechanism to draw and dispense the liquid into containers with high precision.

- **Peristaltic Fillers**: Suitable for sterile and sensitive formulations. Peristaltic fillers use a peristaltic pump mechanism that ensures gentle handling of the liquid, minimizing contamination risk.
- **Overflow Fillers**: Used for free-flowing liquids such as elixirs and emulsions. Overflow fillers ensure uniform fill levels by allowing excess liquid to overflow and recirculate.

**Packaging Process**

Packaging is the process of enclosing and protecting the filled containers to ensure product stability, safety, and compliance with regulatory requirements. The packaging process involves several key steps, including **container selection**, **capping and sealing**, **labeling**, and **secondary packaging**.

**Container Selection**: The choice of container is crucial for maintaining the stability and integrity of the liquid formulation. Common container materials include glass and plastic, each offering specific advantages. **Glass containers** are impermeable, chemically inert, and provide excellent protection against light and moisture. They are often used for sensitive formulations. **Plastic containers** are lightweight, shatterproof, and cost-effective, making them suitable for a wide range of liquid formulations. The container design, such as bottles, vials, or jars, depends on the product's intended use and dosage form.

**Capping and Sealing**: Capping and sealing ensure the container is securely closed, preventing contamination and leakage. Various types of caps and seals are used, including **screw caps**, **snap-on caps**, **child-resistant caps**, and **tamper-evident seals**. The choice of cap and seal depends on the container type and the specific requirements of the formulation. Automated capping machines are commonly used to enhance efficiency and ensure consistent sealing.

**Labeling**: Labeling is a critical step in the packaging process, providing essential information about the product, such as the name, active ingredient concentration, dosage instructions, batch number, expiration date, and regulatory compliance. Labels must be clear, accurate, and durable to withstand storage and handling conditions. Automated labeling machines ensure precise placement and adhesion of labels on containers, enhancing efficiency and consistency.

**Secondary Packaging**: Secondary packaging involves enclosing the primary packaged product in additional packaging materials for added protection, ease of handling, and branding. Common secondary packaging includes **cartons**, **boxes**, and **shrink wrap**. This step helps prevent damage during transportation and storage and provides space for additional information such as patient leaflets and marketing materials.

**Quality Control in Filling and Packaging**

Quality control measures are essential throughout the filling and packaging processes to ensure the final product meets the required standards. Key quality control tests include:

- **Fill Volume Verification**: Ensures each container receives the correct amount of liquid formulation.
- **Leak Testing**: Detects any leaks in the containers or seals to ensure product integrity.
- **Label Accuracy**: Verifies that labels are correctly printed and applied, containing all necessary information.
- **Seal Integrity Testing**: Ensures that caps and seals are properly applied and secure.
- **Visual Inspection**: Checks for any defects or inconsistencies in the filled and packaged product.

## 3.2 Evaluation of Liquid Orals

### 3.2.1 Official Methods in Pharmacopoeia

Pharmacopoeias are official publications containing a list of medicinal drugs, their descriptions, and the standards required for their quality, purity, and strength. They provide standardized methods for the evaluation of liquid oral formulations to ensure consistency, safety, and efficacy. The primary pharmacopoeias include the **United States Pharmacopoeia (USP)**, **British Pharmacopoeia (BP)**, **European Pharmacopoeia (Ph. Eur.)**, and **Indian Pharmacopoeia (IP)**. These publications outline various tests and criteria for evaluating liquid oral formulations such as syrups, elixirs, suspensions, and emulsions. The key evaluation parameters include **appearance**, **identification tests**, **pH determination**, **assay of active ingredients**, **microbial limit tests**, **preservative content**, **viscosity**, **specific gravity**, and **stability studies**.

**Appearance**: The appearance of liquid orals is evaluated to ensure they meet the visual standards specified in the pharmacopoeia. This includes checking for clarity, color, and the presence of any particulate matter. For example, syrups and elixirs should be clear and free from turbidity or sediment, while suspensions and emulsions should exhibit uniform dispersion without phase separation.

**Identification Tests**: These tests confirm the presence of the active ingredient(s) in the liquid oral formulation. Techniques such as **thin-layer chromatography (TLC)**, **high-performance liquid chromatography (HPLC)**, **infrared spectroscopy (IR)**, and **UV-visible spectroscopy** are commonly used. The results are compared to reference standards specified in the pharmacopoeia to ensure the correct active ingredient is present.

**pH Determination**: The pH of liquid oral formulations is measured to ensure it falls within the specified range for stability and patient acceptability. pH meters are used to determine the pH, and the values are compared with the pharmacopoeial standards. Maintaining the correct pH is crucial for the stability of the active ingredient and the overall formulation.

**Assay of Active Ingredients**: The assay measures the concentration of active ingredients in the liquid oral formulation to ensure it meets the specified limits. Analytical methods such as **HPLC**, **gas chromatography (GC)**, and **titration** are used. The results must fall within the acceptable range defined by the pharmacopoeia to ensure the formulation contains the correct amount of the active ingredient.

**Microbial Limit Tests**: These tests evaluate the microbial quality of liquid oral formulations to ensure they are free from harmful microorganisms. The pharmacopoeia specifies acceptable limits for total aerobic microbial count, total yeast and mold count, and the absence of specific pathogens such as **Escherichia coli**, **Staphylococcus aureus**, **Pseudomonas aeruginosa**, and **Salmonella spp.** Techniques such as **plate count methods**, **membrane filtration**, and **rapid microbiological methods** are used to assess microbial contamination.

**Preservative Content**: Preservatives are added to liquid oral formulations to prevent microbial growth. The content of preservatives must be within the specified range to ensure effectiveness without compromising safety. Methods such as **HPLC** and **spectrophotometry** are used to quantify preservative levels, and the results are compared to the pharmacopoeial standards.

**Viscosity**: The viscosity of liquid oral formulations is measured to ensure consistency and ease of administration. Viscosity affects the flow properties and stability of the formulation. Instruments such as **viscometers** and **rheometers** are used to measure viscosity, and the values are compared to the specified range in the pharmacopoeia.

**Specific Gravity**: Specific gravity is the ratio of the density of the liquid formulation to the density of water. It is measured to ensure the formulation's consistency and concentration. Specific gravity is determined using **pycnometers** or **digital density meters**, and the results are compared to the pharmacopoeial standards.

**Stability Studies**: Stability studies are conducted to evaluate the shelf life of liquid oral formulations under various environmental conditions such as temperature, humidity, and light. These studies ensure the formulation remains stable and effective throughout its intended shelf life. The pharmacopoeia provides guidelines for conducting stability studies, including the duration and conditions for testing. The results of stability studies help establish the expiration date and storage conditions for the product.

# FOUR

# CAPSULES

## 4.1 Hard Gelatin Capsules

### 4.1.1 Introduction and Production

**Introduction to Hard Gelatin Capsules**

Hard gelatin capsules are one of the most popular dosage forms for oral drug delivery. They consist of two parts: a body and a cap, which fit together to enclose the drug substance. These capsules are typically made from gelatin, a protein derived from the hydrolysis of collagen obtained from animal skin, bones, and connective tissues. Hard gelatin capsules are preferred for their ability to encapsulate a wide range of substances, including powders, granules, pellets, and even non-aqueous liquids. They offer advantages such as ease of swallowing, flexibility in formulation, and the ability to mask unpleasant tastes and odors of the drug substance.

**Advantages of Hard Gelatin Capsules**

1. **Versatility**: Hard gelatin capsules can encapsulate various forms of medication, including powders, granules, pellets, and non-aqueous liquids.
2. **Patient Compliance**: Capsules are generally easier to swallow than tablets and can effectively mask the taste and odor of the medication.
3. **Customization**: They can be manufactured in different sizes and colors, allowing for product differentiation and branding.
4. **Bioavailability**: Capsules dissolve quickly in the stomach, leading to rapid drug release and absorption.

**Production of Hard Gelatin Capsules**

The production of hard gelatin capsules involves several key steps, including the preparation of gelatin solution, formation of capsule shells, filling, and sealing. The process is highly automated to ensure precision, consistency, and hygiene.

**1. Preparation of Gelatin Solution**

The first step in capsule production is preparing a gelatin solution. Gelatin is derived from animal collagen through hydrolysis and is available in the form of granules or sheets. The gelatin is dissolved in hot water (typically at 60-70°C) to form a homogeneous solution. Plasticizers such as glycerin or sorbitol are added to the gelatin solution to provide flexibility and reduce brittleness of the capsule shells. The solution may also include preservatives, colorants, and opacifiers to achieve the desired appearance and stability of the capsules.

**2. Formation of Capsule Shells**

The formation of capsule shells involves a process known as **dipping**. Stainless steel pins or molds, corresponding to the size of the capsule, are dipped into the gelatin solution. The pins are then rotated to ensure even coating and remove excess gelatin. The coated pins are moved through a series of drying ovens where warm air removes moisture from the gelatin, allowing it to solidify and form a thin, uniform film. Once dried, the gelatin films are stripped off the pins and cut to form the body and cap of the capsules.

**3. Joining and Trimming**

After the gelatin films are formed and cut, the body and cap are joined together temporarily. The capsule halves are aligned and trimmed to ensure they fit together precisely. This step is crucial for maintaining the integrity and uniformity of the capsules.

**4. Filling**

The filling of hard gelatin capsules can be done using various techniques depending on the nature of the drug substance. The most common filling methods include:

- **Powder Filling**: Powders are filled into the capsule body using volumetric or dosator machines, which accurately measure and dispense the powder.
- **Pellet and Granule Filling**: Pellets or granules are filled using similar techniques to powder filling but may require specialized equipment to handle different particle sizes and shapes.

- **Liquid Filling**: Non-aqueous liquids can be filled into capsules using precision liquid filling machines. These machines ensure accurate dosing and prevent leakage.

**5. Sealing**

Once the capsules are filled, the cap is placed over the body, and the two parts are sealed. Sealing can be done using various methods, such as banding (applying a gelatin or polymer band around the joint), heat welding, or using a small amount of water to slightly moisten the cap and body, which then bond together upon drying.

**6. Polishing and Inspection**

The filled and sealed capsules are polished to remove any adhering powder or residues. This step enhances the appearance of the capsules and ensures they are clean and free from contaminants. The capsules undergo rigorous inspection to check for defects such as cracks, deformation, or improper sealing. Automated systems and manual inspections are used to ensure only high-quality capsules proceed to packaging.

**7. Packaging and Storage**

The final step in the production of hard gelatin capsules is packaging. Capsules are counted and filled into suitable containers, such as bottles or blister packs, and sealed. The containers are labeled with the necessary information, including the name of the product, dosage instructions, batch number, and expiration date. Proper storage conditions, such as controlled temperature and humidity, are essential to maintain the stability and shelf life of the capsules.

### 4.1.2 Size of Capsules

**Introduction to Capsule Sizes**

Hard gelatin capsules are available in various sizes to accommodate different dosages and formulations. The size of a capsule is an important consideration in the formulation process as it affects the dosage, ease of swallowing, and overall patient compliance. Capsule sizes are standardized and range from the smallest, size 5, to the largest, size 000. Each size corresponds to a specific volume and weight capacity, which must be matched to the dosage form being encapsulated.

**Standard Capsule Sizes**

The following table outlines the most common capsule sizes along with their approximate volume capacities:

| Capsule Size | Volume Capacity (ml) | Approximate Fill Weight (mg) |
|---|---|---|
| 000 | 1.37 | 950 - 1350 |
| 00 | 0.95 | 650 - 950 |
| 0 | 0.68 | 450 - 680 |
| 1 | 0.50 | 300 - 600 |
| 2 | 0.37 | 250 - 450 |
| 3 | 0.30 | 200 - 300 |
| 4 | 0.21 | 150 - 200 |
| 5 | 0.13 | 100 - 130 |

**Factors Influencing Capsule Size Selection**

**1. Dosage Requirements**: The primary factor influencing capsule size selection is the dosage of the active ingredient. Higher doses typically require larger capsules to accommodate the required volume of the formulation. For low-dose medications, smaller capsules may be sufficient.

**2. Formulation Characteristics**: The physical properties of the formulation, such as bulk density, particle size, and flowability, play a significant role in determining the appropriate capsule size. Powders with low bulk density require larger capsules to achieve the same weight as powders with higher bulk density.

**3. Patient Compliance**: Capsule size affects the ease of swallowing and overall patient compliance. Smaller capsules are generally easier to swallow and are preferred for pediatric and geriatric patients. However, the size must still be large enough to contain the required dose.

**4. Manufacturing Considerations**: The choice of capsule size can impact the manufacturing process, including the equipment used for filling and the efficiency of production. Standardizing capsule sizes within a product line can streamline manufacturing and reduce costs.

**5. Regulatory Requirements**: Regulatory guidelines and pharmacopeial standards may specify certain capsule sizes for specific drugs or dosage forms. Compliance with these regulations is essential to ensure product approval and marketability.

**Filling Capacity and Capsule Size**

The filling capacity of a capsule depends on the size and the density of the material being encapsulated. For instance, a size 0 capsule has a volume capacity of approximately 0.68 ml, which can hold around 450 to 680 mg of a material with average bulk density. Adjusting the density and particle size of the formulation can optimize the fill weight and ensure consistent dosing.

**Special Capsule Sizes and Customization**

In addition to the standard sizes, capsules can be customized to meet specific formulation needs. Custom sizes may be required for unique dosages, specialized formulations, or to differentiate products in the market. Capsule manufacturers offer customization options, including different colors, printing, and branding, to enhance product identification and consumer appeal.

The selection of the appropriate capsule size is a critical aspect of pharmaceutical formulation and manufacturing. It ensures accurate dosing, enhances patient compliance, and optimizes the efficiency of the production process. Understanding the factors that influence capsule size selection and the standard capacities available helps formulators design effective and patient-friendly dosage forms. Advances in capsule technology and manufacturing continue to provide new opportunities for customization and innovation in oral drug delivery.

### 4.1.3 Filling and Finishing Techniques

**Introduction to Filling and Finishing Techniques**

The filling and finishing of hard gelatin capsules are crucial steps in the manufacturing process, ensuring that the final product meets quality standards and regulatory requirements. These processes involve accurately dispensing the drug formulation into the capsules, sealing them, and performing various finishing steps to ensure their integrity, appearance, and stability.

**Filling Techniques**

The filling of hard gelatin capsules can be accomplished using several methods, depending on the type of formulation and the scale of production. The primary filling techniques include:

**1. Manual Filling**: Manual filling is suitable for small-scale production or compounding pharmacies. It involves using simple tools such as scoops, spatulas, or hand-operated filling machines to fill the capsules. Although labor-intensive and less precise, manual filling is cost-effective for limited production runs.

**2. Semi-Automatic Filling**: Semi-automatic filling machines bridge the gap between manual and fully automated processes. These machines use mechanical or pneumatic systems to fill capsules with a higher degree of precision and speed than manual methods. Operators manually load empty capsules into the machine, which then fills and closes them. Semi-automatic machines are ideal for medium-scale production.

**3. Fully Automatic Filling**: Fully automatic capsule filling machines are used for large-scale production, offering high speed, precision, and consistency. These machines can fill thousands of capsules per hour and are equipped with various filling stations to handle different types of formulations, including powders, granules, pellets, tablets, and liquids. Common types of fully automatic filling machines include:

- **Dosator Machines**: These machines use a dosator, a cylindrical tube with a plunger, to measure and fill powder into capsules. The dosator compresses the powder to form a plug, which is then transferred into the capsule body.
- **Tamping Pin Machines**: Tamping pin machines use pins to tamp or press the powder into a dosing disc, forming a compact slug that is then ejected into the capsule body.
- **Piston Fillers**: Piston fillers are used for filling liquid or semi-solid formulations. They use a piston mechanism to accurately measure and dispense the formulation into the capsule.

**Finishing Techniques**

Once the capsules are filled, several finishing steps are necessary to ensure their quality and stability. These steps include sealing, polishing, inspection, and packaging.

**1. Sealing**: Sealing ensures that the capsule contents are securely enclosed, preventing leakage or tampering. Several sealing techniques are used:

- **Banding**: This technique involves applying a gelatin or polymer band around the joint of the capsule body and cap. Banding provides a visible seal and can be used to enhance tamper resistance.
- **Liquid Sealing**: Liquid sealing involves applying a small amount of liquid gelatin or other sealing solution to the capsule joint. The liquid solidifies, forming a secure seal.

- **Heat Sealing**: Heat sealing uses heat to melt a portion of the capsule body and cap, fusing them together. This method is suitable for capsules made from heat-sensitive materials.

**2. Polishing**: Polishing removes any residual powder or formulation from the surface of the capsules, improving their appearance and ensuring cleanliness. Polishing can be done using:

- **Brushing**: Capsules are passed through a series of soft brushes that gently remove any adhering powder.
- **Cloth Polishing**: Capsules are tumbled with a soft cloth to achieve a polished finish.
- **Vacuum Polishing**: Capsules are exposed to a vacuum that removes dust and particles from their surface.

**3. Inspection**: Inspection is a critical step to ensure the quality and consistency of the capsules. It involves checking for defects such as cracks, dents, improper sealing, or incorrect fill volumes. Inspection can be performed manually or using automated systems with cameras and sensors to detect defects.

**4. Packaging**: Packaging protects the capsules from environmental factors such as moisture, light, and air, ensuring their stability and shelf life. Common packaging methods include:

- **Blister Packaging**: Capsules are placed in individual cavities made of plastic or aluminum, sealed with a foil backing. Blister packaging provides excellent protection and allows for easy dispensing of individual doses.
- **Bottle Packaging**: Capsules are filled into bottles, which are then sealed with a tamper-evident cap. Desiccants are often included to control moisture.
- **Strip Packaging**: Capsules are placed between layers of foil or plastic, which are then sealed to form strips. This method provides excellent protection and is often used for unit-dose packaging.

**Quality Control in Filling and Finishing**

Quality control measures are essential throughout the filling and finishing processes to ensure the final product meets regulatory standards and patient expectations. Key quality control tests include:

- **Fill Weight Verification**: Ensures that each capsule contains the correct amount of the active ingredient.
- **Leak Testing**: Detects any leaks in the capsules or seals to ensure product integrity.
- **Visual Inspection**: Checks for any defects or inconsistencies in the filled and finished capsules.
- **Content Uniformity**: Ensures that the active ingredient is uniformly distributed in all capsules within a batch.

The filling and finishing of hard gelatin capsules are critical steps that require precision, consistency, and adherence to quality standards. Advances in filling and finishing technologies continue to improve the efficiency and reliability of these processes, ensuring that pharmaceutical products meet the highest standards of quality and safety.

#### 4.1.4 Special Techniques

The production of hard gelatin capsules involves not only standard filling and finishing processes but also a range of special techniques designed to enhance the functionality, stability, and patient compliance of the final product. These special techniques are employed to address specific formulation challenges, improve the therapeutic profile of the drug, or add unique features to the capsules. Some of the most notable special techniques include **enteric coating**, **sustained-release formulations**, **pellet and multiparticulate filling**, **liquid filling of hard gelatin capsules**, and **capsule-in-capsule technology**.

**1. Enteric Coating**

Enteric coating is a process applied to capsules to protect the drug substance from the acidic environment of the stomach and ensure its release in the more neutral or alkaline environment of the intestines. This technique is particularly useful for drugs that can be degraded by stomach acid or can cause gastric irritation.

- **Application**: Enteric coatings are typically applied using pan coating or fluidized bed coating methods. Polymers such as cellulose acetate phthalate (CAP), hydroxypropyl methylcellulose phthalate (HPMCP), and methacrylic acid copolymers are commonly used for enteric coatings.

- **Benefits**: Protects acid-sensitive drugs, reduces gastric irritation, and allows for targeted drug release in the intestines.

**2. Sustained-Release Formulations**

Sustained-release formulations are designed to release the drug over an extended period, maintaining therapeutic levels in the bloodstream and improving patient compliance by reducing the frequency of dosing.

- **Techniques**: Various methods are used to achieve sustained release, including the incorporation of matrix-forming polymers, coated pellets, and osmotic systems. The choice of technique depends on the drug's properties and the desired release profile.
- **Benefits**: Provides prolonged therapeutic effect, reduces dosing frequency, and improves patient adherence to the medication regimen.

**3. Pellet and Multiparticulate Filling**

Pellet and multiparticulate filling involves filling capsules with small, discrete units such as pellets, granules, or mini-tablets. These units can be coated to modify the drug release profile, allowing for a combination of immediate and sustained-release effects.

- **Application**: Pellets and multiparticulates are typically filled into capsules using specialized filling machines that ensure uniform distribution and precise dosing.
- **Benefits**: Allows for flexible formulation strategies, enables combination therapies, and can enhance drug stability and bioavailability.

**4. Liquid Filling of Hard Gelatin Capsules**

Liquid filling involves encapsulating liquid or semi-solid formulations in hard gelatin capsules. This technique is particularly useful for drugs that are poorly soluble in water or require a liquid medium for stability and absorption.

- **Techniques**: Liquid filling can be achieved using piston fillers, peristaltic pumps, or other precision dosing equipment. The capsules are then sealed using banding or other sealing methods to prevent leakage.
- **Benefits**: Enhances the bioavailability of poorly soluble drugs, allows for the encapsulation of lipid-based formulations, and provides precise

dosing.

**5. Capsule-in-Capsule Technology**

Capsule-in-capsule technology involves placing a smaller capsule or multiple smaller capsules inside a larger outer capsule. This technique can be used to separate incompatible ingredients, create combination therapies, or provide multi-phase release profiles.

- **Application**: Capsule-in-capsule systems are manufactured using specialized equipment that places the inner capsules into the outer capsule before sealing.
- **Benefits**: Enables the separation of incompatible ingredients, facilitates combination therapies, and allows for complex release profiles.

**6. Hot Melt Extrusion (HME) for Capsule Filling**

Hot melt extrusion (HME) is a technique used to improve the solubility and bioavailability of poorly water-soluble drugs by dispersing them in a polymer matrix. The extrudate can then be filled into hard gelatin capsules.

- **Techniques**: The drug and polymer are melted and mixed together using an extruder, then cooled and milled into uniform particles for capsule filling.
- **Benefits**: Enhances drug solubility and bioavailability, provides controlled release properties, and improves the stability of the drug.

**7. Microencapsulation**

Microencapsulation involves coating small particles or droplets of the drug with a protective layer to form microcapsules, which are then filled into hard gelatin capsules. This technique can provide controlled release, protect sensitive drugs, and mask unpleasant tastes.

- **Techniques**: Methods such as coacervation, spray drying, and solvent evaporation are used to create microcapsules.
- **Benefits**: Provides controlled release, enhances the stability of sensitive drugs, and masks unpleasant tastes or odors.

Special techniques in the production of hard gelatin capsules offer numerous advantages in terms of drug delivery, stability, and patient compliance. These techniques enable the development of advanced pharmaceutical formulations that meet specific therapeutic needs and enhance the overall effectiveness of the medication. Advances in technology and innovation continue to expand the possibilities for capsule-based drug delivery systems, providing new opportunities for improving patient outcomes.

### 4.1.5 Manufacturing Defects

Manufacturing defects in hard gelatin capsules can compromise the quality, efficacy, and safety of the final pharmaceutical product. Identifying and addressing these defects is crucial to ensure the production of high-quality capsules that meet regulatory standards and provide therapeutic benefits to patients. Common manufacturing defects in hard gelatin capsules include **weight variation**, **visual defects**, **dissolution issues**, **cross-linking**, **brittleness**, **microbial contamination**, and **improper sealing**.

#### 1. Weight Variation

Weight variation occurs when the filled capsules do not contain the uniform amount of the active ingredient or excipients, leading to inconsistent dosing. This can result from inaccuracies in the filling process or variations in the density and flow properties of the formulation.

- **Causes**: Inconsistent filling machine settings, uneven flow of the formulation, improper calibration of filling equipment.
- **Prevention**: Regular calibration and maintenance of filling machines, use of flow enhancers in the formulation, ensuring uniform particle size distribution.

#### 2. Visual Defects

Visual defects include a range of issues such as cracks, dents, holes, discoloration, and surface imperfections. These defects can affect the capsule's appearance and may indicate underlying quality problems.

- **Causes**: Poor quality raw materials, inadequate drying, mishandling during production, contamination during manufacturing.
- **Prevention**: Using high-quality raw materials, optimizing drying conditions, implementing strict handling protocols, and maintaining a clean manufacturing environment.

#### 3. Dissolution Issues

Dissolution issues arise when the capsule does not release the active ingredient as expected, affecting the drug's bioavailability and therapeutic efficacy. This can result from problems with the capsule shell or the formulation itself.

- **Causes**: Improper formulation, poor-quality gelatin, inadequate disintegration properties, cross-linking of gelatin.
- **Prevention**: Conducting thorough pre-formulation studies, using high-quality gelatin, incorporating disintegrants in the formulation, and monitoring the dissolution profile during development.

**4. Cross-Linking**

Cross-linking of gelatin capsules involves the formation of chemical bonds between gelatin molecules, leading to decreased solubility and delayed drug release. This defect is often caused by reactive impurities or interactions with the formulation.

- **Causes**: Presence of aldehydes or other reactive impurities, interactions with certain drugs or excipients, storage under improper conditions.
- **Prevention**: Using high-purity gelatin, avoiding reactive excipients, incorporating antioxidants, and storing capsules under controlled conditions.

**5. Brittleness**

Brittleness in hard gelatin capsules makes them prone to cracking or breaking during handling and packaging. This defect can compromise the integrity of the capsule and the stability of the drug.

- **Causes**: Low moisture content, improper plasticizer concentration, exposure to extreme environmental conditions.
- **Prevention**: Maintaining optimal moisture levels, using appropriate plasticizers, and storing capsules in a controlled environment.

**6. Microbial Contamination**

Microbial contamination poses a significant risk to the safety and efficacy of hard gelatin capsules. Contaminants can compromise the stability of the formulation and pose health risks to patients.

- **Causes**: Poor hygiene during manufacturing, contaminated raw materials, inadequate sterilization procedures.
- **Prevention**: Implementing stringent hygiene protocols, using high-quality, sterile raw materials, and conducting regular microbial testing.

**7. Improper Sealing**

Improper sealing can lead to capsule leakage, loss of the active ingredient, and contamination. This defect affects the capsule's integrity and can result from issues during the sealing process.

- **Causes**: Inadequate sealing conditions, improper alignment of capsule parts, defective sealing equipment.
- **Prevention**: Regularly maintaining and calibrating sealing equipment, ensuring proper alignment of capsule parts, and optimizing sealing conditions.

**Quality Control and Defect Prevention**

Implementing robust quality control measures throughout the manufacturing process is essential to prevent and identify defects in hard gelatin capsules. Key quality control steps include:

- **Raw Material Testing**: Ensuring the quality and purity of all raw materials used in capsule production.
- **In-Process Monitoring**: Regularly monitoring critical parameters such as fill weight, moisture content, and environmental conditions during manufacturing.
- **Finished Product Testing**: Conducting comprehensive tests on the final product, including weight uniformity, dissolution testing, microbial testing, and visual inspection.
- **Process Validation**: Validating manufacturing processes to ensure they consistently produce capsules that meet predefined quality criteria.
- **Training and SOPs**: Providing thorough training for personnel and implementing standard operating procedures (SOPs) to ensure consistent manufacturing practices.

Manufacturing defects in hard gelatin capsules can significantly impact the quality, efficacy, and safety of the final product. By understanding the common defects and their causes, pharmaceutical manufacturers can implement effective preventive measures and quality control protocols to ensure the production of high-quality capsules. Advances in manufacturing technology and continuous process improvements contribute to minimizing defects and enhancing the overall reliability of capsule-based drug delivery systems.

### 4.1.6 In-Process Quality Control Tests

In-process quality control (IPQC) tests are essential to ensure that hard gelatin capsules meet the required standards throughout the manufacturing process. These tests help identify and rectify any issues early, ensuring consistent quality and compliance with regulatory standards. The key in-process quality control tests for hard gelatin capsules include **appearance inspection**, **weight variation**, **moisture content**, **disintegration time**, **hardness and brittleness**, **microbial contamination**, and **capsule integrity**.

#### 1. Appearance Inspection

**Appearance inspection** involves visually examining the capsules for any defects such as cracks, dents, holes, discoloration, or surface imperfections. Consistency in the appearance of the capsules is crucial for maintaining product quality and patient trust.

- **Procedure**: Capsules are randomly sampled from the production line and inspected under adequate lighting conditions. Any defects or deviations from the standard appearance are recorded and analyzed.
- **Frequency**: This inspection is carried out at multiple stages during production, including after filling and sealing.

#### 2. Weight Variation

**Weight variation** tests ensure that each capsule contains the correct amount of the active ingredient and excipients, providing consistent dosing.

- **Procedure**: A specified number of capsules are weighed individually, and the average weight is calculated. The individual weights are compared to the average weight to determine the variation. The acceptable limits for weight variation are defined by pharmacopeial standards.
- **Frequency**: This test is performed at regular intervals during the filling process to ensure uniformity.

#### 3. Moisture Content

**Moisture content** affects the stability and integrity of gelatin capsules. Maintaining optimal moisture levels is crucial to prevent brittleness or excessive softness.

- **Procedure**: The moisture content is measured using techniques such as **loss on drying (LOD)** or **Karl Fischer titration**. Capsules are sampled and subjected to these tests to determine the moisture content.
- **Frequency**: Regular checks are performed during production, particularly after drying and before packaging.

**4. Disintegration Time**

**Disintegration time** measures how quickly the capsule breaks down in the gastrointestinal tract, which is crucial for the drug's bioavailability.

- **Procedure**: Capsules are placed in a disintegration testing apparatus containing a suitable medium at a specified temperature. The time taken for the capsules to disintegrate completely is recorded and compared to the specified limits.
- **Frequency**: This test is conducted periodically during production to ensure the capsules meet the required disintegration time.

**5. Hardness and Brittleness**

**Hardness and brittleness** tests ensure that capsules can withstand handling, packaging, and transportation without breaking or deforming.

- **Procedure**: The hardness of the capsules is tested using a **hardness tester**, which applies a force until the capsule breaks. Brittleness is assessed by subjecting the capsules to mechanical stress and examining them for cracks or breaks.
- **Frequency**: These tests are performed at different stages of production to monitor the mechanical properties of the capsules.

**6. Microbial Contamination**

**Microbial contamination** tests ensure that the capsules are free from harmful microorganisms, which could compromise the product's safety.

- **Procedure**: Capsules are sampled and tested for microbial contamination using methods such as **plate count**, **membrane filtration**, or **rapid microbiological methods (RMM)**. The tests check for total aerobic microbial count, total yeast and mold count, and the absence of specific pathogens.

- **Frequency**: Regular microbial testing is performed throughout the production process, particularly after critical steps such as filling and sealing.

**7. Capsule Integrity**

**Capsule integrity** tests check for proper sealing and ensure that the capsule contents are securely enclosed.

- **Procedure**: Various methods, including **visual inspection**, **dye ingress test**, and **vacuum leak test**, are used to assess the integrity of the capsules. These tests detect any leaks, improper sealing, or structural defects.
- **Frequency**: Capsule integrity is checked continuously during production, with particular attention during and after the sealing process.

In-process quality control tests are vital to maintaining the high standards required for hard gelatin capsules. These tests help identify potential issues early in the manufacturing process, ensuring that the final product meets all regulatory requirements and quality standards. Implementing robust IPQC protocols contributes to the consistent production of safe, effective, and high-quality pharmaceutical capsules. Advances in analytical techniques and automation continue to enhance the precision and efficiency of in-process quality control, supporting the overall goal of delivering reliable and effective medications to patients.

### 4.1.7 Final Product Quality Control Tests

Final product quality control (FPQC) tests are essential for ensuring that hard gelatin capsules meet the required standards for safety, efficacy, and quality before they are released into the market. These tests encompass various physical, chemical, and microbiological evaluations to confirm that the capsules comply with pharmacopeial specifications and regulatory requirements. Key FPQC tests for hard gelatin capsules include **appearance inspection**, **weight uniformity**, **content uniformity**, **disintegration time**, **dissolution testing**, **moisture content**, **microbial limit testing**, and **stability testing**.

**1. Appearance Inspection**

**Appearance inspection** ensures that the capsules are visually free from defects and have a consistent appearance.

- **Procedure**: Capsules are sampled and examined under adequate lighting for defects such as cracks, dents, discoloration, or improper sealing. The color, shape, and overall appearance are compared to the specified standards.
- **Importance**: Ensures consumer acceptance and identifies any visible defects that might indicate underlying quality issues.

**2. Weight Uniformity**

**Weight uniformity** ensures that each capsule contains a consistent amount of the formulation, which is critical for accurate dosing.

- **Procedure**: A specified number of capsules are individually weighed, and the weights are compared to the average weight to determine uniformity. The acceptable limits are defined by pharmacopeial standards.
- **Importance**: Ensures that each dose delivers the correct amount of active ingredient, contributing to efficacy and safety.

**3. Content Uniformity**

**Content uniformity** measures the amount of active ingredient in each capsule to ensure consistent potency.

- **Procedure**: Capsules are sampled, and the active ingredient is extracted and quantified using analytical techniques such as **high-performance liquid chromatography (HPLC)** or **gas chromatography (GC)**. The content of the active ingredient in each capsule is compared to the specified limits.
- **Importance**: Ensures that each capsule contains the intended amount of active ingredient, maintaining therapeutic effectiveness and patient safety.

**4. Disintegration Time**

**Disintegration time** assesses how quickly the capsule breaks down in the gastrointestinal tract, which is crucial for drug release and absorption.

- **Procedure**: Capsules are placed in a disintegration testing apparatus with a suitable medium at a specified temperature. The time taken for the capsules to disintegrate completely is recorded and compared to pharmacopeial limits.
- **Importance**: Ensures that the capsule disintegrates as expected to release the active ingredient for absorption.

**5. Dissolution Testing**

**Dissolution testing** evaluates the rate and extent to which the active ingredient is released from the capsule into a dissolution medium.

- **Procedure**: Capsules are placed in a dissolution apparatus, and samples of the dissolution medium are taken at specified intervals. The concentration of the active ingredient in the samples is measured using analytical techniques like HPLC or UV spectrophotometry. The dissolution profile is compared to the specified criteria.
- **Importance**: Ensures that the drug is released at the intended rate and extent, which is critical for bioavailability and therapeutic efficacy.

**6. Moisture Content**

**Moisture content** testing ensures that the capsules have the appropriate level of moisture, which affects their stability and integrity.

- **Procedure**: The moisture content is measured using techniques such as **loss on drying (LOD)** or **Karl Fischer titration.** Capsules are sampled and tested to determine their moisture levels.
- **Importance**: Prevents issues such as brittleness or microbial growth that can compromise the quality and stability of the capsules.

**7. Microbial Limit Testing**

**Microbial limit testing** checks for the presence of harmful microorganisms to ensure the capsules are safe for consumption.

- **Procedure**: Capsules are sampled and tested for microbial contamination using methods such as **plate count, membrane filtration**, or **rapid microbiological methods (RMM).** The tests measure the total aerobic microbial count, total yeast and mold count, and the absence of specific pathogens.

- **Importance**: Ensures the microbial safety of the product, preventing potential infections or spoilage.

**8. Stability Testing**

**Stability testing** assesses the capsule's ability to maintain its quality over time under various environmental conditions.

- **Procedure**: Capsules are stored under controlled conditions (e.g., temperature, humidity, light) for specified periods. Samples are taken at predetermined intervals and subjected to various tests, including appearance, assay, dissolution, and microbial testing.
- **Importance**: Determines the shelf life and appropriate storage conditions for the product, ensuring it remains effective and safe throughout its intended use period.

Final product quality control tests are crucial for verifying that hard gelatin capsules meet all necessary standards and specifications before they are released to the market. These tests help ensure the safety, efficacy, and quality of the capsules, thereby protecting patient health and maintaining regulatory compliance. Implementing comprehensive FPQC protocols and using advanced analytical techniques contribute to the consistent production of high-quality pharmaceutical products. Advances in quality control methodologies continue to enhance the precision and reliability of these tests, supporting the overall goal of delivering safe and effective medications to patients.

## 4.2 Soft Gelatin Capsules

### 4.2.1 Nature of Shell and Capsule Content

**Introduction to Soft Gelatin Capsules**

Soft gelatin capsules (softgels) are a popular oral dosage form used for delivering both liquid and semi-solid formulations. They consist of a flexible, gelatin-based shell that encloses the active ingredient along with suitable excipients. Softgels are preferred for their ability to encapsulate a wide range of formulations, including oils, solutions, suspensions, and pastes, offering numerous advantages such as improved bioavailability, enhanced patient compliance, and masking of unpleasant tastes and odors.

**Nature of Shell**

The shell of a soft gelatin capsule is a crucial component that provides structural integrity, protects the encapsulated content, and facilitates ingestion. The key characteristics and composition of the soft gelatin shell include:

**1. Gelatin**: The primary ingredient in the soft gelatin shell is gelatin, a protein derived from the hydrolysis of collagen, which is obtained from animal skin, bones, and connective tissues. Gelatin provides the necessary flexibility and strength to the capsule shell. The type of gelatin used (Type A or Type B) and its bloom strength (a measure of gelatin's firmness) are selected based on the desired properties of the capsule.

**2. Plasticizers**: Plasticizers are added to the gelatin to make the shell flexible and elastic. Common plasticizers include glycerin, sorbitol, and polyethylene glycol. The concentration of plasticizers can vary depending on the required softness and durability of the capsule shell. A typical ratio of gelatin to plasticizer ranges from 1:0.3 to 1:1.

**3. Water**: Water is an essential component of the gelatin solution used to form the capsule shell. It helps dissolve the gelatin and plasticizers and facilitates the formation of a homogenous mixture. During the capsule manufacturing process, water content is reduced to achieve the desired consistency and firmness of the shell.

**4. Colorants and Opacifiers**: Colorants (dyes or pigments) and opacifiers (such as titanium dioxide) are added to the gelatin solution to provide the capsules with an appealing appearance and to differentiate between different products. These additives must be approved for pharmaceutical use and should not affect the stability or efficacy of the encapsulated content.

**5. Preservatives**: Preservatives such as parabens or sorbic acid may be added to the gelatin solution to prevent microbial growth during the manufacturing process and storage. The choice and concentration of preservatives depend on the shelf life and storage conditions of the final product.

**Nature of Capsule Content**

Soft gelatin capsules are versatile and can encapsulate a wide range of formulations. The nature of the capsule content can significantly affect the choice of excipients and the encapsulation process. The key characteristics and types of capsule contents include:

**1. Liquids**: Softgels are commonly used to encapsulate liquid formulations, including solutions, suspensions, and emulsions. These liquids can be aqueous, oily, or a mixture of both. Oils, such as fish oil, evening primrose oil, and vitamin E, are frequently encapsulated in softgels due to their hydrophobic nature and the protective barrier provided by the gelatin shell.

**2. Semi-Solids**: Semi-solid formulations, such as pastes and gels, can also be encapsulated in soft gelatin capsules. These formulations are typically more viscous than liquids and may require specialized filling equipment to ensure accurate dosing.

**3. Solutions**: Solutions are clear, homogeneous mixtures of the active ingredient dissolved in a suitable solvent or mixture of solvents. The solvent system can be composed of water, oils, or other suitable organic solvents. The selection of solvents depends on the solubility of the active ingredient and the desired release profile.

**4. Suspensions**: Suspensions contain solid particles dispersed in a liquid medium. The particle size, density, and stability of the suspension must be carefully controlled to ensure uniformity and prevent sedimentation. Suitable suspending agents and surfactants may be added to maintain the stability of the suspension.

**5. Emulsions**: Emulsions are biphasic systems consisting of two immiscible liquids, typically oil and water, with one liquid dispersed in the other. Emulsions can be oil-in-water (O/W) or water-in-oil (W/O), stabilized by emulsifying agents. The choice of emulsifiers and the ratio of the two phases are critical to the stability and effectiveness of the encapsulated emulsion.

**Excipients in Capsule Content**

The formulation inside a soft gelatin capsule often requires additional excipients to enhance stability, bioavailability, and patient acceptability. Common excipients include:

**1. Solubilizers**: Solubilizers such as surfactants and co-solvents are used to enhance the solubility of poorly soluble drugs, improving their bioavailability. Examples include polysorbates, polyethylene glycols, and propylene glycol.

**2. Stabilizers**: Stabilizers help maintain the chemical and physical stability of the encapsulated content. Antioxidants like vitamin E, butylated hydroxytoluene (BHT), and butylated hydroxyanisole (BHA) are commonly used to prevent oxidative degradation.

**3. Viscosity Modifiers**: Viscosity modifiers, such as glycerin, sorbitol, and polyethylene glycol, are added to adjust the viscosity of the formulation, ensuring uniform filling and preventing leakage.

**4. pH Adjusters**: pH adjusters, such as citric acid or sodium hydroxide, are used to maintain the desired pH of the formulation, ensuring the stability and solubility of the active ingredient.

**5. Preservatives**: Preservatives may be included to prevent microbial contamination, especially in aqueous-based formulations. Common preservatives include parabens and sorbic acid.

The nature of the shell and capsule content in soft gelatin capsules plays a critical role in determining the quality, stability, and efficacy of the final product. The careful selection of gelatin, plasticizers, excipients, and formulation components ensures that the capsules meet the desired specifications and provide effective drug delivery. Advances in softgel technology and formulation continue to expand the possibilities for encapsulating a wide range of therapeutic agents, enhancing patient compliance and therapeutic outcomes.

### 4.2.2 Size of Capsules

**Introduction to Soft Gelatin Capsule Sizes**

Soft gelatin capsules (softgels) come in a variety of sizes to accommodate different dosages and formulations. The size of a capsule is a critical consideration in the formulation process, impacting the dosage, ease of swallowing, and patient compliance. Capsule sizes are standardized and are typically specified by their capacity in terms of volume (milliliters or cubic centimeters) or weight (milligrams).

**Standard Soft Gelatin Capsule Sizes**

The sizes of soft gelatin capsules are designated by numbers, which correspond to their volume capacity. The most common sizes range from small volumes suitable for potent drugs to larger volumes used for dietary supplements and oils. The table below provides an overview of standard soft gelatin capsule sizes along with their approximate volume capacities:

| Capsule Size | Volume Capacity (ml) | Typical Fill Weight (mg) |
|---|---|---|
| 5 | 0.13 | 100 - 150 |
| 4 | 0.21 | 150 - 250 |
| 3 | 0.30 | 200 - 300 |
| 2 | 0.37 | 300 - 400 |
| 1 | 0.50 | 400 - 600 |
| 0 | 0.68 | 600 - 800 |
| 00 | 0.95 | 800 - 1000 |
| 000 | 1.37 | 1000 - 1350 |

**Factors Influencing Capsule Size Selection**

**1. Dosage Requirements**: The primary factor in selecting the capsule size is the required dosage of the active ingredient. Higher doses necessitate larger capsules to accommodate the volume of the drug and excipients. Conversely, potent drugs that require small doses can be encapsulated in smaller capsules.

**2. Formulation Characteristics**: The physical and chemical properties of the formulation, such as density, viscosity, and solubility, influence the choice of capsule size. Formulations with low density require larger capsules to achieve the same weight as denser formulations.

**3. Patient Compliance**: Capsule size affects ease of swallowing and overall patient compliance. Smaller capsules are generally easier to swallow and are preferred for pediatric and geriatric patients. Ensuring the capsule size is manageable for the target patient population is crucial for adherence to the medication regimen.

**4. Manufacturing Considerations**: The choice of capsule size can impact the efficiency of the manufacturing process. Standardizing capsule sizes within a product line can streamline production and reduce costs. Additionally, the compatibility of the capsule size with filling equipment and packaging machinery must be considered.

**5. Regulatory Requirements**: Regulatory guidelines may specify certain capsule sizes for specific drugs or dosage forms. Compliance with these regulations ensures that the product meets the required standards for safety and efficacy.

**Special Capsule Sizes and Customization**

In addition to standard sizes, custom capsule sizes can be produced to meet specific formulation needs or branding requirements. Customization options include:

- **Custom Volumes**: Tailoring the volume capacity to match unique dosage requirements.
- **Shape Variations**: Modifying the shape of the capsules, such as oblong or spherical, to differentiate products or improve patient acceptance.
- **Color and Branding**: Using different colors, printing logos, or adding branding elements to enhance product identification and marketability.

The size of soft gelatin capsules is a critical factor in pharmaceutical formulation and manufacturing. Selecting the appropriate capsule size ensures accurate dosing, enhances patient compliance, and optimizes production efficiency. Understanding the standard sizes and the factors influencing size selection helps formulators design effective and patient-friendly dosage forms. Advances in capsule technology and customization options continue to expand the possibilities for softgel-based drug delivery systems, providing new opportunities for innovation and improvement in therapeutic outcomes.

### 4.2.3 Base Adsorption and Minimum/Gram Factors

**Introduction to Base Adsorption and Minimum/Gram Factors**

In the formulation of soft gelatin capsules, certain properties such as **base adsorption** and **minimum/gram factors** are critical for ensuring the proper encapsulation and performance of the active ingredients. These factors help formulators understand how the active ingredient interacts with the excipients and the capsule shell, impacting the overall quality and efficacy of the final product.

**Base Adsorption**

**Base adsorption** refers to the ability of a powder or a solid to adsorb or hold a certain amount of liquid. In the context of soft gelatin capsules, this concept is essential for determining how much of the liquid excipient (often an oil or another solvent) can be absorbed by the active ingredient and other solid excipients. The base adsorption value influences the choice of excipients and the overall formulation process.

- **Definition**: Base adsorption is typically expressed in terms of the amount of liquid (in grams or milliliters) that can be adsorbed by one gram of the solid ingredient.
- **Importance**: Knowing the base adsorption capacity helps in accurately determining the proportions of liquids and solids in the formulation. It ensures that the mixture has the appropriate consistency for encapsulation and that the active ingredient is uniformly distributed.

**Calculation of Base Adsorption**: To determine the base adsorption capacity, a known amount of the solid ingredient is mixed with varying amounts of the liquid excipient until the mixture reaches a specified consistency or saturation point. The amount of liquid required to achieve this is measured and expressed as the base adsorption value.

**Minimum/Gram Factors**

**Minimum/gram factors** refer to the minimum amount of a liquid that can be effectively used to formulate a stable and uniform suspension or solution of a given active ingredient within a soft gelatin capsule. This factor is crucial for optimizing the formulation to ensure that the capsules are not only effective but also manufacturable at scale.

- **Definition**: The minimum/gram factor is the minimum volume of the liquid medium required per gram of the active ingredient to achieve a stable formulation.
- **Importance**: This factor helps in formulating the correct dosage and ensures that the active ingredient is adequately dissolved or suspended in the liquid medium. It also influences the capsule size and the fill weight.

**Calculation of Minimum/Gram Factor**: To calculate the minimum/gram factor, a series of formulations with varying ratios of liquid medium to active ingredient are prepared and tested for stability, homogeneity, and efficacy. The smallest volume of liquid that can achieve these criteria per gram of active ingredient is determined as the minimum/gram factor.

**Practical Application**

**1. Optimizing Formulation**: By understanding base adsorption and minimum/gram factors, formulators can optimize the ratio of liquid to solid components in the soft gelatin capsule. This ensures that the formulation is both stable and effective.

**2. Ensuring Uniform Distribution**: Proper calculation and adjustment of these factors ensure that the active ingredient is uniformly distributed within the capsule, which is essential for consistent dosing and therapeutic effect.

**3. Capsule Size Determination**: These factors help in determining the appropriate capsule size by ensuring that the volume of the fill material fits within the chosen capsule dimensions without causing leakage or stability issues.

**4. Stability and Bioavailability**: Formulating with the correct base adsorption and minimum/gram factors helps in maintaining the stability of the active ingredient within the capsule, enhancing its bioavailability and therapeutic efficacy.

**Example Calculation**

**Base Adsorption Example**: If a particular active ingredient has a base adsorption capacity of 0.5 ml/g, this means that each gram of the active ingredient can adsorb 0.5 ml of the liquid excipient. Therefore, if 10 grams of the active ingredient are used, they would require 5 ml of the liquid excipient to achieve the desired consistency.

**Minimum/Gram Factor Example**: Suppose the minimum/gram factor for a certain active ingredient is determined to be 1 ml/g. This means that at least 1 ml of the liquid medium is required for each gram of the active ingredient to achieve a stable and homogeneous formulation. For a formulation containing 5 grams of the active ingredient, at least 5 ml of the liquid medium would be needed.

Understanding and applying the concepts of base adsorption and minimum/gram factors are vital for the successful formulation of soft gelatin capsules. These factors ensure the correct proportion of liquid and solid components, leading to stable, effective, and manufacturable products. Advances in formulation science continue to refine these parameters, contributing to the development of high-quality soft gelatin capsules that meet the therapeutic needs of patients.

### 4.2.4 Production Process

The production of soft gelatin capsules involves several critical steps, each designed to ensure the quality and consistency of the final product. The process is highly automated and includes the preparation of the gelatin mass, encapsulation of the fill material, and subsequent drying and finishing steps.

**1. Preparation of the Gelatin Mass**

The gelatin mass forms the capsule shell and is prepared using high-quality gelatin, plasticizers, water, and other additives such as colorants and opacifiers.

- **Gelatin Dissolution**: Gelatin is dissolved in warm water at a controlled temperature. The process is carried out in jacketed kettles equipped with agitators to ensure complete dissolution.
- **Addition of Plasticizers and Additives**: Plasticizers such as glycerin or sorbitol are added to the gelatin solution to provide flexibility. Colorants and opacifiers are added to achieve the desired appearance and opacity.
- **Homogenization**: The mixture is homogenized to ensure uniform distribution of all components. The resulting gelatin mass is kept at a controlled temperature and humidity to maintain its consistency.

**2. Preparation of the Fill Material**

The fill material can be a liquid, semi-solid, or suspension. The preparation process depends on the nature of the active ingredient and the desired release profile.

- **Mixing and Homogenization**: The active ingredient is dissolved or suspended in the appropriate liquid excipient. The mixture is homogenized to ensure uniform distribution of the active ingredient.
- **Deaeration**: The fill material is subjected to deaeration to remove any trapped air, which could affect the encapsulation process and the stability of the capsules.

**3. Encapsulation**

The encapsulation process involves forming the gelatin ribbon, filling it with the prepared fill material, and sealing the capsules.

- **Gelatin Ribbon Formation**: The gelatin mass is fed into a rotary die machine, where it is extruded into two thin ribbons. These ribbons are continuously lubricated to prevent sticking.
- **Filling and Sealing**: The fill material is injected between the two gelatin ribbons as they pass through the rotary die cavities. The ribbons are then pressed together, and the capsules are cut, filled, and sealed simultaneously. This process is highly automated and ensures precise dosing and uniform capsule formation.

**4. Drying**

After encapsulation, the soft gelatin capsules are still pliable and contain excess moisture. The drying process is essential to achieve the desired mechanical strength and stability.

- **Initial Drying**: The capsules are first subjected to an initial drying phase, where they are tumbled in drying drums with controlled temperature and humidity.
- **Final Drying**: The capsules are transferred to drying trays and placed in drying tunnels or rooms with controlled environmental conditions. This phase can take several days, depending on the size of the capsules and the drying conditions.

**5. Finishing and Inspection**

The final steps in the production process involve finishing and quality control to ensure the capsules meet the required standards.

- **Polishing**: The dried capsules are polished to remove any residual lubricant and improve their appearance. This can be done using soft cloths or brushes.
- **Inspection**: Capsules are inspected for defects such as leaks, deformations, or color inconsistencies. Automated inspection systems and manual checks are employed to ensure quality.
- **Sorting and Packaging**: Capsules are sorted based on size and quality and then packaged into appropriate containers, such as bottles or blister packs. Proper labeling and sealing are done to ensure product safety and compliance with regulatory requirements.

### 4.2.5 In-Process Quality Control Tests

In-process quality control (IPQC) tests are critical to ensure that soft gelatin capsules meet the required standards throughout the manufacturing process. These tests help identify and rectify any issues early, ensuring consistent quality and regulatory compliance.

**1. Appearance Inspection**

Appearance inspection involves visually examining the capsules for any defects such as cracks, leaks, discoloration, or deformations.

- **Procedure**: Capsules are randomly sampled and inspected under adequate lighting conditions. Any defects or deviations from the standard appearance are recorded and analyzed.
- **Importance**: Ensures consumer acceptance and identifies any visible defects that might indicate underlying quality issues.

**2. Fill Weight Variation**

Fill weight variation tests ensure that each capsule contains the correct amount of the fill material, providing consistent dosing.

- **Procedure**: A specified number of capsules are individually weighed, and the fill weights are compared to the target weight. The acceptable limits for weight variation are defined by pharmacopeial standards.
- **Importance**: Ensures accurate dosing and consistency in the therapeutic effect.

**3. Gelatin Ribbon Thickness**

The thickness of the gelatin ribbon is critical for the integrity and performance of the capsule shell.

- **Procedure**: The thickness of the gelatin ribbon is measured using micrometers or other precision instruments during the encapsulation process.
- **Importance**: Ensures uniformity and strength of the capsule shell, preventing leaks and breaks.

**4. Seal Integrity**

Seal integrity tests ensure that the capsules are properly sealed and do not leak.

- **Procedure**: Capsules are subjected to vacuum or dye ingress tests to detect any leaks or weak seals. Capsules are also visually inspected for seal integrity.
- **Importance**: Prevents contamination and ensures the stability of the encapsulated content.

**5. Moisture Content**

Moisture content affects the stability and integrity of the gelatin capsules.

- **Procedure**: The moisture content is measured using techniques such as loss on drying (LOD) or Karl Fischer titration. Capsules are sampled at various stages of drying to ensure optimal moisture levels.
- **Importance**: Prevents brittleness or excessive softness of the capsules, ensuring their stability and shelf life.

**6. Disintegration Time**

Disintegration time measures how quickly the capsule breaks down in the gastrointestinal tract, which is crucial for drug release and absorption.

- **Procedure**: Capsules are placed in a disintegration testing apparatus with a suitable medium at a specified temperature. The time taken for the capsules to disintegrate completely is recorded and compared to pharmacopeial limits.
- **Importance**: Ensures that the capsule disintegrates as expected to release the active ingredient for absorption.

**7. Microbial Contamination**

Microbial contamination tests ensure that the capsules are free from harmful microorganisms.

- **Procedure**: Capsules are sampled and tested for microbial contamination using methods such as plate count, membrane filtration, or rapid microbiological methods (RMM). The tests measure the total aerobic microbial count, total yeast and mold count, and the absence of specific pathogens.
- **Importance**: Ensures the microbial safety of the product, preventing potential infections or spoilage.

The production process of soft gelatin capsules involves multiple critical steps, from the preparation of the gelatin mass and fill material to encapsulation, drying, and finishing. In-process quality control tests are essential to ensure that the capsules meet the required standards throughout the manufacturing process. These tests help identify and rectify any issues early, ensuring consistent quality and regulatory compliance.

Advances in manufacturing technology and quality control methodologies continue to enhance the precision and efficiency of these processes, supporting the overall goal of delivering safe and effective soft gelatin capsules to patients.

### 4.2.6 Final Product Quality Control Tests

Final product quality control (FPQC) tests are essential for ensuring that soft gelatin capsules meet the required standards for safety, efficacy, and quality before they are released into the market. These tests encompass various physical, chemical, and microbiological evaluations to confirm that the capsules comply with pharmacopeial specifications and regulatory requirements. Key FPQC tests for soft gelatin capsules include **appearance inspection**, **weight uniformity**, **content uniformity**, **disintegration time**, **dissolution testing**, **moisture content**, **microbial limit testing**, and **stability testing**.

#### 1. Appearance Inspection

Appearance inspection ensures that the capsules are visually free from defects and have a consistent appearance.

- **Procedure**: Capsules are sampled and examined under adequate lighting for defects such as cracks, leaks, discoloration, or deformation. The color, shape, and overall appearance are compared to the specified standards.
- **Importance**: Ensures consumer acceptance and identifies any visible defects that might indicate underlying quality issues.

#### 2. Weight Uniformity

Weight uniformity ensures that each capsule contains a consistent amount of the formulation, which is critical for accurate dosing.

- **Procedure**: A specified number of capsules are individually weighed, and the weights are compared to the average weight to determine uniformity. The acceptable limits are defined by pharmacopeial standards.
- **Importance**: Ensures that each dose delivers the correct amount of active ingredient, contributing to efficacy and safety.

#### 3. Content Uniformity

Content uniformity measures the amount of active ingredient in each capsule to ensure consistent potency.

- **Procedure**: Capsules are sampled, and the active ingredient is extracted and quantified using analytical techniques such as **high-performance liquid chromatography (HPLC)** or **gas chromatography (GC)**. The content of the active ingredient in each capsule is compared to the specified limits.
- **Importance**: Ensures that each capsule contains the intended amount of active ingredient, maintaining therapeutic effectiveness and patient safety.

**4. Disintegration Time**

Disintegration time assesses how quickly the capsule breaks down in the gastrointestinal tract, which is crucial for drug release and absorption.

- **Procedure**: Capsules are placed in a disintegration testing apparatus with a suitable medium at a specified temperature. The time taken for the capsules to disintegrate completely is recorded and compared to pharmacopeial limits.
- **Importance**: Ensures that the capsule disintegrates as expected to release the active ingredient for absorption.

**5. Dissolution Testing**

Dissolution testing evaluates the rate and extent to which the active ingredient is released from the capsule into a dissolution medium.

- **Procedure**: Capsules are placed in a dissolution apparatus, and samples of the dissolution medium are taken at specified intervals. The concentration of the active ingredient in the samples is measured using analytical techniques like HPLC or UV spectrophotometry. The dissolution profile is compared to the specified criteria.
- **Importance**: Ensures that the drug is released at the intended rate and extent, which is critical for bioavailability and therapeutic efficacy.

**6. Moisture Content**

Moisture content testing ensures that the capsules have the appropriate level of moisture, which affects their stability and integrity.

- **Procedure**: The moisture content is measured using techniques such as **loss on drying (LOD)** or **Karl Fischer titration**. Capsules are sampled to determine their moisture levels.

- **Importance**: Prevents brittleness or excessive softness of the capsules, ensuring their stability and shelf life.

**7. Microbial Limit Testing**

Microbial limit testing checks for the presence of harmful microorganisms to ensure the capsules are safe for consumption.

- **Procedure**: Capsules are sampled and tested for microbial contamination using methods such as **plate count**, **membrane filtration**, or **rapid microbiological methods (RMM)**. The tests measure the total aerobic microbial count, total yeast and mold count, and the absence of specific pathogens.
- **Importance**: Ensures the microbial safety of the product, preventing potential infections or spoilage.

**8. Stability Testing**

Stability testing assesses the capsule's ability to maintain its quality over time under various environmental conditions.

- **Procedure**: Capsules are stored under controlled conditions (e.g., temperature, humidity, light) for specified periods. Samples are taken at predetermined intervals and subjected to various tests, including appearance, assay, dissolution, and microbial testing.
- **Importance**: Determines the shelf life and appropriate storage conditions for the product, ensuring it remains effective and safe throughout its intended use period.

### 4.2.7 Packing, Storage, and Stability Testing

Proper packing, storage, and stability testing are crucial to maintaining the quality, efficacy, and safety of soft gelatin capsules throughout their shelf life. These steps ensure that the capsules are protected from environmental factors such as moisture, light, and temperature, which can affect their stability and integrity.

**Packing**

**1. Blister Packaging**

Blister packaging is a common method for packing soft gelatin capsules. It provides excellent protection against moisture, light, and physical damage.

- **Procedure**: Capsules are placed in individual cavities made of plastic or aluminum, sealed with a foil backing. The blister packs are then placed in cartons or boxes for additional protection.
- **Importance**: Blister packaging ensures that each capsule is individually protected, making it easy to monitor usage and maintain product integrity.

**2. Bottle Packaging**

Bottle packaging involves placing capsules in plastic or glass bottles, which are then sealed with tamper-evident caps. Desiccants are often included to control moisture.

- **Procedure**: Capsules are counted and filled into bottles, which are sealed and labeled with necessary information such as the product name, dosage instructions, batch number, and expiration date.
- **Importance**: Bottle packaging provides a convenient and secure way to store and dispense capsules, protecting them from environmental factors.

**3. Strip Packaging**

Strip packaging involves sealing capsules between layers of foil or plastic to form strips. This method provides excellent protection and is often used for unit-dose packaging.

- **Procedure**: Capsules are placed between two layers of packaging material, which are then sealed together to form individual strips.
- **Importance**: Strip packaging provides a high level of protection against moisture and contamination, ensuring the capsules remain intact and effective.

**Storage**

Proper storage conditions are essential to maintain the stability and shelf life of soft gelatin capsules. Key considerations include:

**1. Temperature Control**

- **Recommended Conditions**: Soft gelatin capsules should be stored at controlled room temperature, typically between 15°C and 25°C (59°F and 77°F). Avoid exposure to high temperatures, which can cause the capsules to soften or melt.
- **Importance**: Maintaining the correct temperature prevents degradation of the gelatin shell and the encapsulated content, ensuring the capsules remain effective.

**2. Humidity Control**

- **Recommended Conditions**: Capsules should be stored in a dry environment with controlled humidity levels, typically between 30% and 50% relative humidity. Excessive moisture can cause the capsules to soften, while low humidity can make them brittle.
- **Importance**: Controlling humidity levels prevents changes in the physical properties of the capsules, maintaining their integrity and stability.

**3. Light Protection**

- **Recommended Conditions**: Capsules should be stored in opaque or light-resistant containers to protect them from light exposure, which can cause degradation of the active ingredient and the gelatin shell.
- **Importance**: Protecting capsules from light ensures that the active ingredient remains stable and effective throughout the shelf life.

**Stability Testing**

Stability testing is conducted to evaluate the long-term stability of soft gelatin capsules under various environmental conditions. It involves both accelerated and real-time testing.

**1. Accelerated Stability Testing**

- **Procedure**: Capsules are stored at elevated temperatures (e.g., 40°C ± 2°C) and humidity levels (e.g., 75% ± 5% RH) for a specified period (usually 6 months). Samples are taken at regular intervals and tested for physical, chemical, and microbiological stability.
- **Importance**: Accelerated stability testing provides early indications of potential stability issues, helping to predict the product's shelf life.

### 2. Real-Time Stability Testing

- **Procedure**: Capsules are stored under recommended storage conditions (e.g., 25°C ± 2°C and 60% ± 5% RH) for the duration of the intended shelf life (e.g., 24 to 36 months). Samples are taken at predetermined intervals and tested for stability.
- **Importance**: Real-time stability testing confirms the product's shelf life and ensures that it remains effective and safe throughout its intended use period.

Packing, storage, and stability testing are critical components in the lifecycle of soft gelatin capsules. Proper packing and storage conditions ensure the capsules maintain their quality and efficacy, while comprehensive stability testing provides assurance that the product will remain stable and effective throughout its shelf life. Advances in packaging technology and stability testing methodologies continue to enhance the ability to protect and evaluate soft gelatin capsules, contributing to the overall goal of delivering safe and effective pharmaceutical products to patients.

## 4.3 Pellets

### 4.3.1 Introduction and Formulation Requirements

#### Introduction to Pellets

Pellets are small, free-flowing, spherical or semi-spherical solid dosage forms that contain active pharmaceutical ingredients (APIs) along with suitable excipients. They are commonly used in oral drug delivery systems for their numerous advantages, including uniform size, ease of administration, and controlled drug release properties. Pellets can be administered directly as capsules or tablets, or they can be incorporated into other dosage forms such as sachets and suspensions. They are particularly valuable in creating multiparticulate drug delivery systems, which can provide both immediate and sustained release profiles.

#### Advantages of Pellets

1. **Uniform Size and Shape**: Pellets typically have a uniform size and shape, which ensures consistent flow properties and accurate dosing.
2. **Controlled Release**: Pellets can be formulated to release the drug at different rates, enabling both immediate and sustained release profiles within the same dosage form.

3. **Reduced Dose Dumping**: The multiparticulate nature of pellets reduces the risk of dose dumping compared to single-unit dosage forms.
4. **Versatility**: Pellets can be filled into capsules, compressed into tablets, or used in suspensions, providing flexibility in dosage form design.
5. **Improved Stability**: The small size and spherical shape of pellets can enhance the stability of sensitive drugs by reducing surface exposure.

**Formulation Requirements**

The formulation of pellets involves several key components and considerations to ensure the desired drug release profile, stability, and manufacturability. The primary components of pellet formulations include the active ingredient, binder, filler, disintegrant, and coating materials.

**1. Active Ingredient**

The active ingredient is the therapeutic agent intended to exert the desired pharmacological effect. The selection and concentration of the active ingredient depend on the intended dose and therapeutic goal. It is crucial to ensure that the active ingredient is uniformly distributed within the pellets to achieve consistent dosing.

**2. Binder**

Binders are used to facilitate the agglomeration of powder particles into pellets during the granulation process. They provide the necessary cohesiveness to form stable pellets. Common binders include:

- **Povidone (PVP)**
- **Hydroxypropyl methylcellulose (HPMC)**
- **Starch**

The choice of binder and its concentration can significantly impact the mechanical strength and dissolution properties of the pellets.

**3. Filler**

Fillers, or diluents, are inert substances used to increase the bulk volume of the pellets and improve their flow properties. They help achieve the desired size and weight of the pellets. Common fillers include:

- **Microcrystalline Cellulose (MCC)**
- **Lactose**
- **Dicalcium Phosphate**

Fillers should be compatible with the active ingredient and other excipients to ensure the stability and performance of the pellets.

**4. Disintegrant**

Disintegrants are added to pellet formulations to facilitate the breakup of the pellets upon contact with gastrointestinal fluids, ensuring rapid drug release. Common disintegrants include:

- **Croscarmellose Sodium**
- **Sodium Starch Glycolate**
- **Crospovidone**

The concentration of disintegrants must be optimized to balance the mechanical strength of the pellets and their disintegration time.

**5. Coating Materials**

Coating materials are applied to pellets to modify the drug release profile, enhance stability, and improve the appearance. Coatings can be used to achieve various release profiles, including immediate, sustained, and delayed release. Common coating materials include:

- **Polymers**: Such as ethylcellulose, HPMC, and methacrylic acid copolymers.
- **Plasticizers**: Such as polyethylene glycol (PEG) and triethyl citrate, to improve the flexibility of the coating.
- **Colorants**: To provide a uniform appearance and facilitate product identification.

**Formulation Process**

The formulation of pellets typically involves several key processes, including granulation, spheronization, drying, and coating.

**1. Granulation**

Granulation is the process of agglomerating powder particles into larger granules to form the core of the pellets. This can be achieved through various methods, including:

- **Wet Granulation**: Involves the addition of a liquid binder solution to the powder mixture, followed by mixing to form granules.
- **Extrusion**: The wet mass is extruded through a die to form cylindrical extrudates, which are then cut to the desired length.

**2. Spheronization**

Spheronization is the process of transforming cylindrical extrudates into spherical pellets. The extrudates are placed in a spheronizer, where they are subjected to high-speed rotational motion, causing them to round off into uniform spheres.

**3. Drying**

The wet pellets are dried to remove excess moisture, which is crucial for maintaining their stability and mechanical strength. Drying can be carried out using various methods, such as fluidized bed drying or tray drying.

**4. Coating**

The dried pellets are coated to achieve the desired drug release profile and enhance stability. Coating can be performed using techniques such as:

- **Fluidized Bed Coating**: Pellets are suspended in a fluidized bed and sprayed with the coating solution.
- **Pan Coating**: Pellets are tumbled in a coating pan while the coating solution is applied.

**Quality Control**

Ensuring the quality of pellets involves various in-process and final product quality control tests, including:

- **Particle Size Distribution**: Ensures uniformity in pellet size.
- **Drug Content Uniformity**: Verifies that the active ingredient is evenly distributed.
- **Mechanical Strength**: Assesses the durability of the pellets.
- **Dissolution Testing**: Evaluates the release profile of the active ingredient.
- **Stability Testing**: Ensures the pellets maintain their quality over time.

The formulation of pellets requires careful consideration of various components and processes to ensure the production of high-quality, effective, and stable dosage forms. Advances in pelletization technology and formulation science continue to enhance the capabilities and applications of pellet-based drug delivery systems, offering improved therapeutic outcomes and patient compliance.

**4.3.2 Pelletization Process**

The pelletization process is a critical part of manufacturing pellets, ensuring that they have the appropriate size, shape, and quality for pharmaceutical use. The process involves several key steps: powder blending, wet granulation, extrusion, spheronization, drying, and coating. Each step is carefully controlled to produce uniform and high-quality pellets.

**1. Powder Blending**

**Powder blending** is the first step in the pelletization process, where the active pharmaceutical ingredient (API) and excipients are mixed to achieve a uniform distribution.

- **Procedure**: All powder components, including the active ingredient, binders, fillers, and disintegrants, are accurately weighed and placed in a blender. Common blending equipment includes V-blenders, ribbon blenders, or high-shear mixers. The mixture is blended until a homogenous powder is achieved.
- **Importance**: Ensures uniform distribution of the active ingredient and excipients, which is crucial for consistent pellet quality and drug release.

**2. Wet Granulation**

**Wet granulation** involves the addition of a liquid binder to the powder blend to form granules, which helps in agglomerating the particles and improving their flow properties.

- **Procedure**: The blended powder is transferred to a granulator, where a liquid binder solution (such as water, ethanol, or a polymer solution) is sprayed onto the powder while it is mixed. The amount of binder added is carefully controlled to achieve the desired consistency of the wet mass.
- **Importance**: Enhances the cohesiveness of the powder mixture, allowing it to be formed into granules and subsequently into pellets.

**3. Extrusion**

**Extrusion** is the process of shaping the wet mass into cylindrical extrudates, which will be converted into spherical pellets in the next step.

- **Procedure**: The wet mass is fed into an extruder, where it is forced through a die with cylindrical holes to form extrudates. The diameter of the die holes determines the size of the extrudates. Common types of extruders include screw extruders, ram extruders, and basket extruders.

- **Importance**: Produces uniform cylindrical extrudates with consistent size and shape, which is essential for producing uniform pellets.

**4. Spheronization**

**Spheronization** transforms the cylindrical extrudates into spherical pellets, which are preferred for their uniform size and shape.

- **Procedure**: The extrudates are placed in a spheronizer, which consists of a rotating plate with a rough surface. As the plate rotates, the extrudates are subjected to centrifugal and frictional forces, causing them to round off into spheres. The process parameters, such as rotation speed and duration, are optimized to achieve the desired pellet characteristics.
- **Importance**: Produces spherical pellets with uniform size and shape, which ensures consistent drug release and ease of coating.

**5. Drying**

**Drying** is essential to remove excess moisture from the pellets, ensuring their stability and mechanical strength.

- **Procedure**: The wet pellets are dried using techniques such as fluidized bed drying, tray drying, or vacuum drying. The drying temperature and duration are carefully controlled to avoid degradation of the active ingredient and other components.
- **Importance**: Ensures the pellets are dry and stable, preventing microbial growth and maintaining their mechanical integrity.

**6. Coating**

**Coating** is often applied to pellets to modify the drug release profile, enhance stability, and improve appearance.

- **Procedure**: The dried pellets are coated using techniques such as fluidized bed coating or pan coating. The coating solution, which contains polymers, plasticizers, and other additives, is sprayed onto the pellets while they are suspended or tumbled. Multiple layers of coating may be applied to achieve the desired release characteristics.
- **Importance**: Provides controlled release properties, protects the active ingredient from environmental factors, and enhances the appearance and patient acceptability of the pellets.

**Quality Control During Pelletization**

Throughout the pelletization process, various in-process quality control tests are conducted to ensure the pellets meet the required specifications.

- **Particle Size Distribution**: Ensures uniform size of the pellets, which is critical for consistent drug release and dosage.
- **Moisture Content**: Monitors the moisture levels during drying to ensure the pellets are properly dried.
- **Drug Content Uniformity**: Verifies that the active ingredient is evenly distributed within the pellets.
- **Mechanical Strength**: Assesses the durability of the pellets to withstand handling and packaging processes.
- **Dissolution Testing**: Evaluates the release profile of the active ingredient from the pellets.

The pelletization process is a complex and precise manufacturing method that produces uniform, high-quality pellets suitable for various pharmaceutical applications. Each step, from powder blending to coating, is carefully controlled to ensure the pellets meet stringent quality standards. Advances in pelletization technology and process optimization continue to enhance the efficiency and consistency of pellet production, contributing to the development of effective and reliable pharmaceutical dosage forms.

**4.3.3 Equipment for Manufacture of Pellets**

The manufacture of pellets involves several key pieces of equipment, each designed to perform specific functions in the pelletization process. The choice of equipment can significantly impact the quality, efficiency, and scalability of pellet production. The primary equipment used in the manufacture of pellets includes **blenders**, **granulators**, **extruders**, **spheronizers**, **dryers**, and **coating machines**.

**1. Blenders**

**Blenders** are used to mix the active pharmaceutical ingredients (APIs) and excipients to ensure a uniform powder blend, which is crucial for consistent pellet quality.

- **V-Blenders**: V-blenders consist of a V-shaped container that tumbles the powder blend. They are commonly used for their efficient mixing and ability to handle large volumes.

- **Ribbon Blenders**: Ribbon blenders use a helical ribbon agitator to mix the powders. They are effective for both dry and wet blending processes.
- **High-Shear Mixers**: High-shear mixers provide intense mixing action, which is useful for achieving a uniform blend, especially for cohesive or dense powders.

**2. Granulators**

**Granulators** are used to form granules from the powder blend, which helps improve the flow properties and cohesiveness of the mixture.

- **Fluid Bed Granulators**: These granulators use a fluidized bed of powder particles and spray the binder solution to form granules. They offer excellent control over granule size and moisture content.
- **High-Shear Granulators**: High-shear granulators use rapid mixing and a binder solution to produce dense granules. They are suitable for forming strong granules with good compressibility.

**3. Extruders**

**Extruders** shape the wet granules into cylindrical extrudates, which are then converted into spherical pellets.

- **Screw Extruders**: Screw extruders use a rotating screw to push the wet mass through a die, forming continuous extrudates. They are ideal for high-throughput production.
- **Ram Extruders**: Ram extruders use a piston to force the wet mass through a die. They are suitable for smaller batches and provide precise control over extrudate dimensions.
- **Basket Extruders**: Basket extruders consist of a cylindrical screen (basket) and a rotating blade that forces the wet mass through the screen openings. They are effective for producing uniform extrudates.

**4. Spheronizers**

**Spheronizers** convert cylindrical extrudates into spherical pellets through a combination of centrifugal and frictional forces.

- **Rotary Spheronizers**: These devices have a rotating plate with a rough surface that rounds off the extrudates into spheres. The process parameters, such as rotation speed and duration, can be adjusted to achieve the desired pellet characteristics.

- **Disc Spheronizers**: Disc spheronizers use a rotating disc to produce spherical pellets. They are known for their high efficiency and ability to handle large batches.

**5. Dryers**

**Dryers** remove excess moisture from the pellets, ensuring their stability and mechanical strength.

- **Fluidized Bed Dryers**: Fluidized bed dryers circulate hot air through a bed of pellets, providing uniform drying and preventing agglomeration.
- **Tray Dryers**: Tray dryers spread the pellets on trays and circulate hot air over them. They are suitable for batch drying and offer precise control over drying conditions.
- **Vacuum Dryers**: Vacuum dryers remove moisture under reduced pressure, which is useful for heat-sensitive materials. They provide gentle drying and preserve the integrity of the pellets.

**6. Coating Machines**

**Coating machines** apply a protective or functional coating to the pellets, enhancing their stability, appearance, and release profile.

- **Fluidized Bed Coaters**: These coaters use a fluidized bed of pellets and spray the coating solution onto the moving particles. They offer excellent control over coating thickness and uniformity.
- **Pan Coaters**: Pan coaters tumble the pellets in a rotating pan while the coating solution is applied. They are effective for batch coating and can handle a wide range of pellet sizes.
- **Wurster Coaters**: Wurster coaters are a type of fluidized bed coater that uses a bottom-spray method to apply the coating solution. They are ideal for achieving precise and uniform coatings.

**Supporting Equipment**

In addition to the primary equipment, several supporting pieces of equipment are essential for the efficient production of pellets.

- **Mixers and Stirring Tanks**: Used for preparing the binder and coating solutions.

- **Sieves and Screeners**: Ensure uniform particle size distribution by removing oversized or undersized particles.
- **Conveyors**: Transport materials between different stages of the pelletization process, improving workflow efficiency.
- **Inspection and Quality Control Instruments**: Include tools for measuring particle size, moisture content, mechanical strength, and dissolution rate, ensuring the quality of the final product.

# FIVE

# PARENTERAL PRODUCTS

## 5.1 Introduction to Parenterals

### 5.1.1 Definition, Types, Advantages, and Limitations

**Definition**

**Parenterals** refer to sterile drug products administered by injection, infusion, or implantation directly into the body, bypassing the gastrointestinal tract. These preparations are designed to be introduced into the body through various routes, including intravenous (IV), intramuscular (IM), subcutaneous (SC), and intradermal (ID), among others. Parenteral products are typically available in the form of solutions, suspensions, emulsions, or powders that need reconstitution before administration.

**Types of Parenteral Preparations**

1. **Intravenous (IV) Injections**: Administered directly into the veins, providing rapid onset of action as the drug is immediately available in the bloodstream.
2. **Intramuscular (IM) Injections**: Administered into the muscle tissue, allowing for slower absorption compared to IV injections, providing a sustained effect.
3. **Subcutaneous (SC) Injections**: Administered into the fatty tissue beneath the skin, offering a slower absorption rate than IM injections, suitable for sustained release.
4. **Intradermal (ID) Injections**: Administered into the dermal layer of the skin, primarily used for allergy testing and vaccination.

5. **Intrathecal Injections**: Administered into the cerebrospinal fluid, used for spinal anesthesia and chemotherapy.
6. **Intra-articular Injections**: Administered into joint spaces, used for treating inflammatory conditions and administering local anesthetics.
7. **Epidural Injections**: Administered into the epidural space around the spinal cord, commonly used for pain management and anesthesia.
8. **Implants**: Solid forms placed subcutaneously or intramuscularly, providing long-term drug release.

**Advantages of Parenteral Preparations**

1. **Rapid Onset of Action**: Parenteral administration allows for immediate delivery of the drug into the systemic circulation, providing a quick therapeutic effect. This is particularly crucial in emergency situations where rapid intervention is needed.
2. **Controlled Drug Delivery**: Parenteral routes can provide precise control over drug dosage and delivery, which is essential for drugs with narrow therapeutic windows or those requiring specific plasma concentration levels.
3. **Bypasses Gastrointestinal Tract**: Parenteral administration avoids the gastrointestinal tract, making it suitable for drugs that are poorly absorbed, unstable, or degraded by gastric enzymes and acids.
4. **Suitable for Unconscious or Uncooperative Patients**: Parenteral routes are ideal for patients who cannot take medications orally due to unconsciousness, severe illness, or non-compliance.
5. **Long-acting Formulations**: Implants and depot injections can provide sustained drug release over extended periods, reducing the need for frequent dosing and improving patient compliance.
6. **Local Effects**: Parenteral administration allows for targeted drug delivery to specific sites, such as joints, spinal fluid, or tumors, enhancing therapeutic efficacy and minimizing systemic side effects.

**Limitations of Parenteral Preparations**

1. **Invasive Procedure**: Parenteral administration involves the use of needles or catheters, which can cause pain, discomfort, and potential complications such as infections, bleeding, and tissue damage.

2. **Sterility Requirements**: Parenteral products must be sterile and free from pyrogens, requiring stringent manufacturing processes and quality control measures to ensure safety.
3. **Cost and Complexity**: The production, storage, and administration of parenteral products are more expensive and complex compared to oral formulations, involving specialized equipment and trained personnel.
4. **Limited Shelf Life**: Some parenteral products, particularly those in solution form, may have limited stability and require refrigeration or other specific storage conditions.
5. **Risk of Adverse Reactions**: Rapid administration and high bioavailability of parenteral drugs can increase the risk of adverse reactions, including hypersensitivity, anaphylaxis, and toxic effects.
6. **Professional Administration Required**: Many parenteral routes require administration by healthcare professionals, limiting their use in home settings and increasing the need for healthcare services.

### 5.1.2 Preformulation Factors

**Introduction to Preformulation Factors**

Preformulation is a crucial stage in the development of parenteral products, as it involves the study and characterization of the physicochemical properties of the drug substance and excipients. This stage aims to gather essential information that will influence the formulation, stability, and bioavailability of the final parenteral product. Understanding these properties helps in designing a suitable dosage form, optimizing the formulation, and ensuring the product's safety and efficacy. The key preformulation factors for parenteral products include **solubility**, **stability**, **pH and buffering capacity**, **isotonicity**, **viscosity**, **compatibility with excipients**, **particulate matter**, and **sterility and pyrogen testing.**

**1. Solubility**

**Solubility** is a critical factor in the development of parenteral formulations, as it determines the drug's ability to dissolve in a suitable solvent for injection.

- **Importance**: Adequate solubility ensures that the drug can be formulated into a solution, which is the most preferred form for parenteral administration due to its rapid absorption and predictable bioavailability.

- **Assessment**: Solubility studies involve determining the solubility of the drug in various solvents, including water, saline, and other physiologically compatible vehicles. Techniques such as pH adjustment, cosolvency, complexation, and the use of solubilizing agents (e.g., surfactants, cyclodextrins) can enhance solubility.

**2. Stability**

**Stability** refers to the drug's ability to maintain its chemical integrity and therapeutic efficacy over time under various conditions.

- **Importance**: Ensuring the stability of the drug substance and formulation is essential to provide a safe and effective product with an adequate shelf life.
- **Assessment**: Stability studies assess the physical, chemical, and microbiological stability of the drug under different environmental conditions, such as temperature, humidity, and light. Forced degradation studies and stability-indicating assays help identify potential degradation pathways and establish appropriate storage conditions and shelf life.

**3. pH and Buffering Capacity**

**pH and buffering capacity** are crucial for maintaining the stability and solubility of the drug, as well as ensuring compatibility with the physiological environment.

- **Importance**: The pH of the formulation affects the drug's solubility, stability, and potential for irritation at the injection site. Buffering agents are used to maintain the desired pH and enhance the drug's stability and compatibility.
- **Assessment**: The optimal pH range for the drug and formulation is determined through pH-solubility and pH-stability profiles. Suitable buffering agents (e.g., phosphate, acetate, citrate buffers) are selected to maintain the pH within the desired range.

**4. Isotonicity**

**Isotonicity** refers to the osmotic pressure of the formulation relative to body fluids, which is crucial for minimizing pain and tissue damage upon administration.

- **Importance**: Parenteral formulations must be isotonic with body fluids to prevent osmotic stress, which can cause cell lysis, pain, and irritation at the injection site.
- **Assessment**: Isotonicity is achieved by adjusting the formulation with isotonic agents such as sodium chloride, dextrose, or glycerol. Osmolality measurements are conducted to ensure the formulation is isotonic with physiological fluids.

### 5. Viscosity

**Viscosity** is an important factor affecting the ease of administration and the drug's release profile from the formulation.

- **Importance**: The viscosity of parenteral formulations influences syringeability, injectability, and the flow properties of the formulation. High viscosity can cause difficulty in administration and pain at the injection site.
- **Assessment**: Viscosity is measured using viscometers or rheometers, and appropriate viscosity modifiers (e.g., polyethylene glycol, polysorbates) are added to achieve the desired flow properties.

### 6. Compatibility with Excipients

**Compatibility with excipients** ensures that the drug does not interact adversely with other formulation components, which could affect stability, efficacy, or safety.

- **Importance**: Excipients are used to enhance solubility, stability, and bioavailability, as well as to provide isotonicity and buffering capacity. Incompatibilities can lead to degradation, precipitation, or loss of efficacy.
- **Assessment**: Compatibility studies involve mixing the drug with various excipients and evaluating the physical and chemical stability over time. Techniques such as differential scanning calorimetry (DSC), thermogravimetric analysis (TGA), and high-performance liquid chromatography (HPLC) are used to identify potential incompatibilities.

### 7. Particulate Matter

**Particulate matter** refers to unwanted particles that can be present in parenteral formulations, posing risks such as embolism and inflammation.

- **Importance**: The presence of particulate matter in parenteral formulations is strictly controlled to prevent adverse reactions and ensure patient safety.
- **Assessment**: Particulate matter is measured using methods such as light obscuration particle count test and microscopic particle count test. Filtration and aseptic processing techniques are employed to minimize particulate contamination.

**8. Sterility and Pyrogen Testing**

**Sterility and pyrogen testing** ensure that the parenteral formulation is free from microbial contamination and pyrogens, which can cause severe adverse reactions.

- **Importance**: Sterility is critical for parenteral products to prevent infections. Pyrogens, such as bacterial endotoxins, can induce fever and shock, making their removal essential.
- **Assessment**: Sterility testing is performed using membrane filtration or direct inoculation methods, following pharmacopeial guidelines. Pyrogen testing is conducted using the Limulus Amebocyte Lysate (LAL) test or the rabbit pyrogen test to detect endotoxins.

### 5.1.3 Essential Requirements

The formulation and manufacture of parenteral products are governed by stringent requirements to ensure their safety, efficacy, and quality. These essential requirements encompass various aspects, including sterility, pyrogen-free status, isotonicity, pH, particulate matter control, container-closure integrity, stability, and labeling. Meeting these requirements is critical to producing parenteral products that are safe for patient use and comply with regulatory standards.

**1. Sterility**

**Sterility** is the absence of viable microorganisms in the parenteral product. It is the most critical requirement for parenteral formulations to prevent infections and ensure patient safety.

- **Importance**: Parenteral products bypass the body's natural barriers, making sterility essential to avoid introducing harmful microorganisms into the bloodstream or tissues.

- **Achieving Sterility**: Sterilization methods include steam sterilization (autoclaving), dry heat sterilization, filtration, gas sterilization (ethylene oxide), and radiation. The choice of method depends on the nature of the product and its components.
- **Testing**: Sterility testing is performed using methods such as membrane filtration or direct inoculation, following pharmacopeial guidelines. The test involves incubating the product in a growth medium to check for microbial growth.

**2. Pyrogen-Free Status**

**Pyrogens** are substances that can induce fever when introduced into the body. Parenteral products must be free from pyrogens, particularly bacterial endotoxins.

- **Importance**: Pyrogens, especially endotoxins from Gram-negative bacteria, can cause severe reactions, including fever, shock, and potentially life-threatening complications.
- **Achieving Pyrogen-Free Status**: Manufacturing processes must be designed to minimize endotoxin contamination. This includes using high-quality raw materials, implementing stringent cleaning procedures, and conducting endotoxin removal steps.
- **Testing**: Pyrogen testing is conducted using the Limulus Amebocyte Lysate (LAL) test, which is highly sensitive to endotoxins, or the rabbit pyrogen test.

**3. Isotonicity**

**Isotonicity** refers to the osmotic pressure of the parenteral product, which should be similar to that of body fluids to prevent cellular damage.

- **Importance**: Isotonic solutions prevent osmotic stress on cells, which can cause pain, irritation, and tissue damage at the injection site.
- **Achieving Isotonicity**: Formulations are adjusted using isotonic agents such as sodium chloride, dextrose, or glycerol. The osmolality of the product is measured to ensure it is within the acceptable range for physiological compatibility.
- **Testing**: Osmolality testing is conducted using osmometers to ensure the product is isotonic with body fluids.

### 4. pH

**pH** of the parenteral product should be within a range that is compatible with body fluids and does not cause irritation or instability of the drug.

- **Importance**: The pH affects the solubility, stability, and bioavailability of the drug, as well as the comfort and safety of the patient.
- **Achieving the Desired pH**: Buffer systems (e.g., phosphate, acetate, citrate) are used to maintain the pH within the desired range.
- **Testing**: pH is measured using pH meters to ensure it falls within the specified range for the formulation.

### 5. Particulate Matter Control

**Particulate matter** includes extraneous, mobile, undissolved particles that are unintentionally present in parenteral products.

- **Importance**: Particulate matter can cause serious complications such as embolism, inflammation, and local tissue reactions.
- **Achieving Particulate Matter Control**: The manufacturing environment must be controlled to minimize particulate contamination. This includes using cleanrooms, filtration, and aseptic techniques.
- **Testing**: Particulate matter is measured using light obscuration particle count tests and microscopic particle count tests as specified by pharmacopeial standards.

### 6. Container-Closure Integrity

**Container-closure integrity** ensures that the packaging system adequately protects the parenteral product from contamination and maintains its sterility and stability.

- **Importance**: A robust container-closure system prevents microbial ingress, maintains the product's sterility, and protects it from environmental factors.
- **Achieving Integrity**: Containers and closures are selected based on compatibility with the product and their ability to maintain a sterile barrier. This includes materials like glass vials, plastic containers, and rubber stoppers.
- **Testing**: Container-closure integrity testing methods include dye ingress tests, vacuum decay tests, and microbial ingress tests.

**7. Stability**

**Stability** ensures that the parenteral product retains its quality, efficacy, and safety throughout its shelf life.

- **Importance**: Stability testing confirms that the product remains within its specified limits for potency, purity, and physical characteristics over time.
- **Achieving Stability**: Formulation optimization, appropriate packaging, and controlled storage conditions are essential to maintain stability.
- **Testing**: Stability testing involves subjecting the product to various environmental conditions (e.g., temperature, humidity, light) and conducting periodic assays to monitor changes in its properties.

**8. Labeling**

**Labeling** provides critical information about the parenteral product, including its identity, dosage, administration route, storage conditions, and expiration date.

- **Importance**: Proper labeling ensures safe and effective use of the product by healthcare professionals and patients.
- **Achieving Compliance**: Labels must comply with regulatory requirements and include all necessary information to prevent medication errors and ensure patient safety.
- **Testing**: Labeling compliance is verified through inspections and audits to ensure all regulatory and safety requirements are met.

### 5.1.4 Vehicles and Additives

**Introduction**

In the formulation of parenteral products, the choice of vehicles and additives is crucial for ensuring the stability, efficacy, and safety of the final product. Vehicles are the carriers or solvents in which the active pharmaceutical ingredient (API) is dissolved or suspended, while additives are substances added to the formulation to enhance its properties. The selection of appropriate vehicles and additives depends on the physicochemical properties of the API, the desired therapeutic effect, and the route of administration.

**Vehicles**

**Vehicles** are the primary solvents or carriers used in parenteral formulations. They must be physiologically compatible, non-toxic, and capable of maintaining the stability and solubility of the API.

**1. Aqueous Vehicles**

Aqueous vehicles are the most commonly used solvents in parenteral formulations due to their compatibility with the body's physiological environment.

- **Water for Injection (WFI)**: Water for Injection is sterile, pyrogen-free water used as a solvent for parenteral products. It is used either alone or as a component of other aqueous vehicles.
- **Sodium Chloride Solution**: A 0.9% sodium chloride solution (normal saline) is isotonic with body fluids and commonly used as a vehicle for parenteral drugs.
- **Dextrose Solution**: Aqueous solutions of dextrose (e.g., 5% dextrose) are used as vehicles for drugs, providing an energy source for patients while maintaining isotonicity.
- **Ringer's Solution**: A balanced salt solution containing sodium chloride, potassium chloride, and calcium chloride, used as a vehicle for parenteral nutrition and drug delivery.

**2. Non-Aqueous Vehicles**

Non-aqueous vehicles are used when the API is poorly soluble in water or requires a different solvent environment for stability or solubility.

- **Fixed Oils**: Oils such as soybean oil, sesame oil, and peanut oil are used as vehicles for lipid-soluble drugs. They must be of vegetable origin, non-toxic, and free from rancidity.
- **Polyethylene Glycol (PEG)**: PEGs are water-soluble polymers used as solvents or co-solvents in parenteral formulations. They are available in various molecular weights, providing flexibility in formulation design.
- **Propylene Glycol**: Propylene glycol is a commonly used co-solvent that enhances the solubility of certain drugs. It is miscible with water and other solvents.
- **Glycerin**: Glycerin is used as a solvent and stabilizer in parenteral formulations. It is miscible with water and can enhance the solubility and stability of the API.

**Additives**

**Additives** are substances added to parenteral formulations to enhance their stability, solubility, safety, and efficacy. Common additives include preservatives, antioxidants, buffering agents, solubilizing agents, and tonicity adjusters.

**1. Preservatives**

Preservatives are added to multi-dose parenteral formulations to prevent microbial growth and ensure product safety.

- **Benzyl Alcohol**: A commonly used preservative in parenteral formulations, effective against a wide range of microorganisms.
- **Phenol and Cresol**: These preservatives are used in certain vaccines and injectable formulations for their antimicrobial properties.
- **Parabens (Methylparaben, Propylparaben)**: Parabens are used as preservatives in parenteral formulations, providing broad-spectrum antimicrobial activity.

**2. Antioxidants**

Antioxidants are added to parenteral formulations to prevent oxidative degradation of the API, which can compromise its stability and efficacy.

- **Ascorbic Acid**: Used as an antioxidant to protect APIs from oxidation.
- **Sodium Metabisulfite**: An effective antioxidant that prevents oxidation of susceptible APIs.
- **Butylated Hydroxyanisole (BHA) and Butylated Hydroxytoluene (BHT)**: Lipid-soluble antioxidants used in oil-based parenteral formulations.

**3. Buffering Agents**

Buffering agents are used to maintain the pH of the parenteral formulation within the desired range, ensuring stability and compatibility with the physiological environment.

- **Phosphate Buffers**: Commonly used to maintain the pH of parenteral formulations in the neutral range.
- **Acetate Buffers**: Used to maintain acidic pH in certain formulations.
- **Citrate Buffers**: Employed to achieve and maintain a slightly acidic to neutral pH.

**4. Solubilizing Agents**

Solubilizing agents enhance the solubility of poorly soluble APIs, enabling their formulation into stable and effective parenteral products.

- **Cyclodextrins**: Used to form inclusion complexes with APIs, improving their solubility and stability.
- **Polysorbates (Tween 20, Tween 80)**: Non-ionic surfactants that enhance the solubility of hydrophobic drugs.
- **Polyethylene Glycol (PEG)**: Used as a co-solvent to enhance the solubility of certain APIs.

**5. Tonicity Adjusters**

Tonicity adjusters are added to parenteral formulations to ensure they are isotonic with body fluids, preventing cellular damage and discomfort at the injection site.

- **Sodium Chloride**: Used to adjust the tonicity of parenteral formulations.
- **Dextrose**: Commonly used to achieve isotonicity in parenteral solutions.
- **Glycerin**: Can be used to adjust the tonicity of formulations while also acting as a solvent and stabilizer.

### 5.1.5 Importance of Isotonicity

**Introduction to Isotonicity**

**Isotonicity** refers to the osmotic pressure exerted by a solution compared to the osmotic pressure of body fluids such as blood plasma and cellular fluids. An isotonic solution has the same osmotic pressure as body fluids, which is essential for maintaining cellular integrity and function. In the context of parenteral formulations, ensuring isotonicity is crucial to prevent adverse reactions and ensure patient safety.

**Significance of Isotonicity in Parenteral Products**

**1. Prevention of Cellular Damage**

- **Osmotic Balance**: Isotonic solutions maintain osmotic balance between the parenteral solution and body fluids, preventing the movement of water into or out of cells. This balance is vital to maintain cell structure and function.
- **Hypertonic Solutions**: Solutions with higher osmotic pressure than body fluids cause water to move out of cells, leading to cell shrinkage and

potential damage (crenation).

- **Hypotonic Solutions**: Solutions with lower osmotic pressure than body fluids cause water to move into cells, leading to cell swelling and possible rupture (lysis).

**2. Reduction of Pain and Irritation at the Injection Site**

- **Pain Reduction**: Isotonic solutions minimize pain and irritation at the injection site by preventing osmotic stress on tissues. Hypertonic or hypotonic solutions can cause discomfort and pain due to the movement of water across cell membranes.
- **Tissue Compatibility**: Maintaining isotonicity ensures that the parenteral solution is compatible with tissues, reducing the risk of inflammation and irritation.

**3. Ensuring Drug Efficacy and Safety**

- **Drug Stability**: Isotonic solutions can help maintain the stability of the drug by preventing changes in the formulation that could occur due to osmotic imbalances.
- **Controlled Drug Release**: For certain controlled-release formulations, isotonicity ensures that the drug is released at a consistent rate, providing predictable therapeutic effects.

**4. Maintaining Blood Flow and Circulation**

- **Avoiding Hemolysis**: Isotonic solutions prevent hemolysis, the destruction of red blood cells, which can occur with hypotonic solutions. Hemolysis can lead to serious complications such as anemia and kidney damage.
- **Maintaining Circulatory Function**: Isotonic solutions help maintain normal blood flow and circulation by preventing the aggregation of blood cells and ensuring proper blood viscosity.

**5. Compatibility with Infusion Systems and Devices**

- **Device Functionality**: Ensuring isotonicity is important for the proper functioning of infusion systems and devices, such as intravenous catheters and pumps. Osmotic imbalances can affect the flow rate and stability of the infusion.

- **Minimizing Complications**: Isotonic solutions reduce the risk of complications associated with the use of infusion devices, such as phlebitis (inflammation of the veins) and infiltration (leakage of the solution into surrounding tissues).

**Achieving and Testing Isotonicity**

**1. Formulation Adjustments**

- **Osmolality Agents**: Tonicity adjusters such as sodium chloride, dextrose, and glycerin are used to adjust the osmolality of parenteral solutions to match that of body fluids.
- **Buffer Systems**: Buffer systems may also be employed to maintain the desired pH while ensuring isotonicity.

**2. Testing Methods**

- **Osmolality Testing**: The osmolality of the formulation is measured using osmometry techniques to ensure it falls within the desired range for isotonicity.
- **Freezing Point Depression**: This method measures the freezing point of the solution, which correlates with its osmolality. An isotonic solution has a freezing point depression similar to that of body fluids.
- **Vapor Pressure Osmometry**: This technique measures the vapor pressure of the solution to determine its osmolality.

**Clinical Considerations**

**1. Patient-Specific Needs**

- **Tailored Solutions**: In certain clinical situations, the isotonicity of parenteral solutions may need to be adjusted based on patient-specific needs, such as in patients with altered fluid balance or electrolyte imbalances.

**2. Monitoring and Management**

- **Monitoring**: Continuous monitoring of patients receiving parenteral therapy is essential to ensure that the solution remains isotonic and to detect any signs of osmotic imbalances.
- **Intervention**: If osmotic imbalances are detected, appropriate interventions such as adjusting the formulation or changing the infusion rate may be required.

## 5.2 Production Procedures

### 5.2.1 Production Facilities and Controls

**Introduction to Production Facilities and Controls**

The production of parenteral products requires highly controlled environments to ensure sterility, safety, and efficacy. Production facilities must be designed and maintained to minimize the risk of contamination and ensure compliance with regulatory standards. This involves stringent controls over the manufacturing environment, equipment, personnel, and processes.

**Production Facilities**

**1. Cleanrooms**

**Cleanrooms** are specialized environments with controlled levels of contamination, designed to maintain sterility during the production of parenteral products.

- **Classifications**: Cleanrooms are classified based on the number of particles per cubic meter, as specified by standards such as ISO 14644-1. Common classifications for parenteral production include ISO Class 5 (Class 100) for critical areas and ISO Class 7 (Class 10,000) for less critical areas.
- **Design and Layout**: Cleanrooms are designed with smooth, non-porous surfaces to facilitate cleaning and minimize particle accumulation. The layout should minimize personnel movement and reduce the risk of cross-contamination.
- **Air Quality**: High-efficiency particulate air (HEPA) filters are used to maintain air quality by removing particles and microorganisms from the air. Laminar airflow systems ensure a unidirectional flow of filtered air to prevent contamination.

**2. Equipment and Utilities**

**Equipment and utilities** used in the production of parenteral products must be designed for easy cleaning, sterilization, and maintenance.

- **Sterilization Equipment**: Autoclaves, dry heat ovens, and gas sterilizers are used to sterilize equipment, containers, and closures.
- **Water Systems**: Water for Injection (WFI) systems provide sterile, pyrogen-free water used in formulations and cleaning processes. The water must be continuously monitored and tested for compliance.
- **HVAC Systems**: Heating, ventilation, and air conditioning (HVAC) systems control temperature, humidity, and air quality in the production areas. Regular maintenance and validation ensure their effectiveness.

**3. Environmental Monitoring**

**Environmental monitoring** is essential to ensure that the cleanroom environment remains within specified limits for particulate and microbial contamination.

- **Air Sampling**: Regular air sampling is conducted using impaction, filtration, or sedimentation methods to detect airborne particles and microorganisms.
- **Surface Monitoring**: Surfaces, equipment, and personnel are routinely monitored using contact plates, swabs, or settle plates to detect microbial contamination.
- **Temperature and Humidity Control**: Continuous monitoring of temperature and humidity ensures that the production environment remains within specified limits.

**Controls**

**1. Personnel Controls**

**Personnel controls** are crucial to minimize contamination risks associated with human activity in the production environment.

- **Training**: All personnel involved in the production of parenteral products must receive comprehensive training in aseptic techniques, cleanroom behavior, and hygiene practices.
- **Gowning Procedures**: Personnel must follow strict gowning procedures, including wearing sterile gowns, gloves, masks, and shoe covers. Gowning should be performed in designated areas to prevent

contamination.

- **Access Control**: Access to cleanrooms and critical areas should be restricted to authorized personnel only. Entry and exit procedures must be followed to maintain the integrity of the cleanroom environment.

**2. Process Controls**

**Process controls** ensure that all manufacturing processes are consistently performed according to validated procedures and specifications.

- **Standard Operating Procedures (SOPs)**: Detailed SOPs must be in place for all production processes, including cleaning, sterilization, formulation, filling, and packaging.
- **Batch Records**: Comprehensive batch records document every step of the production process, ensuring traceability and accountability. Any deviations from the process must be recorded and investigated.
- **Validation**: All processes, equipment, and systems must be validated to demonstrate their reliability and consistency in producing sterile products. This includes process validation, equipment qualification, and cleaning validation.

**3. Quality Control**

**Quality control (QC)** involves rigorous testing of raw materials, in-process materials, and finished products to ensure compliance with specifications and regulatory requirements.

- **Raw Material Testing**: All raw materials must be tested for identity, purity, potency, and microbial contamination before use in production.
- **In-Process Testing**: In-process testing monitors critical parameters such as pH, osmolality, and particulate matter during production to ensure that the process remains within control limits.
- **Finished Product Testing**: Finished products undergo comprehensive testing, including sterility testing, pyrogen testing, and potency assays, to confirm their quality and safety.

### 5.2.2 Aseptic Processing

**Introduction to Aseptic Processing**

Aseptic processing involves the handling of sterile drug products and components in a controlled environment to prevent microbial contamination. It is essential for products that cannot be terminally sterilized and require aseptic techniques to maintain sterility throughout the manufacturing process.

**Key Elements of Aseptic Processing**

**1. Sterile Materials and Equipment**

- **Sterilization Methods**: Equipment, containers, closures, and other materials are sterilized using methods such as autoclaving, dry heat sterilization, ethylene oxide gas sterilization, and gamma irradiation. The choice of method depends on the nature of the materials and their compatibility with the sterilization process.
- **Sterile Filtration**: Liquid drug products are often sterilized by filtration through a 0.22-micron filter to remove microorganisms. The integrity of the filter must be validated before and after use.

**2. Aseptic Technique**

- **Aseptic Assembly**: All aseptic operations, including the assembly of sterile components and the filling of sterile products, must be performed using aseptic techniques to prevent contamination.
- **Laminar Flow Hoods**: Laminar flow hoods or isolators provide a sterile environment for aseptic processing. HEPA-filtered air flows unidirectionally to protect the product from contamination.
- **Personnel Practices**: Personnel must follow strict aseptic techniques, including minimizing movement, avoiding direct contact with sterile surfaces, and performing manipulations in a manner that reduces the risk of contamination.

**3. Environmental Monitoring**

- **Continuous Monitoring**: Continuous environmental monitoring is essential to detect any changes in the cleanroom environment that could compromise sterility. This includes monitoring airborne particles, microbial contamination, temperature, and humidity.
- **Interventions**: Any interventions or disturbances in the aseptic processing area must be minimized and carefully controlled. If an

intervention is necessary, it should be documented, and additional environmental monitoring should be conducted.

**4. Aseptic Filling**

- **Filling Operations**: Aseptic filling involves transferring the sterile drug product into sterile containers in a controlled environment. Automated filling machines with aseptic features are commonly used to minimize human intervention and reduce contamination risk.
- **Container Closure**: The filled containers must be immediately and securely closed using sterile closures to maintain sterility. This includes capping, stoppering, or sealing the containers in a sterile environment.

**5. Validation and Qualification**

- **Process Validation**: Aseptic processing must be validated to ensure that it consistently produces sterile products. This includes media fill simulations, where a microbiological growth medium is used to simulate the product and filling process, to detect potential contamination.
- **Equipment Qualification**: All equipment used in aseptic processing must be qualified to ensure it operates correctly and consistently. This includes installation qualification (IQ), operational qualification (OQ), and performance qualification (PQ).

**6. Quality Assurance**

- **Sterility Testing**: Sterility testing is performed on samples of the finished product to confirm that they are free from viable microorganisms. This is typically done using direct inoculation or membrane filtration methods.
- **Endotoxin Testing**: Parenteral products must be tested for bacterial endotoxins to ensure they are pyrogen-free. The Limulus Amebocyte Lysate (LAL) test is commonly used for this purpose.
- **Environmental Control**: Strict control and monitoring of the aseptic processing environment are essential to ensure that all conditions meet the required standards for sterility.

## 5.3 Formulation of Injections

### 5.3.1 Sterile Powders

**Introduction to Sterile Powders**

Sterile powders are lyophilized or freeze-dried forms of medications intended for parenteral administration. These powders are reconstituted with a suitable solvent before injection. The formulation of sterile powders is crucial for drugs that are unstable in solution form or require long-term storage stability. Sterile powders offer advantages such as extended shelf life, stability, and ease of transportation.

**Formulation Considerations for Sterile Powders**

**1. Choice of Drug and Excipients**

- **Active Pharmaceutical Ingredient (API)**: The selection of the API is based on its therapeutic effect, stability, and compatibility with excipients.
- **Excipients**: Common excipients include bulking agents (e.g., mannitol, lactose), stabilizers (e.g., albumin, glycine), and buffers (e.g., phosphate, citrate). These excipients help maintain the stability and integrity of the API during the freeze-drying process and subsequent storage.

**2. Preparation of Solution**

- **Solubilization**: The API and excipients are dissolved in a suitable solvent, typically Water for Injection (WFI). The solution must be clear and free from particulate matter.
- **pH Adjustment**: The pH of the solution is adjusted to the optimal range for the stability of the API and the desired therapeutic effect. Buffering agents are used to maintain this pH during the freeze-drying process and storage.

**3. Sterilization**

- **Filtration**: The solution is sterilized by filtration through a 0.22-micron filter to remove any microorganisms. This step ensures the sterility of the solution before it is filled into vials.
- **Aseptic Processing**: The sterilized solution is transferred aseptically into sterile vials under laminar airflow conditions to prevent contamination.

**4. Freeze-Drying (Lyophilization)**

- **Filling**: The sterilized solution is filled into vials, and the fill volume is accurately controlled to ensure uniformity.
- **Freezing**: The filled vials are rapidly frozen at low temperatures to solidify the solution. This step is critical for forming a solid matrix that will be stable during the drying process.
- **Primary Drying (Sublimation)**: The frozen vials are placed in a freeze-dryer, and a vacuum is applied. Heat is supplied to sublime the ice directly from solid to vapor without passing through the liquid phase, removing most of the water content.
- **Secondary Drying (Desorption)**: The temperature is gradually increased to remove any remaining bound water, ensuring the final product has minimal moisture content.

**5. Sealing and Packaging**

- **Sealing**: The vials are sealed with sterile rubber stoppers and aluminum caps to maintain sterility and protect the lyophilized product from moisture and contamination.
- **Packaging**: The sealed vials are labeled and packaged in suitable containers to protect them during storage and transportation. Appropriate labeling includes the drug name, dosage, reconstitution instructions, storage conditions, and expiration date.

**6. Quality Control**

- **Sterility Testing**: Sterility tests are performed to confirm that the final product is free from microbial contamination.
- **Moisture Content**: The residual moisture content is measured to ensure it is within acceptable limits, which is critical for the stability of the lyophilized product.
- **Reconstitution Time**: The time required to reconstitute the powder with the solvent is tested to ensure it meets the specified criteria for clinical use.
- **Potency and Purity**: The potency and purity of the reconstituted product are tested to ensure it meets the required specifications for therapeutic efficacy and safety.

### 5.3.2 Large Volume Parenterals

**Introduction to Large Volume Parenterals**

Large volume parenterals (LVPs) are sterile solutions typically administered intravenously in volumes of 100 ml or more. They are used for fluid replacement, electrolyte balance, and as vehicles for delivering medications. Common examples include saline solutions, dextrose solutions, and nutrient solutions.

**Formulation Considerations for Large Volume Parenterals**

**1. Choice of Solution**

- **Types of LVPs**: Common LVPs include isotonic saline (0.9% sodium chloride), dextrose solutions (e.g., 5% dextrose in water), Ringer's solution, and lactated Ringer's solution.
- **Compatibility**: The formulation must be compatible with the patient's physiology and other medications that may be co-administered.

**2. Composition**

- **Active Ingredients**: Depending on the intended use, LVPs may contain electrolytes (e.g., sodium, potassium, calcium), nutrients (e.g., amino acids, vitamins), or medications (e.g., antibiotics, analgesics).
- **Solvent**: The primary solvent for LVPs is Water for Injection (WFI), which is sterile and pyrogen-free.

**3. Sterilization**

- **Aseptic Preparation**: The solution is prepared aseptically to prevent contamination. All ingredients and equipment used must be sterile.
- **Terminal Sterilization**: LVPs are often terminally sterilized using methods such as autoclaving, which involves steam sterilization at high temperatures and pressures to ensure sterility.

**4. Packaging**

- **Containers**: LVPs are typically packaged in glass or plastic containers, such as bottles, bags, or flexible pouches. The choice of container depends on factors like compatibility, ease of use, and storage requirements.

- **Sealing**: Containers are sealed with sterile closures, such as rubber stoppers or plastic ports, to maintain sterility and allow for easy administration.

**5. Quality Control**

- **Sterility Testing**: LVPs undergo sterility testing to confirm the absence of microbial contamination.
- **Particulate Matter**: The presence of particulate matter is tested using methods such as light obscuration particle count test and microscopic particle count test to ensure the solution is free from visible particles.
- **Pyrogen Testing**: Pyrogen testing, typically using the Limulus Amebocyte Lysate (LAL) test, is performed to ensure the solution is free from pyrogens.
- **Osmolality and pH**: The osmolality and pH of the solution are tested to ensure they are within acceptable ranges for physiological compatibility.
- **Potency and Purity**: The concentration and purity of the active ingredients are tested to ensure they meet the specified requirements.

**6. Storage and Stability**

- **Storage Conditions**: LVPs should be stored under controlled conditions, typically at room temperature or refrigerated, depending on the formulation. Storage conditions should prevent exposure to light and extreme temperatures.
- **Shelf Life**: Stability studies are conducted to determine the shelf life of the product, ensuring it remains stable and effective throughout its intended use period.

### 5.3.3 Lyophilized Products

**Introduction to Lyophilized Products**

Lyophilized products, also known as freeze-dried products, are pharmaceuticals that have been dehydrated by a process called lyophilization. This technique is particularly beneficial for drugs that are unstable in liquid form. Lyophilization helps improve the stability, shelf life, and transportability of pharmaceuticals. These products are reconstituted with a suitable solvent before administration, typically as injections.

**Advantages of Lyophilization**

1. **Enhanced Stability**: Lyophilization removes water from the product, which significantly improves the stability of drugs that are sensitive to hydrolysis and other degradation processes in aqueous solutions.
2. **Extended Shelf Life**: Lyophilized products have a longer shelf life compared to their liquid counterparts, making them suitable for long-term storage.
3. **Ease of Transportation**: Dehydrated products are lighter and easier to transport, especially for drugs that need to be shipped over long distances or to remote areas.
4. **Rapid Reconstitution**: Lyophilized products can be quickly reconstituted with a sterile solvent, providing a ready-to-use solution for injection.

**Lyophilization Process**

The lyophilization process involves three main stages: freezing, primary drying (sublimation), and secondary drying (desorption). Each stage is carefully controlled to ensure the production of a high-quality, stable product.

**1. Freezing**

**Freezing** is the initial stage of lyophilization, where the solution containing the drug and excipients is frozen to form a solid matrix.

- **Procedure**: The solution is filled into vials and cooled rapidly to temperatures below the eutectic point or glass transition temperature. This ensures the formation of a solid ice matrix.
- **Importance**: Proper freezing is crucial for creating a uniform and stable structure that facilitates effective sublimation during the primary drying phase.

**2. Primary Drying (Sublimation)**

**Primary drying** involves the removal of the frozen solvent (usually water) by sublimation under vacuum.

- **Procedure**: The frozen vials are placed in a freeze-dryer, and a vacuum is applied. The temperature is gradually increased to provide the energy needed for sublimation. Ice transitions directly from solid to vapor without passing through the liquid phase.
- **Importance**: This stage removes most of the water content and requires careful control to avoid melting the product. Effective primary drying

results in a porous structure that allows for efficient secondary drying.

**3. Secondary Drying (Desorption)**

**Secondary drying** removes any residual water molecules bound to the product.

- **Procedure**: The temperature is increased further under continued vacuum conditions to desorb the remaining bound water.
- **Importance**: Secondary drying ensures the final product has minimal moisture content, which is essential for stability during storage.

**Formulation Considerations**

**1. Selection of Excipients**

- **Bulking Agents**: Substances like mannitol, lactose, or sucrose are added to provide bulk to the product, ensuring a uniform and easily handleable cake after lyophilization.
- **Stabilizers**: These agents, such as glycine or trehalose, help stabilize the drug during the freeze-drying process and subsequent storage.
- **Buffers**: Buffers such as citrate or phosphate are used to maintain the pH of the solution, which is critical for the stability of the drug.

**2. Optimization of Lyophilization Cycle**

- **Freezing Rate**: The rate at which the solution is frozen can affect the size and distribution of ice crystals, impacting the efficiency of sublimation and the quality of the final product.
- **Primary Drying Parameters**: The temperature and pressure conditions must be optimized to ensure effective sublimation without collapsing the product structure.
- **Secondary Drying Parameters**: The final drying temperature and duration must be carefully controlled to achieve the desired residual moisture content.

**Quality Control**

**1. Residual Moisture Content**

- **Importance**: The residual moisture content must be within specified limits to ensure the stability and shelf life of the lyophilized product.
- **Testing**: Methods such as Karl Fischer titration or gravimetric analysis are used to measure the moisture content.

**2. Reconstitution Time**

- **Importance**: The product should reconstitute rapidly and completely in the specified solvent to ensure ease of use in clinical settings.
- **Testing**: The reconstitution time is measured by adding the solvent to the lyophilized cake and recording the time taken for complete dissolution.

**3. Sterility**

- **Importance**: Sterility is crucial for parenteral products to prevent infections.
- **Testing**: Sterility testing is performed according to pharmacopeial standards to ensure the absence of viable microorganisms.

**4. Potency and Purity**

- **Importance**: The potency and purity of the reconstituted product must meet the specified requirements to ensure therapeutic efficacy and safety.
- **Testing**: Analytical methods such as high-performance liquid chromatography (HPLC) are used to determine the potency and purity of the product.

**5. Appearance**

- **Importance**: The lyophilized cake should have a uniform appearance without signs of collapse or shrinkage, which can indicate issues during the lyophilization process.
- **Testing**: Visual inspection is performed to assess the appearance of the lyophilized product.

**Packaging and Storage**

**1. Packaging**

- **Vials and Stoppers**: Lyophilized products are typically packaged in glass vials sealed with rubber stoppers and aluminum caps to maintain sterility and protect the product from moisture.
- **Labeling**: Vials are labeled with essential information, including the drug name, dosage, reconstitution instructions, storage conditions, and expiration date.

**2. Storage Conditions**

- **Temperature**: Lyophilized products should be stored at controlled temperatures, usually at room temperature or refrigerated, depending on the stability of the drug.
- **Humidity**: Packaging should protect the product from moisture, as increased humidity can compromise the stability of the lyophilized cake.

## 5.4 Containers and Closures

### 5.4.1 Selection of Containers

**Introduction to Container Selection**

The selection of appropriate containers is critical in the formulation of parenteral products to ensure their stability, sterility, and compatibility. The choice of container depends on various factors, including the nature of the drug, the type of parenteral product, storage conditions, and regulatory requirements. Common containers for parenteral products include ampoules, vials, prefilled syringes, and infusion bags.

**Types of Containers**

**1. Ampoules**

- **Material**: Ampoules are typically made of glass, which can be either clear or amber-colored to protect light-sensitive drugs.
- **Usage**: Ampoules are used for single-dose parenteral products. They provide a hermetic seal that ensures sterility and protection from contamination.
- **Advantages**: Complete sealing prevents contamination, and the glass material offers excellent chemical resistance.
- **Disadvantages**: Ampoules require careful handling to avoid breakage and contamination during opening.

**2. Vials**

- **Material**: Vials are made of glass or plastic and come in various sizes. Glass vials are more common due to their chemical resistance.
- **Usage**: Vials can be used for single-dose or multi-dose parenteral products. They are sealed with rubber stoppers and aluminum caps.
- **Advantages**: Vials are versatile and can accommodate a wide range of drug formulations. They are suitable for both liquid and lyophilized products.
- **Disadvantages**: The rubber stopper can interact with the drug, potentially causing stability issues. Proper sterilization and handling are required to maintain sterility.

### 3. Prefilled Syringes

- **Material**: Prefilled syringes are made of glass or plastic, with plastic being more common due to its breakage resistance.
- **Usage**: Prefilled syringes are used for single-dose administration, offering convenience and reducing the risk of dosing errors.
- **Advantages**: Prefilled syringes are user-friendly, reduce preparation time, and minimize the risk of contamination.
- **Disadvantages**: They are generally more expensive than vials and ampoules and have limited volume capacity.

### 4. Infusion Bags

- **Material**: Infusion bags are typically made of plastic materials such as polyvinyl chloride (PVC), ethylene-vinyl acetate (EVA), or polypropylene (PP).
- **Usage**: Infusion bags are used for large volume parenteral solutions administered intravenously.
- **Advantages**: Infusion bags are lightweight, flexible, and can accommodate large volumes of fluids. They are suitable for a variety of intravenous therapies.
- **Disadvantages**: Some plastic materials can leach plasticizers into the solution, potentially causing compatibility issues with certain drugs.

### Selection Criteria

### 1. Compatibility

- **Chemical Compatibility**: The container material must not interact with the drug formulation, causing degradation or loss of potency.
- **Physical Compatibility**: The container must be able to withstand sterilization processes and storage conditions without compromising its integrity.

**2. Protection**

- **Light Protection**: For light-sensitive drugs, amber-colored glass or opaque plastic containers are used to protect the drug from light-induced degradation.
- **Moisture Protection**: The container must protect the drug from moisture, which can affect the stability of the formulation, especially for lyophilized products.

**3. Sterility**

- **Sterile Barrier**: The container must provide a sterile barrier to prevent microbial contamination during storage and use.
- **Sealing Integrity**: Proper sealing of the container is essential to maintain sterility. Rubber stoppers, crimp caps, and break-off tops are commonly used sealing methods.

**4. Ease of Use**

- **Administration**: The container should facilitate easy and accurate administration of the drug, minimizing the risk of dosing errors.
- **Handling**: The container should be easy to handle, especially in clinical settings where quick access to the drug is required.

**5. Regulatory Compliance**

- **Standards**: The container must comply with regulatory standards such as those set by the United States Pharmacopeia (USP), European Pharmacopoeia (Ph. Eur.), and other relevant authorities.
- **Documentation**: Proper documentation of the container's compatibility, sterility, and quality control measures must be maintained to meet regulatory requirements.

### 5.4.2 Filling and Sealing of Ampoules and Vials

**Introduction to Filling and Sealing**

The filling and sealing of ampoules and vials are critical steps in the manufacturing of parenteral products. These processes must be carried out under aseptic conditions to ensure the sterility and integrity of the final product. The choice of filling and sealing methods depends on the type of container, the nature of the drug product, and the production scale.

**Filling Processes**

**1. Ampoule Filling**

- **Aseptic Filling**: Ampoules are filled with the drug solution using automated aseptic filling machines. The filling process must be carried out in a controlled environment, typically under laminar airflow to prevent contamination.
- **Volume Control**: Precision filling nozzles are used to ensure accurate filling volumes, which is critical for maintaining dosage accuracy.

**2. Vial Filling**

- **Aseptic Filling**: Vials are filled aseptically using automated filling lines. The filling environment must be controlled to maintain sterility, and the equipment must be regularly validated.
- **Lyophilized Products**: For lyophilized products, the solution is filled into vials, which are then partially stoppered before being transferred to the lyophilizer. After lyophilization, the vials are fully stoppered and sealed.

**Sealing Processes**

**1. Ampoule Sealing**

- **Flame Sealing**: After filling, the open end of the ampoule is flame-sealed using a high-temperature flame. The glass is melted and fused to form a hermetic seal, ensuring sterility.
- **Inspection**: Sealed ampoules are inspected for defects such as cracks or incomplete seals, which could compromise sterility.

**2. Vial Sealing**

- **Stoppering**: After filling, vials are sealed with sterile rubber stoppers. For lyophilized products, the stoppers are partially inserted before lyophilization and fully inserted afterward.
- **Capping**: Vials are then sealed with aluminum crimp caps, which provide an additional layer of protection and ensure the integrity of the rubber stopper.

**Quality Control**

- **Sterility Testing**: Sterility tests are performed on samples to ensure that the filling and sealing processes have maintained the sterility of the product.
- **Leak Testing**: Sealed containers are subjected to leak testing to ensure the integrity of the seal. Common methods include vacuum decay, dye ingress, and helium leak testing.
- **Visual Inspection**: Filled and sealed ampoules and vials are visually inspected for defects such as particulate matter, fill volume accuracy, and sealing integrity.

### 5.4.3 Infusion Fluids

**Introduction to Infusion Fluids**

Infusion fluids are sterile solutions administered intravenously in large volumes. They are used to maintain hydration, provide electrolytes, deliver medications, and support nutritional needs. The formulation, packaging, and administration of infusion fluids require careful consideration to ensure safety and efficacy.

**Formulation of Infusion Fluids**

**1. Types of Infusion Fluids**

- **Crystalloids**: Solutions containing small molecules such as sodium chloride, dextrose, and lactate. Common examples include normal saline (0.9% sodium chloride) and Ringer's lactate.
- **Colloids**: Solutions containing larger molecules such as proteins or starches, which remain in the vascular compartment longer. Examples include albumin solutions and hydroxyethyl starch.

**2. Composition**

- **Electrolytes**: Infusion fluids often contain electrolytes such as sodium, potassium, calcium, and magnesium to maintain electrolyte balance.
- **Carbohydrates**: Dextrose is commonly added to provide an energy source.
- **Buffers**: Buffers such as lactate or acetate are added to help maintain the acid-base balance.

**Packaging of Infusion Fluids**

**1. Infusion Bags**

- **Material**: Infusion bags are typically made of plastic materials such as polyvinyl chloride (PVC), ethylene-vinyl acetate (EVA), or polypropylene (PP).
- **Features**: Infusion bags are designed with ports for adding medications and connecting to infusion sets. They are flexible and collapse as the fluid is infused, eliminating the need for air vents.

**2. Bottles**

- **Material**: Glass or plastic bottles can also be used for infusion fluids. Glass bottles are chemically inert but heavier and more prone to breakage.
- **Features**: Bottles are sealed with rubber stoppers and aluminum caps, providing a secure barrier against contamination.

**Administration of Infusion Fluids**

**1. Intravenous Infusion**

- **IV Sets**: Infusion fluids are administered using intravenous (IV) sets, which include tubing, drip chambers, and flow regulators.
- **Pumps**: Electronic infusion pumps are often used to control the flow rate accurately, ensuring precise delivery of the fluid.

**2. Additives**

- **Medication Addition**: Medications can be added to infusion fluids through the medication port. This must be done aseptically to prevent contamination.

- **Compatibility**: Compatibility of the medication with the infusion fluid must be verified to prevent precipitation or degradation.

**Quality Control and Safety**

**1. Sterility**

- **Importance**: Infusion fluids must be sterile to prevent infections.
- **Testing**: Sterility testing is conducted on samples to ensure the absence of microbial contamination.

**2. Particulate Matter**

- **Importance**: Infusion fluids must be free from visible and sub-visible particles to prevent complications such as embolism.
- **Testing**: Particulate matter testing is performed using light obscuration and microscopic methods.

**3. Pyrogen Testing**

- **Importance**: Infusion fluids must be free from pyrogens to prevent febrile reactions.
- **Testing**: Pyrogen testing is conducted using the Limulus Amebocyte Lysate (LAL) test or the rabbit pyrogen test.

**4. Stability Testing**

- **Importance**: Stability testing ensures that the infusion fluid remains effective and safe throughout its shelf life.
- **Testing**: Stability studies include tests for physical and chemical stability, sterility, and container integrity.

## 5.5 Quality Control Tests

### 5.5.1 For Parenteral Products

Quality control (QC) tests are essential in ensuring the safety, efficacy, and consistency of parenteral products. These tests encompass a wide range of parameters, including sterility, pyrogenicity, particulate matter, potency, and stability, among others. Adhering to stringent QC protocols ensures that parenteral products meet the necessary regulatory requirements and provide therapeutic benefits without causing harm to patients.

**1. Sterility Testing**

**Sterility testing** is performed to ensure that parenteral products are free from viable microorganisms. This is crucial as any contamination can lead to severe infections in patients.

- **Methods**: Common methods include membrane filtration and direct inoculation.
    - **Membrane Filtration**: The product is filtered through a membrane that captures any microorganisms. The membrane is then incubated in a suitable growth medium to detect microbial growth.
    - **Direct Inoculation**: The product is directly inoculated into a growth medium and incubated to detect any microbial contamination.
- **Incubation Conditions**: Incubation typically occurs at 20-25°C for fungi and at 30-35°C for bacteria, for a period of 14 days.

**2. Pyrogen Testing**

**Pyrogen testing** ensures that the parenteral product is free from pyrogens, substances that can cause fever when administered to patients.

- **Methods**: The two main tests are the **Rabbit Pyrogen Test** and the **Limulus Amebocyte Lysate (LAL) Test**.
    - **Rabbit Pyrogen Test**: The product is injected into rabbits, and their body temperatures are monitored. An increase in temperature indicates the presence of pyrogens.
    - **LAL Test**: This in vitro test uses the blood of horseshoe crabs, which coagulates in the presence of bacterial endotoxins. It is more sensitive and specific than the rabbit test.

**3. Particulate Matter Testing**

**Particulate matter testing** ensures that parenteral solutions are free from visible and sub-visible particles that could cause harm if injected.

- **Methods**: Common methods include light obscuration and microscopic particle count tests.

- **Light Obscuration**: This automated method detects particles based on the amount of light blocked as the solution passes through a light beam.
- **Microscopic Particle Count Test**: This method involves manually counting particles under a microscope.

**4. Potency and Purity Testing**

**Potency and purity testing** confirm that the active pharmaceutical ingredient (API) is present in the correct concentration and free from impurities.

- **Methods**: High-performance liquid chromatography (HPLC), gas chromatography (GC), and mass spectrometry (MS) are commonly used analytical techniques.

  - **HPLC**: Separates and quantifies the components of the product to ensure the correct concentration of the API and detect any impurities.
  - **GC**: Used for volatile compounds, providing precise quantification of the API and impurities.
  - **MS**: Identifies and quantifies the API and impurities based on their mass-to-charge ratio.

**5. Stability Testing**

**Stability testing** assesses the product's ability to maintain its quality, safety, and efficacy over time under various environmental conditions.

- **Methods**: Stability studies involve storing the product under different conditions and periodically testing for potency, purity, sterility, and physical properties.

  - **Storage Conditions**: Common conditions include accelerated stability testing (e.g., 40°C and 75% RH) and long-term stability testing (e.g., 25°C and 60% RH).
  - **Testing Parameters**: Parameters such as potency, pH, particulate matter, and sterility are tested at specified intervals to ensure the product remains stable throughout its shelf life.

**6. pH and Osmolality Testing**

**pH and osmolality testing** ensure that the parenteral product is physiologically compatible with the body, preventing irritation or damage upon administration.

- **pH Testing**: The pH of the product is measured using a pH meter to ensure it is within the specified range.
- **Osmolality Testing**: Osmolality is measured using an osmometer to ensure the solution is isotonic with body fluids.

**7. Container-Closure Integrity Testing**

**Container-closure integrity testing** ensures that the packaging system maintains the sterility and stability of the parenteral product throughout its shelf life.

- **Methods**: Common methods include dye ingress, vacuum decay, and helium leak testing.
    - **Dye Ingress**: The container is immersed in a dye solution, and any ingress of dye indicates a compromised seal.
    - **Vacuum Decay**: Detects leaks by measuring the pressure change in a vacuum chamber containing the sealed container.
    - **Helium Leak Testing**: Uses helium as a tracer gas to detect minute leaks in the container closure system.

**8. Visual Inspection**

**Visual inspection** is a critical QC step to detect visible defects such as particulate contamination, discoloration, or improper sealing.

- **Methods**: Manual or automated inspection systems are used to examine each container for defects.
    - **Manual Inspection**: Trained personnel inspect the containers under controlled lighting conditions.
    - **Automated Inspection**: High-speed machines equipped with cameras and sensors detect defects in containers.

**9. Endotoxin Testing**

**Endotoxin testing** is crucial to ensure the product is free from bacterial endotoxins, which can cause severe reactions in patients.

- **Methods**: The Limulus Amebocyte Lysate (LAL) test is the most commonly used method for detecting endotoxins.
    - **LAL Test**: Uses the blood extract of horseshoe crabs, which coagulates in the presence of endotoxins. The test is highly sensitive and specific for endotoxins.

# SIX

# OPHTHALMIC PREPARATIONS

## 6.1 Introduction and Formulation Considerations

### Introduction

The formulation of ophthalmic products, including eye drops and eye ointments, requires careful consideration to ensure safety, efficacy, and patient comfort. These products must be sterile, non-irritating, and compatible with the delicate tissues of the eye. The primary goals of ophthalmic formulations are to deliver the active pharmaceutical ingredient (API) effectively to the intended site of action and to maintain stability and sterility throughout the product's shelf life.

### 6.1.1 Formulation of Eye Drops

**Introduction to Eye Drops**

Eye drops are sterile liquid preparations designed for instillation into the eye. They are commonly used to treat various ocular conditions, including infections, allergies, glaucoma, and dry eye. The formulation of eye drops must ensure that the API is delivered efficiently, remains stable, and does not cause irritation or discomfort.

**Key Considerations in Formulating Eye Drops**

**1. Sterility**

- **Importance**: Sterility is crucial to prevent eye infections. All components and the final product must be sterile.
- **Sterilization Methods**: Common methods include autoclaving, sterile filtration, and aseptic processing.

**2. pH and Buffering**

- **Importance**: The pH of eye drops should be close to the physiological pH of tears (approximately 7.4) to minimize irritation.
- **Buffering Agents**: Buffers such as phosphate, citrate, and borate are used to maintain the pH within the desired range.

**3. Isotonicity**

- **Importance**: Eye drops should be isotonic with the natural fluids of the eye to avoid causing discomfort or osmotic stress.
- **Tonicity Adjusters**: Sodium chloride, dextrose, and boric acid are commonly used to adjust the tonicity of the formulation.

**4. Viscosity**

- **Importance**: The viscosity of eye drops affects their residence time in the eye. Slightly viscous solutions can improve contact time and bioavailability without causing blurring.
- **Viscosity Enhancers**: Agents such as methylcellulose, hydroxypropyl methylcellulose (HPMC), and polyvinyl alcohol are used to adjust viscosity.

**5. Preservatives**

- **Importance**: Multi-dose containers of eye drops require preservatives to prevent microbial contamination during use.
- **Common Preservatives**: Benzalkonium chloride, chlorobutanol, and thimerosal are commonly used. Preservative-free formulations are preferred for patients with sensitivities or when using unit-dose packaging.

**6. Solubility**

- **Importance**: The API must be adequately soluble in the chosen solvent to ensure uniform dosing.
- **Solubilizing Agents**: Surfactants such as polysorbates (Tween 20, Tween 80) and cyclodextrins can enhance solubility.

**7. Stability**

- **Importance**: The formulation must remain stable throughout its shelf life, with the API maintaining its potency and effectiveness.
- **Stabilizers**: Antioxidants such as sodium metabisulfite and chelating agents like edetate disodium (EDTA) are used to enhance stability.

**Example Formulation for Eye Drops**

- **API**: 0.5% w/v Timolol maleate
- **Buffer**: Phosphate buffer to maintain pH 7.4
- **Tonicity Adjuster**: Sodium chloride
- **Viscosity Enhancer**: Hydroxypropyl methylcellulose (HPMC)
- **Preservative**: Benzalkonium chloride 0.01%
- **Solvent**: Water for Injection (WFI)
- **Stabilizer**: Sodium metabisulfite

**Preparation Steps**

1. **Dissolve** the API, buffer, tonicity adjuster, viscosity enhancer, preservative, and stabilizer in WFI.
2. **Adjust the pH** to 7.4 if necessary.
3. **Filter** the solution through a 0.22-micron filter to ensure sterility.
4. **Aseptically fill** into sterile dropper bottles.
5. **Seal and label** the bottles, indicating storage conditions and expiration date.

**6.1.2 Formulation of Eye Ointments**

**Introduction to Eye Ointments**

Eye ointments are semi-solid preparations designed for application to the eye or eyelid. They provide prolonged contact time with the ocular surface, making them suitable for delivering drugs that benefit from extended exposure. Eye ointments are typically used to treat infections, inflammation, and dry eye conditions.

**Key Considerations in Formulating Eye Ointments**

**1. Base Selection**

- **Importance**: The base must be non-irritating, provide adequate drug release, and be stable.
- **Common Bases**: Petrolatum, mineral oil, and lanolin are frequently used as bases for eye ointments.

**2. Sterility**

- **Importance**: Sterility is essential to prevent eye infections.
- **Sterilization Methods**: Sterilization of the ointment base and aseptic processing of the final product are required. Terminal sterilization by heat is often used if compatible with the API and base.

**3. pH and Buffering**

- **Importance**: While ointments are not aqueous, any aqueous phase should be buffered to a pH close to that of tears.
- **Buffering Agents**: Similar to those used in eye drops, if an aqueous phase is present.

**4. Particle Size**

- **Importance**: The API must be finely milled to ensure comfort and prevent irritation.
- **Milling**: APIs are micronized to achieve the desired particle size, typically less than 10 microns.

**5. Preservatives**

- **Importance**: Multi-dose containers may require preservatives, although many eye ointments are packaged in single-use tubes to avoid the need for preservatives.
- **Common Preservatives**: Similar to those used in eye drops if required.

**6. Viscosity and Spreadability**

- **Importance**: The ointment must have suitable viscosity to stay in place while providing ease of application and comfort.

- **Adjusting Viscosity**: Adjusted by the ratio of different components in the base.

**Example Formulation for Eye Ointments**

- **API**: 1% w/w Erythromycin
- **Base**: White petrolatum and mineral oil (90:10 ratio)
- **Preservative**: None (single-use tube)
- **Stabilizer**: As needed based on API stability

**Preparation Steps**

1. **Sterilize** the base components (petrolatum and mineral oil) by heat.
2. **Micronize** the API to achieve the desired particle size.
3. **Mix** the sterilized base with the micronized API under aseptic conditions.
4. **Fill** the ointment into sterile, single-use tubes.
5. **Seal and label** the tubes, indicating storage conditions and expiration date.

### 6.1.3 Formulation of Eye Lotions

**Introduction to Eye Lotions**

Eye lotions, also known as eyewashes, are sterile aqueous solutions used for cleansing the eyes. They are commonly employed to remove foreign particles, soothe irritation, and provide relief from discomfort caused by environmental factors such as dust, smoke, or allergens. Eye lotions must be formulated to ensure safety, efficacy, and patient comfort.

**Key Considerations in Formulating Eye Lotions**

**1. Sterility**

- **Importance**: Sterility is essential to prevent introducing infections into the eye.
- **Sterilization Methods**: The solution must be sterile, typically achieved through filtration and aseptic processing.

**2. pH and Buffering**

- **Importance**: The pH should be close to the physiological pH of tears (approximately 7.4) to avoid irritation.
- **Buffering Agents**: Buffers such as phosphate or borate buffers are used to maintain the pH within the desired range.

### 3. Isotonicity

- **Importance**: The solution should be isotonic with natural tears to prevent osmotic stress on the eye tissues.
- **Tonicity Adjusters**: Sodium chloride, dextrose, and boric acid are used to adjust the tonicity.

### 4. Viscosity

- **Importance**: While eye lotions are typically less viscous than eye drops, slight viscosity can help improve contact time with the ocular surface.
- **Viscosity Enhancers**: Agents like hydroxypropyl methylcellulose (HPMC) or polyvinyl alcohol may be used if needed.

### 5. Preservatives

- **Importance**: Multi-dose containers require preservatives to prevent microbial contamination during use.
- **Common Preservatives**: Benzalkonium chloride, chlorobutanol, or thimerosal. Preservative-free formulations are preferable for patients with sensitivities.

### 6. Antimicrobial Agents

- **Optional**: Some eye lotions may contain antimicrobial agents for specific therapeutic purposes, such as treating minor eye infections.

### Example Formulation for Eye Lotions

- **API**: None (basic eyewash)
- **Buffer**: Phosphate buffer to maintain pH 7.4
- **Tonicity Adjuster**: Sodium chloride
- **Viscosity Enhancer**: Hydroxypropyl methylcellulose (optional)

- **Preservative**: Benzalkonium chloride 0.01%
- **Solvent**: Water for Injection (WFI)

**Preparation Steps**

1. **Dissolve** the buffer, tonicity adjuster, viscosity enhancer (if used), and preservative in WFI.
2. **Adjust the pH** to 7.4 if necessary.
3. **Filter** the solution through a 0.22-micron filter to ensure sterility.
4. **Aseptically fill** into sterile containers.
5. **Seal and label** the containers, indicating storage conditions and expiration date.

### 6.1.4 Methods of Preparation

**Introduction**

The preparation of ophthalmic products, including eye drops, eye ointments, and eye lotions, involves various steps to ensure their safety, efficacy, and sterility. The following methods outline the general procedures for preparing these products in a controlled and sterile environment.

**Methods of Preparation for Eye Drops**

**1. Solution Preparation**

- **Weigh and Measure**: Accurately weigh the API and excipients and measure the required volume of solvent (WFI).
- **Dissolution**: Dissolve the API and excipients in the solvent. Ensure complete dissolution by stirring and, if necessary, adjusting the pH using suitable acids or bases.
- **Filtration**: Sterilize the solution by passing it through a 0.22-micron filter to remove any microorganisms.

**2. Aseptic Filling**

- **Filling**: Aseptically fill the sterile solution into sterile dropper bottles under laminar airflow conditions to prevent contamination.
- **Sealing**: Seal the bottles with sterile droppers and caps.
- **Labeling**: Label the bottles with relevant information, including drug name, concentration, usage instructions, storage conditions, and expiration date.

**Methods of Preparation for Eye Ointments**

**1. Base Sterilization**

- **Weigh and Measure**: Accurately weigh the base components (e.g., petrolatum, mineral oil) and measure the required amount of API.
- **Sterilization**: Sterilize the base by heat, typically using an autoclave or dry heat sterilizer.

**2. API Incorporation**

- **Micronization**: Micronize the API to achieve a fine particle size, typically less than 10 microns, to ensure comfort and prevent irritation.
- **Mixing**: Under aseptic conditions, incorporate the micronized API into the sterilized base using a sterile spatula or mixer. Ensure uniform distribution of the API throughout the base.

**3. Aseptic Filling**

- **Filling**: Aseptically fill the prepared ointment into sterile tubes under laminar airflow conditions.
- **Sealing**: Seal the tubes using sterile caps or crimping machines.
- **Labeling**: Label the tubes with relevant information, including drug name, concentration, usage instructions, storage conditions, and expiration date.

**Methods of Preparation for Eye Lotions**

**1. Solution Preparation**

- **Weigh and Measure**: Accurately weigh the excipients and measure the required volume of solvent (WFI).
- **Dissolution**: Dissolve the excipients in the solvent. Ensure complete dissolution by stirring and adjusting the pH using suitable acids or bases.
- **Filtration**: Sterilize the solution by passing it through a 0.22-micron filter to remove any microorganisms.

**2. Aseptic Filling**

- **Filling**: Aseptically fill the sterile solution into sterile containers under laminar airflow conditions to prevent contamination.
- **Sealing**: Seal the containers with sterile caps or lids.
- **Labeling**: Label the containers with relevant information, including product name, usage instructions, storage conditions, and expiration date.

**Quality Control and Assurance**

- **Sterility Testing**: Perform sterility tests on samples to ensure the product is free from microbial contamination.
- **pH and Osmolality Testing**: Test the pH and osmolality to ensure they are within the specified ranges for physiological compatibility.
- **Particulate Matter Testing**: For eye drops and eye lotions, test for the presence of particulate matter to ensure the solution is clear and free from particles.
- **Potency and Purity Testing**: Test the potency and purity of the API to ensure it meets the specified requirements.
- **Stability Testing**: Conduct stability studies to determine the shelf life of the product and ensure it remains effective and safe throughout its intended use period.

### 6.1.5 Labeling and Containers

**Introduction to Labeling and Containers**

Proper labeling and suitable containers are essential for the safe and effective use of ophthalmic preparations. The labeling provides crucial information about the product, while the container ensures the product's stability, sterility, and ease of use. Both elements must comply with regulatory standards to ensure patient safety and compliance.

**Labeling Requirements**

**1. Product Information**

- **Drug Name and Concentration**: Clearly state the name of the drug and its concentration to avoid dosing errors.
- **Dosage Instructions**: Provide detailed instructions on how to use the product, including the dosage, frequency, and duration of use.
- **Storage Conditions**: Indicate the recommended storage conditions, such as temperature and protection from light.

- **Expiration Date**: Clearly display the expiration date to ensure the product is used within its shelf life.

**2. Safety Information**

- **Warnings and Precautions**: Include any necessary warnings, such as potential side effects, interactions with other medications, and contraindications.
- **Sterility and Handling**: Instructions on how to maintain sterility, particularly for multi-dose containers, and advice on what to do if the product becomes contaminated.

**3. Regulatory Compliance**

- **Batch Number and Manufacturer Information**: Include the batch number and information about the manufacturer to ensure traceability.
- **Regulatory Statements**: Ensure compliance with regulatory requirements, such as those from the FDA, EMA, or other relevant authorities.

**Container Requirements**
**1. Material**

- **Compatibility**: The container material must be compatible with the ophthalmic formulation, not interacting chemically or physically with the drug.
- **Protection**: The material should protect the product from light, air, and moisture, which can degrade the formulation.

**2. Types of Containers**

- **Dropper Bottles**: Commonly used for eye drops. These bottles must be made from materials that do not react with the contents and are easy to use.
- **Tubes**: Typically used for eye ointments. The tubes should ensure that the ointment remains sterile and stable throughout its shelf life.
- **Single-Use Containers**: Preferred for preservative-free formulations to ensure sterility for each dose.

**3. Design Features**

- **User-Friendly**: The container should be easy to handle and use, especially for patients with limited dexterity or visual impairments.
- **Tamper-Evident**: Containers should have tamper-evident features to ensure the product's integrity before use.
- **Sterility Maintenance**: For multi-dose containers, features such as one-way valves can help maintain sterility during use.

### 6.1.6 Evaluation of Ophthalmic Preparations

**Introduction to Evaluation**

The evaluation of ophthalmic preparations involves a series of tests and assessments to ensure that the products meet the required standards for safety, efficacy, and quality. These evaluations are conducted during the development phase and continue throughout the product's lifecycle.

**Key Evaluation Tests**

**1. Sterility Testing**

- **Importance**: Ensures the ophthalmic product is free from microbial contamination.
- **Methods**: Common methods include membrane filtration and direct inoculation. Products are incubated in a suitable growth medium to detect microbial growth.

**2. pH Testing**

- **Importance**: Ensures the product's pH is compatible with the eye, typically close to the physiological pH of tears (approximately 7.4).
- **Methods**: pH meters are used to measure the pH of the product.

**3. Isotonicity Testing**

- **Importance**: Ensures the solution is isotonic with natural tears to avoid causing irritation or osmotic stress.
- **Methods**: Osmolality measurements are conducted using osmometers.

**4. Viscosity Testing**

- **Importance**: Determines the flow characteristics of the product, which can affect its residence time in the eye and patient comfort.
- **Methods**: Viscometers or rheometers are used to measure the viscosity of the formulation.

**5. Particulate Matter Testing**

- **Importance**: Ensures the solution is free from visible and sub-visible particles that could cause irritation or damage to the eye.
- **Methods**: Light obscuration and microscopic particle count tests are commonly used.

**6. Stability Testing**

- **Importance**: Assesses the product's ability to maintain its quality, safety, and efficacy over time.
- **Methods**: Stability studies are conducted under various environmental conditions (e.g., temperature, humidity, light) to evaluate the product's shelf life and determine appropriate storage conditions.

**7. Drug Content and Uniformity**

- **Importance**: Ensures that each dose delivers the correct amount of the active ingredient.
- **Methods**: High-performance liquid chromatography (HPLC) and other analytical techniques are used to measure the drug content and ensure uniformity across batches.

**8. Preservative Efficacy Testing**

- **Importance**: For multi-dose containers, ensures that the preservative system effectively prevents microbial growth throughout the product's use.
- **Methods**: Preservative efficacy tests (PET) are conducted to assess the antimicrobial effectiveness of the preservative system.

**9. Irritation Testing**

- **Importance**: Ensures the product does not cause irritation or discomfort when used as intended.
- **Methods**: In vivo testing, such as the Draize test, and in vitro alternatives are used to evaluate potential irritation.

**10. Reconstitution Time (for Powders)**

- **Importance**: For lyophilized products, ensures that the product can be easily and quickly reconstituted before use.
- **Methods**: The time required to dissolve the powder completely in the solvent is measured.

# SEVEN

# COSMETICS

## 7.1 Formulation and Preparation

### 7.1.1 Lipsticks

**Introduction to Lipstick Formulation**

Lipsticks are a widely used cosmetic product designed to impart color, texture, and protection to the lips. The formulation of lipsticks involves a careful selection of ingredients to achieve the desired properties such as color, consistency, spreadability, and longevity. A successful lipstick formulation must also ensure safety, stability, and ease of application.

**Key Components in Lipstick Formulation**

**1. Waxes**

- **Purpose**: Provide structure and rigidity to the lipstick, ensuring it maintains its shape.
- **Common Waxes**: Beeswax, carnauba wax, candelilla wax, and paraffin wax.
- **Characteristics**: Waxes vary in melting points and hardness, which can be adjusted to achieve the desired texture and stability.

**2. Oils**

- **Purpose**: Provide emolliency, smooth application, and moisturization.
- **Common Oils**: Castor oil, mineral oil, lanolin, and vegetable oils such as olive oil and coconut oil.
- **Characteristics**: Oils affect the shine, texture, and spreadability of the lipstick.

### 3. Pigments

- **Purpose**: Impart color to the lipstick.
- **Types of Pigments**: Organic and inorganic pigments, such as iron oxides, titanium dioxide, and D&C dyes.
- **Characteristics**: Pigments must be finely ground and evenly dispersed to ensure uniform color and coverage.

### 4. Emollients and Moisturizers

- **Purpose**: Enhance the feel of the lipstick on the lips and provide moisturization.
- **Common Ingredients**: Shea butter, cocoa butter, and vitamin E.
- **Characteristics**: These ingredients contribute to the smoothness and hydrating properties of the lipstick.

### 5. Preservatives and Antioxidants

- **Purpose**: Prevent microbial growth and oxidation of the formulation.
- **Common Preservatives**: Parabens and phenoxyethanol.
- **Common Antioxidants**: BHT (butylated hydroxytoluene) and tocopherol (vitamin E).

### 6. Fragrances and Flavors

- **Purpose**: Enhance the sensory experience of using the lipstick.
- **Common Additives**: Natural and synthetic fragrances, and flavors such as vanilla or mint.

## Formulation Process for Lipsticks

### 1. Melting and Mixing

- **Procedure**: Waxes are melted in a jacketed kettle at controlled temperatures. Oils and emollients are added to the melted waxes and mixed thoroughly.
- **Importance**: Ensures a homogeneous mixture, which is critical for the consistency and performance of the final product.

**2. Pigment Dispersion**

- **Procedure**: Pigments are finely ground and added to the wax-oil mixture. High-shear mixers or roller mills are used to ensure even dispersion of pigments.
- **Importance**: Achieves uniform color and smooth texture in the lipstick.

**3. Molding and Cooling**

- **Procedure**: The molten mixture is poured into lipstick molds and allowed to cool and solidify. This can be done using cooling tunnels or refrigerated trays.
- **Importance**: Ensures the lipstick forms correctly with the desired shape and texture.

**4. Flavors and Fragrances Addition**

- **Procedure**: After cooling, flavors and fragrances are added to the lipstick base. This is done at lower temperatures to prevent the volatilization of these sensitive ingredients.
- **Importance**: Enhances the user experience without compromising the stability of the formulation.

**5. Molding into Final Packaging**

- **Procedure**: The solidified lipsticks are removed from the molds and inserted into lipstick tubes or other final packaging formats.
- **Importance**: Ensures the product is ready for consumer use, with an emphasis on ease of application and aesthetic appeal.

**Quality Control Tests for Lipsticks**
**1. Melting Point**

- **Purpose**: Ensures the lipstick remains solid at room temperature but melts upon application to the lips.
- **Method**: The melting point is determined using a capillary melting point apparatus or differential scanning calorimetry (DSC).

**2. Color Consistency**

- **Purpose**: Ensures uniform color throughout the batch.
- **Method**: Visual inspection and colorimetric analysis are used to verify color consistency.

**3. Stability Testing**

- **Purpose**: Ensures the product maintains its properties over time under various environmental conditions.
- **Method**: Stability tests include exposure to high and low temperatures, humidity, and light to assess any changes in texture, color, or odor.

**4. Microbial Testing**

- **Purpose**: Ensures the product is free from microbial contamination.
- **Method**: Microbiological tests such as total viable count (TVC) and specific pathogen testing are conducted.

**5. Sensory Evaluation**

- **Purpose**: Ensures the lipstick provides a pleasant sensory experience in terms of application, feel, and scent.
- **Method**: Sensory evaluation panels assess the product for texture, smoothness, and overall user experience.

**Example Formulation for a Basic Lipstick**

- **Waxes**: 10% Beeswax, 10% Carnauba wax
- **Oils**: 40% Castor oil, 10% Mineral oil
- **Pigments**: 5% Iron oxide pigments, 1% Titanium dioxide
- **Emollients**: 10% Shea butter
- **Preservatives**: 0.1% Methylparaben
- **Antioxidants**: 0.05% BHT
- **Fragrances/Flavors**: 0.5% Vanilla flavor

**Preparation Steps**

1. **Melting and Mixing**: Melt the beeswax and carnauba wax in a jacketed kettle. Add the castor oil, mineral oil, and shea butter, and mix thoroughly.
2. **Pigment Dispersion**: Add the pigments to the mixture and use a high-shear mixer to ensure even dispersion.
3. **Cooling and Solidification**: Pour the molten mixture into lipstick molds and allow it to cool and solidify.
4. **Addition of Fragrances/Flavors**: Add the vanilla flavor to the cooled mixture, mix well, and mold into final packaging.

**7.1 Formulation and Preparation**

**7.1.2 Shampoos**

**Introduction to Shampoo Formulation**

Shampoos are liquid formulations designed to cleanse the hair and scalp by removing dirt, oil, and other impurities. An effective shampoo must not only cleanse but also provide conditioning, be gentle on the scalp, and have a pleasing fragrance and appearance. The formulation of shampoos involves a careful selection of ingredients to balance cleansing power with mildness, conditioning properties, and aesthetic appeal.

**Key Components in Shampoo Formulation**

**1. Surfactants**

- **Purpose**: Surfactants are the primary cleansing agents in shampoos. They lower the surface tension of water, allowing it to more effectively emulsify and remove oils and dirt.
- **Common Surfactants**: Sodium lauryl sulfate (SLS), sodium laureth sulfate (SLES), ammonium lauryl sulfate, and cocamidopropyl betaine.
- **Characteristics**: Surfactants vary in their cleansing strength and mildness. A combination of surfactants is often used to balance cleansing efficacy and gentleness.

**2. Conditioning Agents**

- **Purpose**: Conditioning agents improve the texture and manageability of hair, providing smoothness, shine, and reducing static.
- **Common Conditioning Agents**: Silicone derivatives (e.g., dimethicone), quaternary ammonium compounds (e.g., polyquaternium), and natural oils (e.g., argan oil, jojoba oil).

- **Characteristics**: These agents form a thin film on the hair shaft, providing protection and enhancing the hair's appearance.

**3. Thickeners**

- **Purpose**: Thickeners increase the viscosity of the shampoo, making it easier to handle and apply.
- **Common Thickeners**: Xanthan gum, hydroxyethylcellulose, and carbomers.
- **Characteristics**: Thickeners also contribute to the product's texture and stability.

**4. Preservatives**

- **Purpose**: Preservatives prevent microbial growth in the shampoo, ensuring it remains safe and effective during storage and use.
- **Common Preservatives**: Parabens, phenoxyethanol, and methylisothiazolinone.
- **Characteristics**: Effective at low concentrations and stable across the product's pH range.

**5. pH Adjusters**

- **Purpose**: pH adjusters maintain the shampoo's pH at a level that is compatible with the scalp and hair, typically between 4.5 and 5.5.
- **Common pH Adjusters**: Citric acid, sodium hydroxide, and triethanolamine.
- **Characteristics**: Maintain the pH balance to prevent irritation and ensure product stability.

**6. Fragrances and Colorants**

- **Purpose**: Enhance the sensory appeal of the shampoo, providing a pleasant fragrance and an attractive appearance.
- **Common Additives**: Essential oils, synthetic fragrances, and colorants such as FD&C dyes.
- **Characteristics**: Should be non-irritating and stable within the formulation.

**7. Active Ingredients**

- **Purpose**: Provide additional benefits such as dandruff control, hair strengthening, or moisturizing.
- **Common Actives**: Zinc pyrithione (anti-dandruff), panthenol (pro-vitamin B5), keratin, and botanical extracts.
- **Characteristics**: Active ingredients should be compatible with the base formulation and remain effective during the product's shelf life.

**Formulation Process for Shampoos**

**1. Mixing Surfactants**

- **Procedure**: Primary surfactants are mixed with water to form the base of the shampoo. Secondary surfactants and co-surfactants are then added to the mixture.
- **Importance**: Ensures thorough dissolution and even distribution of surfactants, providing the cleansing power of the shampoo.

**2. Adding Conditioning Agents and Thickeners**

- **Procedure**: Conditioning agents and thickeners are added to the surfactant mixture. The mixture is stirred continuously to ensure homogeneity.
- **Importance**: Achieves the desired viscosity and conditioning properties.

**3. Incorporating Preservatives and pH Adjusters**

- **Procedure**: Preservatives are added to protect the product from microbial contamination. pH adjusters are then used to adjust the formulation's pH to the desired range.
- **Importance**: Ensures the shampoo is safe, stable, and gentle on the scalp and hair.

**4. Adding Fragrances, Colorants, and Active Ingredients**

- **Procedure**: Fragrances, colorants, and active ingredients are added last to prevent volatilization or degradation during the mixing process.

- **Importance**: Enhances the sensory appeal and adds specific benefits to the shampoo.

**5. Homogenization and Packaging**

- **Procedure**: The final mixture is homogenized to ensure uniformity. The shampoo is then filled into bottles and sealed.
- **Importance**: Ensures consistency in each bottle and prepares the product for distribution.

**Quality Control Tests for Shampoos**

**1. Viscosity Testing**

- **Purpose**: Ensures the shampoo has the appropriate thickness for ease of application.
- **Method**: Viscometers are used to measure the viscosity of the shampoo.

**2. pH Testing**

- **Purpose**: Confirms the pH is within the desired range to prevent irritation and ensure stability.
- **Method**: pH meters are used to measure the pH of the product.

**3. Stability Testing**

- **Purpose**: Assesses the product's ability to maintain its properties over time.
- **Method**: Stability studies under various environmental conditions (e.g., temperature, humidity) are conducted to evaluate changes in texture, color, and scent.

**4. Microbial Testing**

- **Purpose**: Ensures the shampoo is free from harmful microorganisms.
- **Method**: Microbiological tests such as total viable count (TVC) and specific pathogen testing are conducted.

**5. Sensory Evaluation**

- **Purpose**: Evaluates the product's feel, fragrance, and ease of use.
- **Method**: Sensory panels assess the shampoo for lather, scent, and overall user experience.

**Example Formulation for a Basic Shampoo**

- **Surfactants**: 15% Sodium laureth sulfate (SLES), 5% Cocamidopropyl betaine
- **Conditioning Agents**: 2% Dimethicone
- **Thickeners**: 1% Xanthan gum
- **Preservatives**: 0.1% Phenoxyethanol
- **pH Adjusters**: Citric acid to adjust pH to 5.0
- **Fragrances and Colorants**: 0.5% Fragrance, colorant as needed
- **Active Ingredients**: 1% Panthenol
- **Solvent**: Water to 100%

**Preparation Steps**

1. **Mixing Surfactants**: Dissolve SLES and cocamidopropyl betaine in water, stirring continuously.
2. **Adding Conditioning Agents and Thickeners**: Add dimethicone and xanthan gum to the mixture, ensuring even distribution.
3. **Incorporating Preservatives and pH Adjusters**: Add phenoxyethanol and adjust the pH with citric acid.
4. **Adding Fragrances, Colorants, and Active Ingredients**: Mix in the fragrance, colorant, and panthenol.
5. **Homogenization and Packaging**: Homogenize the final mixture and fill into bottles.

## 7.1 Formulation and Preparation

### 7.1.3 Cold Cream

#### Introduction to Cold Cream Formulation

Cold cream is a type of water-in-oil (W/O) emulsion widely used as a moisturizer, cleanser, and makeup remover. It provides a cooling sensation upon application, which is soothing to the skin. The formulation of cold cream requires a careful balance of oil and water phases, along with emulsifiers and other functional ingredients to ensure stability, texture, and efficacy.

**Key Components in Cold Cream Formulation**

**1. Oil Phase**

- **Purpose**: Provides emolliency, creating a barrier that helps to lock in moisture and protect the skin.
- **Common Oils**: Mineral oil, petrolatum, lanolin, and natural oils like almond oil, olive oil, and jojoba oil.
- **Characteristics**: The choice of oils affects the cream's texture, spreadability, and moisturizing properties.

**2. Water Phase**

- **Purpose**: Hydrates the skin and serves as a medium for water-soluble ingredients.
- **Common Ingredients**: Purified water, humectants (e.g., glycerin, propylene glycol), and botanical extracts.
- **Characteristics**: Humectants attract water to the skin, enhancing its hydration effect.

**3. Emulsifiers**

- **Purpose**: Stabilize the emulsion by reducing the surface tension between the oil and water phases.
- **Common Emulsifiers**: Beeswax, borax, sorbitan stearate, and cetyl alcohol.
- **Characteristics**: Emulsifiers determine the stability, texture, and feel of the cream.

**4. Stabilizers and Thickeners**

- **Purpose**: Enhance the texture and stability of the cream, preventing separation of the oil and water phases.
- **Common Stabilizers/Thickeners**: Stearic acid, cetyl alcohol, and carbomers.
- **Characteristics**: These ingredients help maintain the desired consistency and improve the cream's stability.

**5. Preservatives**

- **Purpose**: Prevent microbial growth to ensure the product's safety and longevity.
- **Common Preservatives**: Parabens (e.g., methylparaben, propylparaben), phenoxyethanol, and sorbic acid.
- **Characteristics**: Effective at low concentrations and stable across the product's pH range.

**6. Fragrances and Colorants**

- **Purpose**: Enhance the sensory appeal of the cream, providing a pleasant fragrance and an attractive appearance.
- **Common Additives**: Essential oils, synthetic fragrances, and cosmetic-grade colorants.
- **Characteristics**: Should be non-irritating and stable within the formulation.

**7. Active Ingredients**

- **Purpose**: Provide additional skin benefits such as soothing, anti-aging, or brightening effects.
- **Common Actives**: Vitamin E (tocopherol), aloe vera extract, and niacinamide.
- **Characteristics**: Active ingredients should be compatible with the base formulation and remain effective during the product's shelf life.

**Formulation Process for Cold Cream**

**1. Preparation of the Oil Phase**

- **Procedure**: Melt the oil phase ingredients (e.g., mineral oil, petrolatum, beeswax, emulsifiers) in a jacketed kettle or a double boiler. Heat until all components are fully melted and mixed.
- **Importance**: Ensures a homogeneous oil phase, which is critical for the stability of the emulsion.

**2. Preparation of the Water Phase**

- **Procedure**: Heat the water phase ingredients (e.g., purified water, humectants) in a separate vessel. Ensure the temperature is similar to that of the oil phase to facilitate emulsification.

- **Importance**: Prepares the water phase for effective blending with the oil phase.

### 3. Emulsification

- **Procedure**: Slowly add the heated water phase to the oil phase with continuous stirring. Use a high-shear mixer or homogenizer to create a stable emulsion.
- **Importance**: Proper emulsification is crucial to achieving a stable and uniform cold cream.

### 4. Cooling and Incorporation of Actives

- **Procedure**: Once the emulsion is formed, allow it to cool while stirring gently. Add temperature-sensitive ingredients such as fragrances, colorants, and active ingredients during the cooling phase.
- **Importance**: Prevents the degradation of heat-sensitive components and ensures uniform distribution.

### 5. Homogenization and Packaging

- **Procedure**: After cooling, homogenize the cream to ensure a smooth and consistent texture. Fill the cream into suitable containers such as jars or tubes.
- **Importance**: Ensures consistency in each container and prepares the product for distribution.

### Quality Control Tests for Cold Cream

### 1. Stability Testing

- **Purpose**: Assesses the product's ability to maintain its properties over time.
- **Method**: Stability studies under various environmental conditions (e.g., temperature, humidity) are conducted to evaluate changes in texture, color, and scent.

### 2. Microbial Testing

- **Purpose**: Ensures the product is free from harmful microorganisms.
- **Method**: Microbiological tests such as total viable count (TVC) and specific pathogen testing are conducted.

### 3. pH Testing

- **Purpose**: Confirms the pH is within the desired range to prevent irritation and ensure stability.
- **Method**: pH meters are used to measure the pH of the product.

### 4. Sensory Evaluation

- **Purpose**: Evaluates the product's feel, fragrance, and ease of use.
- **Method**: Sensory panels assess the cream for texture, spreadability, and overall user experience.

### 5. Emulsion Stability Testing

- **Purpose**: Ensures the emulsion remains stable without phase separation.
- **Method**: Centrifugation and freeze-thaw cycles are used to test the stability of the emulsion.

### Example Formulation for a Basic Cold Cream

- **Oil Phase**: 20% Mineral oil, 15% Petrolatum, 5% Beeswax, 3% Cetyl alcohol
- **Water Phase**: 55% Purified water, 2% Glycerin
- **Emulsifiers**: 2% Borax
- **Preservatives**: 0.1% Methylparaben, 0.1% Propylparaben
- **Fragrances/Colorants**: 0.5% Lavender essential oil, colorant as needed
- **Active Ingredients**: 1% Vitamin E (tocopherol)

### Preparation Steps

1. **Oil Phase Preparation**: Melt the mineral oil, petrolatum, beeswax, and cetyl alcohol in a jacketed kettle.
2. **Water Phase Preparation**: Heat the purified water and glycerin in a separate vessel, adding borax.

3. **Emulsification**: Slowly add the water phase to the oil phase while continuously stirring with a high-shear mixer.
4. **Cooling and Additives**: Allow the emulsion to cool, then add the vitamin E and lavender essential oil.
5. **Homogenization and Packaging**: Homogenize the mixture for a smooth texture and fill into jars or tubes.

## 7.1 Formulation and Preparation

### 7.1.4 Vanishing Cream

#### Introduction to Vanishing Cream Formulation

Vanishing creams are lightweight, oil-in-water (O/W) emulsions that provide a matte finish on the skin. They are named "vanishing" because they are quickly absorbed by the skin, leaving no greasy residue. These creams are commonly used as moisturizers and base products for makeup. The formulation of vanishing creams requires a balance of ingredients to achieve the desired aesthetic properties, skin feel, and efficacy.

#### Key Components in Vanishing Cream Formulation

**1. Water Phase**

- **Purpose**: Provides hydration to the skin and acts as the continuous phase in the emulsion.
- **Common Ingredients**: Purified water, humectants (e.g., glycerin, propylene glycol), and botanical extracts.
- **Characteristics**: Ensures the cream is light and easily absorbed.

**2. Oil Phase**

- **Purpose**: Provides emolliency, creating a smooth, protective layer on the skin.
- **Common Oils**: Stearic acid, myristic acid, isopropyl myristate, and light esters.
- **Characteristics**: Light oils and esters are used to avoid a greasy feel and ensure a matte finish.

**3. Emulsifiers**

- **Purpose**: Stabilize the oil-in-water emulsion by reducing the surface tension between the oil and water phases.

- **Common Emulsifiers**: Potassium stearate, sodium stearate, and glyceryl stearate.
- **Characteristics**: Emulsifiers must be carefully chosen to ensure a stable and homogenous product.

**4. Thickeners and Stabilizers**

- **Purpose**: Enhance the texture and stability of the cream, preventing phase separation.
- **Common Thickeners**: Carbomers, xanthan gum, and cetyl alcohol.
- **Characteristics**: Contribute to the cream's consistency and spreadability.

**5. Preservatives**

- **Purpose**: Prevent microbial growth to ensure the product's safety and longevity.
- **Common Preservatives**: Parabens (e.g., methylparaben, propylparaben), phenoxyethanol, and sorbic acid.
- **Characteristics**: Effective at low concentrations and stable across the product's pH range.

**6. pH Adjusters**

- **Purpose**: Maintain the cream's pH within a range that is compatible with the skin, typically between 5.0 and 7.0.
- **Common pH Adjusters**: Citric acid, sodium hydroxide, and triethanolamine.
- **Characteristics**: Ensures the product is gentle on the skin and stable.

**7. Fragrances and Colorants**

- **Purpose**: Enhance the sensory appeal of the cream, providing a pleasant fragrance and an attractive appearance.
- **Common Additives**: Essential oils, synthetic fragrances, and cosmetic-grade colorants.
- **Characteristics**: Should be non-irritating and stable within the formulation.

**8. Active Ingredients**

- **Purpose**: Provide additional skin benefits such as moisturizing, anti-aging, or soothing effects.
- **Common Actives**: Niacinamide, panthenol (pro-vitamin B5), and botanical extracts like aloe vera.
- **Characteristics**: Active ingredients should be compatible with the base formulation and remain effective during the product's shelf life.

**Formulation Process for Vanishing Cream**

**1. Preparation of the Water Phase**

- **Procedure**: Heat the water phase ingredients (e.g., purified water, humectants) in a jacketed kettle. Ensure the temperature is similar to that of the oil phase to facilitate emulsification.
- **Importance**: Prepares the water phase for effective blending with the oil phase.

**2. Preparation of the Oil Phase**

- **Procedure**: Melt the oil phase ingredients (e.g., stearic acid, myristic acid, emulsifiers) in a separate vessel. Heat until all components are fully melted and mixed.
- **Importance**: Ensures a homogeneous oil phase, which is critical for the stability of the emulsion.

**3. Emulsification**

- **Procedure**: Slowly add the heated water phase to the oil phase with continuous stirring. Use a high-shear mixer or homogenizer to create a stable emulsion.
- **Importance**: Proper emulsification is crucial to achieving a stable and uniform vanishing cream.

**4. Cooling and Incorporation of Actives**

- **Procedure**: Once the emulsion is formed, allow it to cool while stirring gently. Add temperature-sensitive ingredients such as fragrances, colorants, and active ingredients during the cooling phase.

- **Importance**: Prevents the degradation of heat-sensitive components and ensures uniform distribution.

**5. Homogenization and Packaging**

- **Procedure**: After cooling, homogenize the cream to ensure a smooth and consistent texture. Fill the cream into suitable containers such as jars or tubes.
- **Importance**: Ensures consistency in each container and prepares the product for distribution.

**Quality Control Tests for Vanishing Cream**

**1. Stability Testing**

- **Purpose**: Assesses the product's ability to maintain its properties over time.
- **Method**: Stability studies under various environmental conditions (e.g., temperature, humidity) are conducted to evaluate changes in texture, color, and scent.

**2. Microbial Testing**

- **Purpose**: Ensures the product is free from harmful microorganisms.
- **Method**: Microbiological tests such as total viable count (TVC) and specific pathogen testing are conducted.

**3. pH Testing**

- **Purpose**: Confirms the pH is within the desired range to prevent irritation and ensure stability.
- **Method**: pH meters are used to measure the pH of the product.

**4. Sensory Evaluation**

- **Purpose**: Evaluates the product's feel, fragrance, and ease of use.
- **Method**: Sensory panels assess the cream for texture, spreadability, and overall user experience.

### 5. Emulsion Stability Testing

- **Purpose**: Ensures the emulsion remains stable without phase separation.
- **Method**: Centrifugation and freeze-thaw cycles are used to test the stability of the emulsion.

### Example Formulation for a Basic Vanishing Cream

- **Water Phase**: 70% Purified water, 5% Glycerin
- **Oil Phase**: 10% Stearic acid, 5% Isopropyl myristate, 2% Cetyl alcohol
- **Emulsifiers**: 2% Potassium stearate
- **Preservatives**: 0.1% Methylparaben, 0.1% Propylparaben
- **pH Adjusters**: Citric acid to adjust pH to 6.0
- **Fragrances/Colorants**: 0.5% Lavender essential oil, colorant as needed
- **Active Ingredients**: 1% Niacinamide, 1% Panthenol

### Preparation Steps

1. **Water Phase Preparation**: Heat the purified water and glycerin in a jacketed kettle.
2. **Oil Phase Preparation**: Melt the stearic acid, isopropyl myristate, and cetyl alcohol in a separate vessel. Add potassium stearate.
3. **Emulsification**: Slowly add the water phase to the oil phase while continuously stirring with a high-shear mixer.
4. **Cooling and Additives**: Allow the emulsion to cool, then add niacinamide, panthenol, and lavender essential oil.
5. **Homogenization and Packaging**: Homogenize the mixture for a smooth texture and fill into jars or tubes.

## 7.1 Formulation and Preparation

### 7.1.5 Toothpastes

### Introduction to Toothpaste Formulation

Toothpastes are essential oral care products designed to clean teeth, maintain oral hygiene, and provide additional benefits such as fresh breath, whitening, and protection against dental issues like cavities and gum disease. The formulation of toothpaste involves a balanced combination of ingredients to ensure effective cleaning, safety, and consumer appeal.

### Key Components in Toothpaste Formulation

**1. Abrasives**

- **Purpose**: Abrasives help remove plaque, stains, and food particles from the teeth.
- **Common Abrasives**: Calcium carbonate, hydrated silica, dicalcium phosphate dihydrate, and sodium bicarbonate.
- **Characteristics**: Abrasives must be hard enough to clean teeth effectively but not so abrasive as to damage enamel.

**2. Fluoride Compounds**

- **Purpose**: Fluoride strengthens tooth enamel and helps prevent dental caries (cavities).
- **Common Fluorides**: Sodium fluoride, stannous fluoride, and sodium monofluorophosphate.
- **Characteristics**: Effective at low concentrations and compatible with other toothpaste ingredients.

**3. Humectants**

- **Purpose**: Humectants retain moisture in the toothpaste, preventing it from drying out.
- **Common Humectants**: Glycerin, sorbitol, and propylene glycol.
- **Characteristics**: Provide a smooth texture and help maintain stability.

**4. Detergents**

- **Purpose**: Detergents create foam, helping to distribute the toothpaste in the mouth and enhance cleaning.
- **Common Detergents**: Sodium lauryl sulfate (SLS), cocamidopropyl betaine.
- **Characteristics**: Must be mild to avoid irritation of the oral mucosa.

**5. Binders and Thickeners**

- **Purpose**: Binders and thickeners provide the desired consistency and stability to the toothpaste.

- **Common Binders/Thickeners**: Carboxymethyl cellulose (CMC), xanthan gum, and carrageenan.
- **Characteristics**: Ensure the toothpaste maintains its shape and does not separate.

**6. Flavors and Sweeteners**

- **Purpose**: Enhance the taste and overall sensory experience of using the toothpaste.
- **Common Flavors/Sweeteners**: Peppermint, spearmint, menthol, saccharin, and xylitol.
- **Characteristics**: Should be non-cariogenic (not promoting cavities) and provide a pleasant flavor.

**7. Preservatives**

- **Purpose**: Prevent microbial growth and ensure the product's safety and longevity.
- **Common Preservatives**: Sodium benzoate, methylparaben.
- **Characteristics**: Effective at low concentrations and stable within the formulation.

**8. Active Ingredients**

- **Purpose**: Provide additional therapeutic benefits, such as anti-tartar, anti-gingivitis, and whitening effects.
- **Common Actives**: Triclosan (anti-bacterial), pyrophosphates (anti-tartar), hydrogen peroxide (whitening).
- **Characteristics**: Must be compatible with the base formulation and effective during the product's shelf life.

**Formulation Process for Toothpastes**

**1. Preparation of the Abrasive and Humectant Mixture**

- **Procedure**: The abrasive (e.g., hydrated silica) is mixed with humectants (e.g., glycerin, sorbitol) in a mixer to form a homogeneous paste.
- **Importance**: Ensures even distribution of abrasives and humectants, providing the desired texture and cleaning efficacy.

**2. Addition of Detergents and Binders**

- **Procedure**: Detergents (e.g., SLS) and binders/thickeners (e.g., CMC) are added to the abrasive-humectant mixture and mixed thoroughly.
- **Importance**: Ensures the formation of a stable, consistent toothpaste base.

**3. Incorporation of Fluoride Compounds**

- **Procedure**: Fluoride compounds (e.g., sodium fluoride) are added and mixed to ensure even distribution throughout the toothpaste.
- **Importance**: Provides the necessary fluoride content for cavity prevention.

**4. Addition of Flavors, Sweeteners, and Preservatives**

- **Procedure**: Flavors, sweeteners, and preservatives are added to the mixture, ensuring they are evenly distributed.
- **Importance**: Enhances the sensory appeal and shelf life of the toothpaste.

**5. Incorporation of Active Ingredients**

- **Procedure**: Active ingredients (e.g., triclosan, pyrophosphates) are added last to preserve their effectiveness and ensure uniform distribution.
- **Importance**: Provides the desired therapeutic benefits and ensures product efficacy.

**6. Homogenization and Packaging**

- **Procedure**: The final mixture is homogenized to ensure a smooth and consistent texture. The toothpaste is then filled into tubes or other suitable containers.
- **Importance**: Ensures consistency in each tube and prepares the product for distribution.

**Quality Control Tests for Toothpastes**

**1. Abrasivity Testing**

- **Purpose**: Ensures the abrasive level is effective for cleaning but safe for enamel.
- **Method**: Tests such as the Radioactive Dentin Abrasion (RDA) test are conducted to measure abrasivity.

**2. Fluoride Availability**

- **Purpose**: Confirms the availability of fluoride in the formulation for cavity prevention.
- **Method**: Ion-selective electrodes are used to measure fluoride concentration.

**3. Viscosity Testing**

- **Purpose**: Ensures the toothpaste has the appropriate consistency for ease of use.
- **Method**: Viscometers are used to measure the viscosity of the toothpaste.

**4. Stability Testing**

- **Purpose**: Assesses the product's ability to maintain its properties over time.
- **Method**: Stability studies under various environmental conditions (e.g., temperature, humidity) are conducted to evaluate changes in texture, color, and scent.

**5. Microbial Testing**

- **Purpose**: Ensures the product is free from harmful microorganisms.
- **Method**: Microbiological tests such as total viable count (TVC) and specific pathogen testing are conducted.

**6. Sensory Evaluation**

- **Purpose**: Evaluates the product's taste, texture, and overall user experience.
- **Method**: Sensory panels assess the toothpaste for flavor, mouthfeel, and overall acceptability.

**Example Formulation for a Basic Toothpaste**

- **Abrasives**: 30% Hydrated silica
- **Humectants**: 20% Glycerin, 20% Sorbitol
- **Detergents**: 1.5% Sodium lauryl sulfate (SLS)
- **Binders/Thickeners**: 1% Carboxymethyl cellulose (CMC)
- **Fluoride Compounds**: 0.24% Sodium fluoride
- **Flavors/Sweeteners**: 0.8% Peppermint flavor, 0.2% Saccharin
- **Preservatives**: 0.1% Sodium benzoate
- **Active Ingredients**: 0.3% Triclosan (anti-bacterial)

**Preparation Steps**

1. **Abrasive and Humectant Mixture**: Mix hydrated silica with glycerin and sorbitol in a mixer.
2. **Detergents and Binders**: Add SLS and CMC to the mixture and mix thoroughly.
3. **Fluoride Compounds**: Incorporate sodium fluoride and ensure even distribution.
4. **Flavors, Sweeteners, and Preservatives**: Add peppermint flavor, saccharin, and sodium benzoate, mixing well.
5. **Active Ingredients**: Add triclosan and homogenize the mixture.
6. **Homogenization and Packaging**: Homogenize the final mixture and fill into tubes.

## 7.1 Formulation and Preparation

### 7.1.6 Hair Dyes

**Introduction to Hair Dye Formulation**

Hair dyes are cosmetic products used to change the color of hair. They are available in various forms, including temporary, semi-permanent, and permanent dyes. The formulation of hair dyes involves a combination of colorants, developers, conditioning agents, and other functional ingredients to ensure effective coloring, safety, and hair care benefits. Permanent hair dyes typically involve a chemical reaction to achieve long-lasting color, while temporary and semi-permanent dyes deposit color on the hair surface without altering the hair's structure.

**Key Components in Hair Dye Formulation**

**1. Colorants**

- **Purpose**: Provide the desired hair color.
- **Types**:
    - **Temporary Dyes**: Large molecules that coat the hair surface and wash out after one or two shampoos.
    - **Semi-Permanent Dyes**: Smaller molecules that partially penetrate the hair shaft and last for several washes.
    - **Permanent Dyes**: Small molecules that penetrate the hair shaft and undergo a chemical reaction (usually oxidation) to form larger, colored molecules that are trapped inside the hair.
- **Common Colorants**: Aromatic amines (e.g., p-phenylenediamine), nitro dyes, and azo dyes for permanent color; direct dyes like HC Blue No. 2 and Basic Red 76 for temporary and semi-permanent color.

**2. Developers**

- **Purpose**: Oxidize the colorants in permanent hair dyes, facilitating the formation of the final color.
- **Common Developers**: Hydrogen peroxide (H2O2) is the most widely used developer.
- **Concentration**: Varies depending on the desired lightening effect and color intensity, typically ranging from 3% to 12%.

**3. Alkalizers**

- **Purpose**: Open the hair cuticle to allow color penetration and activate the developer.
- **Common Alkalizers**: Ammonia, ethanolamine.
- **Characteristics**: The choice of alkalizer affects the formulation's pH and hair lightening effect.

**4. Conditioning Agents**

- **Purpose**: Protect the hair during the coloring process, providing softness, shine, and manageability.
- **Common Conditioning Agents**: Silicones (e.g., dimethicone), quaternary ammonium compounds (e.g., cetrimonium chloride), and natural oils

(e.g., argan oil, coconut oil).

- **Characteristics**: Conditioning agents help counteract the potential damaging effects of the dyeing process.

**5. Thickeners and Stabilizers**

- **Purpose**: Ensure the proper consistency of the dye for easy application and prevent separation of ingredients.
- **Common Thickeners**: Xanthan gum, hydroxyethylcellulose, carbomers.
- **Characteristics**: Provide a creamy texture that is easy to apply and adheres well to the hair.

**6. Preservatives**

- **Purpose**: Prevent microbial growth and ensure the product's safety and longevity.
- **Common Preservatives**: Parabens (e.g., methylparaben, propylparaben), phenoxyethanol.
- **Characteristics**: Effective at low concentrations and stable within the formulation.

**7. Fragrances**

- **Purpose**: Mask the odor of chemicals and enhance the sensory experience of using the product.
- **Common Fragrances**: Natural and synthetic fragrances, essential oils.
- **Characteristics**: Should be non-irritating and stable within the formulation.

**Formulation Process for Hair Dyes**

**1. Preparation of the Base Cream**

- **Procedure**: Mix the conditioning agents, thickeners, and stabilizers in a mixer to form a homogeneous base cream.
- **Importance**: Ensures a consistent texture and base for the dye formulation.

**2. Addition of Colorants and Alkalizers**

- **Procedure**: Add the colorants and alkalizers to the base cream, mixing thoroughly to ensure even distribution.
- **Importance**: Achieves uniform color development and effective penetration into the hair.

### 3. Incorporation of Developers

- **Procedure**: For permanent dyes, the developer (e.g., hydrogen peroxide) is mixed with the dye base immediately before application. For other types, developers are incorporated during the manufacturing process.
- **Importance**: Activates the colorants for permanent color formulations.

### 4. Addition of Fragrances and Preservatives

- **Procedure**: Add fragrances and preservatives last to avoid degradation and ensure they are evenly distributed.
- **Importance**: Enhances the product's sensory appeal and shelf life.

### 5. Homogenization and Packaging

- **Procedure**: Homogenize the final mixture to ensure a smooth and consistent texture. Fill the dye into suitable containers such as tubes or bottles.
- **Importance**: Ensures consistency in each container and prepares the product for distribution.

## Quality Control Tests for Hair Dyes

### 1. Color Consistency

- **Purpose**: Ensures uniform color across batches.
- **Method**: Visual inspection and colorimetric analysis are used to verify color consistency.

### 2. pH Testing

- **Purpose**: Confirms the pH is within the desired range for effective dyeing and hair safety.
- **Method**: pH meters are used to measure the pH of the product.

### 3. Stability Testing

- **Purpose**: Assesses the product's ability to maintain its properties over time.
- **Method**: Stability studies under various environmental conditions (e.g., temperature, humidity) are conducted to evaluate changes in texture, color, and scent.

### 4. Microbial Testing

- **Purpose**: Ensures the product is free from harmful microorganisms.
- **Method**: Microbiological tests such as total viable count (TVC) and specific pathogen testing are conducted.

### 5. Sensory Evaluation

- **Purpose**: Evaluates the product's feel, fragrance, and overall user experience.
- **Method**: Sensory panels assess the dye for ease of application, smell, and overall acceptability.

### Example Formulation for a Basic Permanent Hair Dye

- **Base Cream**:
    - 10% Stearic acid
    - 5% Cetyl alcohol
    - 15% Glycerin
    - 5% Dimethicone
    - 60% Purified water
- **Colorants**:
    - 1% p-Phenylenediamine
    - 0.5% Resorcinol
- **Alkalizers**:

  - 2% Ammonia

- **Developers**:
  - 6% Hydrogen peroxide (mixed at the time of use)

- **Preservatives**:
  - 0.1% Methylparaben
  - 0.1% Propylparaben

- **Fragrances**:
  - 0.5% Fragrance blend

**Preparation Steps**

1. **Base Cream Preparation**: Mix stearic acid, cetyl alcohol, glycerin, dimethicone, and purified water in a mixer to form the base cream.
2. **Addition of Colorants and Alkalizers**: Add p-phenylenediamine, resorcinol, and ammonia to the base cream, mixing thoroughly.
3. **Incorporation of Developers**: For permanent dyes, mix hydrogen peroxide with the dye base immediately before application.
4. **Addition of Fragrances and Preservatives**: Add fragrance blend and preservatives, mixing well.
5. **Homogenization and Packaging**: Homogenize the final mixture and fill into tubes or bottles.

## 7.1 Formulation and Preparation

### 7.1.7 Sunscreens

#### Introduction to Sunscreen Formulation

Sunscreens are topical formulations designed to protect the skin from the harmful effects of ultraviolet (UV) radiation. They contain active ingredients that either absorb, reflect, or scatter UV rays, preventing sunburn and long-term skin damage. The formulation of sunscreens involves a careful balance of UV filters, emollients, emulsifiers, and other functional ingredients to ensure effective protection, stability, and user comfort.

**Key Components in Sunscreen Formulation**

**1. UV Filters**

- **Purpose**: Provide protection against UVA and UVB radiation.
- **Types**:
    - **Chemical (Organic) Filters**: Absorb UV radiation. Examples include avobenzone, octinoxate, octocrylene, and oxybenzone.
    - **Physical (Inorganic) Filters**: Reflect and scatter UV radiation. Examples include zinc oxide and titanium dioxide.
- **Characteristics**: Effective UV filters should be photostable, non-irritating, and provide broad-spectrum protection.

**2. Emollients**

- **Purpose**: Provide moisturizing benefits and improve the spreadability and feel of the sunscreen.
- **Common Emollients**: Cetyl alcohol, stearyl alcohol, isopropyl myristate, and various oils (e.g., mineral oil, coconut oil).
- **Characteristics**: Emollients help to form a uniform film on the skin, enhancing protection and comfort.

**3. Emulsifiers**

- **Purpose**: Stabilize the formulation by enabling the mixing of oil and water phases in emulsions.
- **Common Emulsifiers**: Glyceryl stearate, PEG-100 stearate, and sorbitan oleate.
- **Characteristics**: Emulsifiers ensure the stability and consistency of the sunscreen.

**4. Thickeners and Stabilizers**

- **Purpose**: Enhance the viscosity and stability of the sunscreen formulation.
- **Common Thickeners/Stabilizers**: Xanthan gum, carbomers, and hydroxyethylcellulose.

- **Characteristics**: These ingredients help maintain the desired texture and prevent separation of ingredients.

**5. Preservatives**

- **Purpose**: Prevent microbial growth and ensure the product's safety and longevity.
- **Common Preservatives**: Parabens (e.g., methylparaben, propylparaben), phenoxyethanol, and benzyl alcohol.
- **Characteristics**: Effective at low concentrations and stable within the formulation.

**6. Antioxidants**

- **Purpose**: Protect the skin from free radical damage and enhance the stability of the formulation.
- **Common Antioxidants**: Vitamin E (tocopherol), vitamin C (ascorbic acid), and green tea extract.
- **Characteristics**: Antioxidants provide additional skin benefits and help protect the active ingredients from degradation.

**7. Fragrances and Colorants**

- **Purpose**: Enhance the sensory appeal of the sunscreen, providing a pleasant fragrance and an attractive appearance.
- **Common Additives**: Essential oils, synthetic fragrances, and cosmetic-grade colorants.
- **Characteristics**: Should be non-irritating and stable within the formulation.

**Formulation Process for Sunscreens**

**1. Preparation of the Oil Phase**

- **Procedure**: Mix the oil phase ingredients (e.g., emollients, emulsifiers, UV filters) in a jacketed kettle or double boiler. Heat until all components are fully melted and mixed.
- **Importance**: Ensures a homogeneous oil phase, which is critical for the stability of the emulsion.

**2. Preparation of the Water Phase**

- **Procedure**: Heat the water phase ingredients (e.g., purified water, thickeners) in a separate vessel. Ensure the temperature is similar to that of the oil phase to facilitate emulsification.
- **Importance**: Prepares the water phase for effective blending with the oil phase.

**3. Emulsification**

- **Procedure**: Slowly add the heated water phase to the oil phase with continuous stirring. Use a high-shear mixer or homogenizer to create a stable emulsion.
- **Importance**: Proper emulsification is crucial to achieving a stable and uniform sunscreen formulation.

**4. Cooling and Incorporation of Actives**

- **Procedure**: Once the emulsion is formed, allow it to cool while stirring gently. Add temperature-sensitive ingredients such as antioxidants, fragrances, and preservatives during the cooling phase.
- **Importance**: Prevents the degradation of heat-sensitive components and ensures uniform distribution.

**5. Homogenization and Packaging**

- **Procedure**: After cooling, homogenize the sunscreen to ensure a smooth and consistent texture. Fill the sunscreen into suitable containers such as tubes or bottles.
- **Importance**: Ensures consistency in each container and prepares the product for distribution.

**Quality Control Tests for Sunscreens**
**1. Sun Protection Factor (SPF) Testing**

- **Purpose**: Measures the level of protection provided against UVB radiation.

- **Method**: In vivo or in vitro testing methods, including the use of human volunteers or specialized equipment (e.g., UV transmittance analyzers).

**2. Broad-Spectrum Testing**

- **Purpose**: Confirms the product provides protection against both UVA and UVB radiation.
- **Method**: In vitro testing methods, such as the critical wavelength method.

**3. Water Resistance Testing**

- **Purpose**: Assesses the sunscreen's ability to maintain its effectiveness after exposure to water.
- **Method**: In vivo testing with human volunteers who immerse in water for specified periods.

**4. Stability Testing**

- **Purpose**: Assesses the product's ability to maintain its properties over time.
- **Method**: Stability studies under various environmental conditions (e.g., temperature, humidity) are conducted to evaluate changes in texture, color, and scent.

**5. Microbial Testing**

- **Purpose**: Ensures the product is free from harmful microorganisms.
- **Method**: Microbiological tests such as total viable count (TVC) and specific pathogen testing are conducted.

**6. Sensory Evaluation**

- **Purpose**: Evaluates the product's feel, fragrance, and overall user experience.
- **Method**: Sensory panels assess the sunscreen for texture, spreadability, and overall acceptability.

**Example Formulation for a Basic Sunscreen**

- **Oil Phase**:
    - 10% Octocrylene (UV filter)
    - 5% Avobenzone (UV filter)
    - 7% C12-15 Alkyl Benzoate (emollient)
    - 3% Glyceryl Stearate (emulsifier)
    - 3% PEG-100 Stearate (emulsifier)
- **Water Phase**:
    - 60% Purified water
    - 2% Glycerin (humectant)
    - 1% Carbomer (thickener)
- **Preservatives**:
    - 0.1% Methylparaben
    - 0.1% Propylparaben
- **Antioxidants**:
    - 1% Vitamin E (tocopherol)
- **Fragrances**:
    - 0.5% Fragrance blend

**Preparation Steps**

1. **Oil Phase Preparation**: Mix octocrylene, avobenzone, C12-15 alkyl benzoate, glyceryl stearate, and PEG-100 stearate in a jacketed kettle until fully melted and mixed.
2. **Water Phase Preparation**: Heat purified water and glycerin in a separate vessel, adding carbomer.
3. **Emulsification**: Slowly add the water phase to the oil phase while continuously stirring with a high-shear mixer.

4. **Cooling and Additives**: Allow the emulsion to cool, then add vitamin E and the fragrance blend.
5. **Homogenization and Packaging**: Homogenize the mixture for a smooth texture and fill into tubes or bottles.

# EIGHT

# PHARMACEUTICAL AEROSOLS

## 8.1 Definition and Types of Aerosol Systems

### Introduction to Aerosol Systems

Aerosol systems are pressurized containers that release a fine spray of liquid, solid, or gas particles when activated. These systems are widely used in various industries, including pharmaceuticals, cosmetics, household products, and food. The formulation and delivery method of aerosols are designed to ensure the effective dispersion of the product. Aerosol systems can be classified based on the type of propellant used and the intended application.

### Types of Aerosol Systems

1. **Pharmaceutical Aerosols**: Used for delivering medications directly to the lungs (e.g., inhalers), skin (e.g., topical sprays), or nasal passages (e.g., nasal sprays).
2. **Cosmetic Aerosols**: Used for personal care products such as deodorants, hairsprays, and perfumes.
3. **Household Aerosols**: Used for products like air fresheners, insecticides, and cleaning agents.
4. **Food Aerosols**: Used for products like whipped cream and cooking sprays.

### 8.1.1 Propellants

### Introduction to Propellants

Propellants are crucial components of aerosol systems, responsible for expelling the product from the container and creating a fine mist. They are selected based on their physical and chemical properties, safety, and compatibility with the product. Propellants can be classified into two main categories: liquefied gases and compressed gases.

**Types of Propellants**

**1. Liquefied Gas Propellants**

- **Definition**: These are gases that are converted into liquids under high pressure. When the pressure is released (e.g., when the aerosol valve is activated), the liquid propellant vaporizes, creating pressure that expels the product.
- **Common Liquefied Gas Propellants**:
    - **Hydrocarbons**: Propane, butane, isobutane.
    - **Chlorofluorocarbons (CFCs)**: Once common but now largely phased out due to their ozone-depleting effects.
    - **Hydrofluorocarbons (HFCs)**: Such as HFC-134a and HFC-152a, which are used as replacements for CFCs due to their lower environmental impact.

**Advantages**:

- Provide consistent pressure throughout the product's life.
- Allow for the formulation of a wide range of products with varying viscosities.
- Effective in creating fine sprays and foams.

**Disadvantages**:

- Environmental concerns (e.g., global warming potential of HFCs).
- Flammability concerns with hydrocarbons.
- Regulatory restrictions on certain types of propellants (e.g., CFCs).

**2. Compressed Gas Propellants**

- **Definition**: These are gases that are compressed and stored under high pressure in their gaseous state. When the aerosol valve is activated, the compressed gas expands, forcing the product out.

- **Common Compressed Gas Propellants**:
    - **Carbon dioxide ($CO_2$)**: Widely used in food aerosols and certain medical applications.
    - **Nitrogen ($N_2$)**: Commonly used in food products and some household aerosols.
    - **Nitrous oxide ($N_2O$)**: Used in food aerosols like whipped cream dispensers.

**Advantages**:

- Environmentally friendly, with low global warming potential.
- Non-flammable, enhancing safety.
- Inert gases like nitrogen are chemically stable and do not react with the product.

**Disadvantages**:

- Provide decreasing pressure as the product is used, which can affect the consistency of spray delivery.
- Limited solubility in the product, which may restrict their use in certain formulations.

**Selection Criteria for Propellants**

- **Product Compatibility**: The propellant must be compatible with the product formulation to prevent chemical reactions or degradation.
- **Environmental Impact**: Consideration of the propellant's effect on the environment, including ozone depletion potential and global warming potential.
- **Safety**: The propellant should be non-toxic and non-flammable or have controlled flammability.
- **Performance**: The propellant should provide consistent pressure and effective delivery of the product throughout its use.

**Example Formulation for a Cosmetic Aerosol (Hairspray)**

- **Active Ingredients**: Film-forming agents (e.g., polyvinylpyrrolidone, vinyl acetate).
- **Solvents**: Ethanol, water.
- **Propellant**: Hydrocarbon blend (e.g., butane, propane).
- **Additives**: Fragrances, conditioning agents.

**Preparation Steps**

1. **Blend the active ingredients and solvents**: Mix the film-forming agents with ethanol and water to create a homogeneous solution.
2. **Add additives**: Incorporate fragrances and conditioning agents.
3. **Fill the container**: Pour the prepared solution into the aerosol container.
4. **Introduce the propellant**: Under controlled conditions, add the hydrocarbon propellant to the container.
5. **Seal and test**: Seal the container with an aerosol valve and test for proper function and safety.

**8.1 Definition and Types of Aerosol Systems**

**Introduction to Aerosol Systems**

Aerosol systems are versatile delivery mechanisms used across various industries to dispense products in the form of fine sprays, foams, or powders. The effectiveness and safety of these systems depend significantly on the choice of containers, which must maintain the integrity and pressure of the contents while ensuring ease of use and safety.

**8.1.2 Containers**

**Introduction to Aerosol Containers**

Aerosol containers are specially designed to withstand the pressure of the propellants and protect the product from contamination and degradation. These containers come in various materials and designs, each suited to specific types of products and propellants. The selection of the right container is crucial for the functionality, safety, and stability of the aerosol product.

**Types of Aerosol Containers**

**1. Tinplate Containers**

- **Material**: Made from thin sheets of steel coated with tin to prevent rusting.
- **Characteristics**:

- **Durability**: Strong and resistant to internal pressure.
- **Compatibility**: Suitable for a wide range of products, including paints, lubricants, and household products.
- **Cost**: Generally cost-effective.
- **Protection**: Tin coating provides a barrier against corrosion.

- **Uses**: Commonly used for products that require high durability and protection, such as industrial and household aerosols.

**2. Aluminum Containers**

- **Material**: Made from pure aluminum or aluminum alloys.
- **Characteristics**:

  - **Lightweight**: Easier to handle and transport.
  - **Non-Corrosive**: Naturally resistant to rust and corrosion.
  - **Recyclability**: Environmentally friendly and easily recyclable.
  - **Flexibility**: Can be molded into various shapes and sizes.

- **Uses**: Widely used for personal care products (e.g., deodorants, hairsprays) and food aerosols due to their non-reactivity and attractive appearance.

**3. Stainless Steel Containers**

- **Material**: Made from high-grade stainless steel.
- **Characteristics**:

  - **High Strength**: Extremely durable and can withstand high internal pressures.
  - **Chemical Resistance**: Resistant to a wide range of chemicals.
  - **Cost**: More expensive compared to tinplate and aluminum.
  - **Aesthetic Appeal**: Provides a premium look.

- **Uses**: Used for specialized applications where high strength and chemical resistance are essential, such as certain pharmaceutical and industrial products.

**4. Glass Containers**

- **Material**: Made from treated glass to enhance strength and pressure resistance.
- **Characteristics**:
    - **Inertness**: Chemically inert and does not react with the contents.
    - **Transparency**: Allows visibility of the product.
    - **Weight**: Heavier and more fragile compared to metal containers.
    - **Aesthetic Appeal**: Provides a high-quality, premium look.
- **Uses**: Used for high-end personal care products, perfumes, and pharmaceutical aerosols where product visibility and chemical inertness are important.

**5. Plastic Containers**

- **Material**: Made from high-density polyethylene (HDPE), polyethylene terephthalate (PET), or other durable plastics.
- **Characteristics**:
    - **Lightweight**: Easy to handle and transport.
    - **Durability**: Resistant to shattering.
    - **Cost**: Generally less expensive than metal containers.
    - **Environmental Impact**: Concerns about plastic waste and recyclability.
- **Uses**: Used for a variety of products, including household cleaners, food aerosols, and some personal care items.

**Design Features of Aerosol Containers**

**1. Valve Systems**

- **Types**: Continuous spray valves, metered dose valves, foam valves.
- **Purpose**: Regulate the flow of the product and ensure precise delivery.
- **Materials**: Typically made from metal or plastic components.

**2. Actuators**

- **Types**: Button, trigger, and twist actuators.
- **Purpose**: Provide a mechanism for the user to activate the aerosol spray.
- **Design**: Ergonomically designed for ease of use.

**3. Dip Tubes**

- **Purpose**: Draw the product from the bottom of the container to the valve.
- **Materials**: Typically made from flexible plastics.

**4. Linings and Coatings**

- **Purpose**: Protect the container and the product from interacting, especially important for metal containers.
- **Materials**: Epoxy, vinyl, and other protective coatings.

**Selection Criteria for Aerosol Containers**

**1. Product Compatibility**

- The container material must be compatible with both the product and the propellant to prevent reactions that could degrade the product or damage the container.

**2. Pressure Resistance**

- The container must withstand the internal pressure exerted by the propellant, ensuring safety during storage and use.

**3. Environmental Impact**

- Consideration of the container's recyclability and environmental footprint is crucial, especially with increasing regulatory and consumer focus on sustainability.

**4. Cost**

- The cost of the container affects the overall product pricing and must be balanced with the desired quality and performance.

**5. Aesthetic Appeal**

- For consumer products, the appearance of the container can influence purchasing decisions. Transparent, sleek, or uniquely shaped containers can add to the product's appeal.

**Example of an Aerosol Container for a Cosmetic Product (Deodorant)**

- **Container Type**: Aluminum container
- **Valve System**: Continuous spray valve
- **Actuator**: Button actuator
- **Dip Tube**: Flexible plastic dip tube
- **Lining/Coating**: Epoxy lining to prevent interaction between the aluminum and the deodorant formulation

**Preparation Steps**

1. **Container Selection**: Choose an aluminum container for its lightweight and non-reactive properties.
2. **Valve and Actuator Assembly**: Attach a continuous spray valve and a button actuator to ensure easy and consistent application.
3. **Filling**: Fill the container with the deodorant formulation and propellant under controlled conditions.
4. **Sealing**: Secure the valve assembly to prevent leakage.
5. **Quality Testing**: Test the container for pressure resistance, spray consistency, and overall performance.

**8.1 Definition and Types of Aerosol Systems**

**Introduction to Aerosol Systems**

Aerosol systems are sophisticated delivery mechanisms that rely on the interaction between the product, propellant, and container. One of the most crucial components of these systems is the valve, which controls the release of the product. Valves must ensure consistent, controlled dispensing and maintain the integrity and safety of the aerosol product.

**8.1.3 Valves**

**Introduction to Aerosol Valves**

Valves are integral to aerosol systems, providing the mechanism by which the product is dispensed. The design and functionality of valves determine the efficiency, safety, and user experience of the aerosol product. Valves must be robust, reliable, and compatible with both the propellant and the product formulation.

**Types of Aerosol Valves**

**1. Continuous Spray Valves**

- **Definition**: Valves that allow a continuous flow of the product as long as the actuator is pressed.
- **Common Uses**: Hairsprays, deodorants, air fresheners.
- **Characteristics**: Provide a steady, continuous spray pattern; suitable for products that need even application over a large area.

**2. Metered Dose Valves**

- **Definition**: Valves that dispense a precise, pre-measured amount of product with each activation.
- **Common Uses**: Pharmaceutical inhalers, nasal sprays, some air fresheners.
- **Characteristics**: Ensure accurate dosing; crucial for medications and products where precise application is essential.

**3. Foam Valves**

- **Definition**: Valves designed to dispense the product as a foam.
- **Common Uses**: Shaving creams, hair mousses, medical foams.
- **Characteristics**: Produce a foamy consistency; typically used with formulations that expand when released.

**4. Tilt Valve**

- **Definition**: Valves that operate by tilting the actuator to release the product.
- **Common Uses**: Furniture polishes, spray paints.
- **Characteristics**: Allow for multi-directional spraying; useful for reaching difficult angles and surfaces.

**Components of Aerosol Valves**

**1. Actuator**

- **Function**: The part of the valve that the user presses to release the product.
- **Design Variations**: Button actuators, trigger actuators, twist actuators.
- **Material**: Typically made from plastic; designed for ergonomic handling and ease of use.

**2. Stem**

- **Function**: Connects the actuator to the valve body and directs the flow of the product.
- **Material**: Usually made from plastic or metal; must be durable and resistant to the product's formulation.

**3. Gasket**

- **Function**: Seals the valve to prevent leakage around the stem.
- **Material**: Made from rubber or elastomeric materials; must be compatible with both the product and the propellant.

**4. Spring**

- **Function**: Returns the actuator to its original position after being pressed, closing the valve.
- **Material**: Typically made from stainless steel; must be corrosion-resistant and durable.

**5. Housing**

- **Function**: Encloses the internal components of the valve.
- **Material**: Often made from metal or high-strength plastic; must withstand internal pressures and ensure durability.

**6. Dip Tube**

- **Function**: Draws the product from the bottom of the container to the valve.
- **Material**: Made from flexible plastic; length and diameter vary based on the container size and product viscosity.

**Selection Criteria for Aerosol Valves**

**1. Compatibility with Product and Propellant**

- The valve materials must be chemically compatible with both the product formulation and the propellant to prevent degradation and ensure safety.

**2. Dispensing Requirements**

- The type of product and its intended use determine the choice of valve. For example, metered dose valves are essential for pharmaceuticals, while continuous spray valves are ideal for hair and body sprays.

**3. User Experience**

- Valves should be easy to operate, providing a smooth and consistent spray or foam. Ergonomic designs enhance user comfort and convenience.

**4. Environmental Considerations**

- Valves should be designed to minimize environmental impact. Recyclable materials and components that reduce propellant emissions are preferred.

**Example of an Aerosol Valve for a Pharmaceutical Inhaler**

- **Valve Type**: Metered dose valve
- **Components**:
  - **Actuator**: Button actuator with a precise dose mechanism
  - **Stem**: High-strength plastic
  - **Gasket**: Elastomer compatible with the inhaler formulation
  - **Spring**: Stainless steel
  - **Housing**: Metal
  - **Dip Tube**: Short, wide-diameter plastic tube

**Preparation Steps**

1. **Component Selection**: Choose materials for each component that are compatible with the pharmaceutical formulation and propellant.
2. **Assembly**: Assemble the valve components under sterile conditions to prevent contamination.
3. **Testing**: Test the valve for proper function, ensuring accurate dosing and consistent spray patterns.
4. **Integration**: Attach the valve to the filled inhaler canister, ensuring a secure fit and seal.
5. **Quality Assurance**: Perform final checks for leakage, dose accuracy, and overall performance.

## 8.2 Formulation and Manufacture

### Introduction to Formulation and Manufacture

The formulation and manufacture of aerosol products involve a series of carefully controlled processes to ensure the final product is effective, safe, and stable. This includes selecting appropriate ingredients, understanding their interactions, and employing precise manufacturing techniques to produce a high-quality aerosol product.

### 8.2.1 Formulation Aspects

#### 1. Active Ingredients

- **Purpose**: Provide the primary function of the aerosol product, such as medication delivery, deodorizing, or insect control.
- **Selection Criteria**: Stability, compatibility with propellants and other ingredients, efficacy at low concentrations.
- **Examples**: Bronchodilators for inhalers, aluminum chlorohydrate for antiperspirants, insecticides for bug sprays.

#### 2. Propellants

- **Purpose**: Create the pressure needed to expel the product from the container and form a fine mist or spray.
- **Types**:
  - **Liquefied Gas Propellants**: Hydrocarbons (propane, butane), HFCs (hydrofluorocarbons).
  - **Compressed Gas Propellants**: Carbon dioxide, nitrogen, nitrous oxide.

- **Selection Criteria**: Safety, environmental impact, compatibility with the product, desired spray characteristics.

### 3. Solvents

- **Purpose**: Dissolve or disperse the active ingredients, adjust the viscosity, and enhance the spray properties.
- **Common Solvents**: Ethanol, isopropanol, acetone, water.
- **Selection Criteria**: Solubility of the active ingredients, evaporation rate, safety, and environmental considerations.

### 4. Surfactants

- **Purpose**: Stabilize the formulation, improve the dispersion of active ingredients, and enhance the spray quality.
- **Types**: Nonionic, anionic, cationic, and amphoteric surfactants.
- **Selection Criteria**: Compatibility with other ingredients, desired foam or spray characteristics, and skin tolerance.

### 5. Antioxidants

- **Purpose**: Prevent oxidation of sensitive ingredients, extending the shelf life of the product.
- **Common Antioxidants**: Butylated hydroxytoluene (BHT), tocopherols (vitamin E), ascorbic acid (vitamin C).
- **Selection Criteria**: Stability, compatibility with the formulation, and efficacy at low concentrations.

### 6. Fragrances and Colorants

- **Purpose**: Enhance the sensory appeal of the product, providing a pleasant smell and appearance.
- **Selection Criteria**: Stability, compatibility with the formulation, and user safety.

### 7. Preservatives

- **Purpose**: Prevent microbial contamination, ensuring product safety during storage and use.
- **Common Preservatives**: Parabens, phenoxyethanol, benzalkonium chloride.
- **Selection Criteria**: Efficacy against a broad spectrum of microorganisms, stability, and safety.

### 8.2.2 Manufacturing Process

#### 1. Preparation of the Formulation

- **Mixing**: Active ingredients, solvents, surfactants, and other additives are mixed in precise proportions to form a homogeneous mixture.
- **Temperature Control**: Maintain appropriate temperatures to ensure proper mixing and solubility of ingredients.

#### 2. Filling the Container

- **Filling the Product**: The prepared formulation is filled into the aerosol container using specialized filling machines. For liquid formulations, this step ensures the correct volume of the product is added to each container.
- **Propellant Addition**: Propellants are added to the container, either through cold filling or pressure filling techniques.
    - **Cold Filling**: The formulation and propellant are cooled to low temperatures, allowing them to be mixed and filled into the container in a liquid state.
    - **Pressure Filling**: The container is filled with the formulation, and then the propellant is added under high pressure.

#### 3. Valve and Actuator Assembly

- **Valve Attachment**: The valve is securely crimped onto the container to prevent leakage and ensure proper dispensing.
- **Actuator Placement**: The actuator is attached to the valve, completing the assembly of the aerosol delivery system.

#### 4. Testing and Quality Control

- **Leak Testing**: Containers are tested for leaks to ensure the integrity of the seal and the safety of the product.
- **Spray Pattern Testing**: The spray pattern and delivery rate are tested to ensure consistency and proper function.
- **Stability Testing**: Stability tests are conducted to ensure the product maintains its efficacy and safety over its intended shelf life.

### 5. Labeling and Packaging

- **Labeling**: Each container is labeled with relevant product information, including ingredients, usage instructions, safety warnings, and regulatory compliance information.
- **Packaging**: Labeled containers are packaged into boxes or cases for distribution. Secondary packaging may include additional safety seals or tamper-evident features.

**Example of the Manufacturing Process for a Pharmaceutical Aerosol (Inhaler)**

1. **Formulation Preparation**:

    - **Active Ingredient**: Albuterol sulfate.
    - **Propellant**: HFC-134a.
    - **Solvent**: Ethanol.
    - **Mixing**: Combine albuterol sulfate with ethanol to dissolve, then add HFC-134a under controlled conditions.

2. **Filling**:

    - **Cold Filling**: Cool the formulation and propellant, then fill into the canister.

3. **Valve and Actuator Assembly**:

    - Attach the valve to the canister and crimp it securely.
    - Place the actuator on the valve.

4. **Quality Control**:

- Conduct leak tests to ensure the integrity of the canister.
- Perform spray pattern and dose uniformity tests to confirm proper function.

5. **Labeling and Packaging**:

   - Label each inhaler with dosage information, usage instructions, and safety warnings.
   - Package labeled inhalers into boxes for distribution.

### 8.3 Evaluation and Quality Control

**Introduction to Evaluation and Quality Control**

Evaluation and quality control are critical aspects of aerosol product development and manufacturing. They ensure that the products meet the required standards for safety, efficacy, and consistency. This section outlines the key testing methods and stability studies employed in the evaluation and quality control of aerosol systems.

#### 8.3.1 Testing Methods

**1. Leak Testing**

- **Purpose**: Ensure that the aerosol container is sealed properly and does not leak under normal conditions.
- **Methods**:

  - **Water Bath Test**: Containers are submerged in a water bath at a specified temperature, and any leaks are detected by observing bubbles.
  - **Pressure Decay Test**: Measures the loss of pressure in the container over time to identify leaks.
  - **Helium Leak Test**: Uses helium gas and a mass spectrometer to detect very small leaks.

**2. Spray Pattern and Particle Size Analysis**

- **Purpose**: Evaluate the spray characteristics and ensure consistent delivery of the product.
- **Methods**:

- **Spray Pattern Analysis**: The spray is directed onto a piece of paper or a pattern analyzer to visualize the distribution and symmetry of the spray.
- **Particle Size Analysis**: Laser diffraction or cascade impactors measure the size distribution of particles in the aerosol spray.

**3. Valve Functionality Testing**

- **Purpose**: Ensure that the valve operates correctly and delivers the product as intended.
- **Methods**:
  - **Actuation Force Test**: Measures the force required to actuate the valve.
  - **Dose Uniformity Test**: Ensures consistent dosing with each actuation, especially important for pharmaceutical aerosols.

**4. Content Uniformity**

- **Purpose**: Ensure that each aerosol container delivers a consistent amount of the active ingredient.
- **Methods**:
  - **Gravimetric Analysis**: Weighing the container before and after dispensing a known number of doses.
  - **Chemical Analysis**: Using techniques like HPLC (High-Performance Liquid Chromatography) to measure the active ingredient content.

**5. Pressure Testing**

- **Purpose**: Ensure that the container can withstand the internal pressure of the propellant without deforming or bursting.
- **Methods**:
  - **Burst Pressure Test**: Increasing the internal pressure until the container bursts, to determine its maximum pressure capacity.
  - **Internal Pressure Test**: Measuring the pressure inside the container at different temperatures to ensure safety under various conditions.

**6. Compatibility Testing**

- **Purpose**: Ensure that the propellant and the product formulation are compatible with the container materials.
- **Methods**:
    - **Chemical Resistance Test**: Evaluating the container materials for any signs of degradation or reaction with the product.
    - **Physical Compatibility Test**: Assessing changes in the physical properties of the container (e.g., color, flexibility) over time.

**8.3.2 Stability Studies**

**1. Accelerated Stability Testing**

- **Purpose**: Predict the long-term stability of the aerosol product by exposing it to elevated temperatures and humidity.
- **Methods**:
    - **Temperature and Humidity Chambers**: Storing the product at elevated temperatures (e.g., 40°C) and high humidity (e.g., 75% RH) for a specific period.
    - **Analysis**: Regularly analyzing the product for changes in physical, chemical, and performance characteristics.

**2. Long-Term Stability Testing**

- **Purpose**: Evaluate the stability of the aerosol product under normal storage conditions over its intended shelf life.
- **Methods**:
    - **Standard Storage Conditions**: Storing the product at room temperature (e.g., 25°C) and controlled humidity.
    - **Analysis**: Periodic testing for physical, chemical, and performance characteristics over an extended period (e.g., 12-24 months).

**3. Photostability Testing**

- **Purpose**: Assess the stability of the aerosol product when exposed to light.
- **Methods**:
    - **Light Exposure Chambers**: Exposing the product to UV and visible light to simulate sunlight exposure.
    - **Analysis**: Evaluating any changes in the product's appearance, potency, and performance.

**4. Freeze-Thaw Stability Testing**

- **Purpose**: Ensure that the aerosol product remains stable through temperature fluctuations, such as freezing and thawing cycles.
- **Methods**:
    - **Cyclic Temperature Testing**: Subjecting the product to repeated cycles of freezing and thawing.
    - **Analysis**: Checking for any changes in the product's physical and chemical properties after the cycles.

**5. Microbial Stability Testing**

- **Purpose**: Ensure the aerosol product remains free from microbial contamination over its shelf life.
- **Methods**:
    - **Microbial Limit Tests**: Testing the product for the presence of specific microorganisms.
    - **Preservative Efficacy Testing**: Assessing the effectiveness of preservatives in the formulation to inhibit microbial growth.

**Example of a Stability Study for a Cosmetic Aerosol (Hairspray)**

1. **Accelerated Stability Testing**:
    - Store the product at 40°C and 75% RH for 6 months.
    - Test for changes in spray pattern, particle size, and active ingredient concentration monthly.

2. **Long-Term Stability Testing**:
   - Store the product at 25°C and 60% RH for 24 months.
   - Test for physical appearance, spray characteristics, and chemical stability every 3 months.
3. **Photostability Testing**:
   - Expose the product to UV and visible light for 2 weeks.
   - Evaluate changes in color, odor, and chemical composition.
4. **Freeze-Thaw Stability Testing**:
   - Subject the product to 10 freeze-thaw cycles (-20°C to 25°C).
   - Assess any physical changes and test spray performance.

# NINE

# Packaging Materials Science

## 9.1 Materials Used for Packaging

### Introduction to Packaging Materials

Packaging materials are critical in preserving the quality, stability, and safety of products, particularly in the pharmaceutical, cosmetic, and food industries. The choice of packaging material affects the product's shelf life, usability, and environmental impact. This section explores the various types of materials used for packaging and their properties.

### 9.1.1 Types and Properties

**1. Glass**

**Types**:

- **Type I**: Borosilicate glass, used for products that require high chemical resistance.
- **Type II**: Treated soda-lime glass, used for products that need moderate chemical resistance.
- **Type III**: Soda-lime glass, used for products that do not require high chemical resistance.

**Properties**:

- **Chemical Inertness**: High resistance to chemicals, making it suitable for sensitive products.
- **Transparency**: Allows visibility of the product, which is beneficial for consumer inspection.

- **Barrier Properties**: Excellent barrier against gases and moisture, protecting the product from contamination and degradation.
- **Rigidity and Strength**: Provides robust protection but is brittle and can break easily if dropped.

**Uses**:

- Pharmaceuticals (ampoules, vials)
- Food and beverages (jars, bottles)
- Cosmetics (perfume bottles)

**2. Plastics**

**Types**:

- **Polyethylene (PE)**: Includes high-density polyethylene (HDPE) and low-density polyethylene (LDPE).
- **Polypropylene (PP)**: Known for its high melting point and durability.
- **Polyethylene Terephthalate (PET)**: Widely used for its strength and clarity.
- **Polyvinyl Chloride (PVC)**: Used for its versatility but less preferred due to environmental concerns.
- **Polystyrene (PS)**: Used for its rigidity and ease of molding.

**Properties**:

- **Lightweight**: Easier to handle and transport.
- **Durability**: Resistant to breakage and can withstand impact.
- **Versatility**: Can be molded into various shapes and sizes.
- **Chemical Resistance**: Varies by type but generally resistant to many chemicals.
- **Barrier Properties**: Provides varying degrees of protection against moisture, gases, and light.

**Uses**:

- Pharmaceuticals (bottles, blister packs)
- Food and beverages (containers, bottles)
- Cosmetics (tubes, jars)

**3. Metals**

**Types:**

- **Aluminum**: Lightweight, non-reactive, and recyclable.
- **Tinplate**: Made from steel coated with tin, used for its strength and corrosion resistance.
- **Stainless Steel**: Highly durable and resistant to corrosion.

**Properties:**

- **Strength and Durability**: Provides robust protection against physical damage.
- **Barrier Properties**: Excellent barrier against light, moisture, and gases.
- **Recyclability**: Highly recyclable, reducing environmental impact.
- **Conductivity**: Conducts heat, which can be a drawback for certain products.

**Uses:**

- Pharmaceuticals (tubes, cans)
- Food and beverages (cans, foil wraps)
- Cosmetics (aerosol cans, compact cases)

**4. Paper and Paperboard**

**Types:**

- **Paper**: Used for labels, leaflets, and lightweight packaging.
- **Paperboard**: Thicker and stronger, used for boxes and cartons.
- **Corrugated Fiberboard**: Used for shipping and secondary packaging due to its strength.

**Properties:**

- **Sustainability**: Biodegradable and recyclable, making it environmentally friendly.
- **Printability**: Easy to print on, allowing for high-quality graphics and labeling.

- **Strength**: Provides good protection, especially when laminated or treated.
- **Barrier Properties**: Generally poor barrier to moisture and gases unless coated or laminated.

**Uses**:

- Pharmaceuticals (cartons, labels)
- Food and beverages (boxes, cartons)
- Cosmetics (packaging boxes, cartons)

**5. Flexible Packaging**
**Types**:

- **Foils**: Aluminum foil for its excellent barrier properties.
- **Films**: Plastic films like polyethylene and polypropylene.
- **Laminates**: Multi-layer materials combining different films and foils.

**Properties**:

- **Flexibility**: Can conform to the shape of the product, reducing space and material usage.
- **Barrier Properties**: Provides excellent protection against moisture, gases, and light when using high-barrier materials.
- **Lightweight**: Reduces shipping costs and environmental impact.
- **Convenience**: Often used for single-use or easy-open packaging.

**Uses**:

- Pharmaceuticals (sachets, blister packs)
- Food and beverages (pouches, wraps)
- Cosmetics (sample packs, pouches)

**Example of Packaging Material Selection for a Pharmaceutical Product (Tablets)**

1. **Primary Packaging**: Blister packs made from PVC (plastic) and aluminum foil.

- **PVC**: Provides a rigid and transparent casing for individual tablets.
- **Aluminum Foil**: Acts as a barrier against moisture and light, protecting the tablets.

2. **Secondary Packaging**: Paperboard carton.

   - **Paperboard**: Offers additional protection and provides space for labeling and information.

3. **Tertiary Packaging**: Corrugated fiberboard for shipping.

   - **Corrugated Fiberboard**: Ensures safe transport and handling.

**9.2 Factors Influencing Choice of Containers**

**Introduction to Factors Influencing Choice of Containers**

Selecting the appropriate container for a product is a critical decision that affects the product's stability, safety, and marketability. Various factors must be considered to ensure that the container meets all necessary requirements, including legal, regulatory, and practical considerations. This section focuses on these influencing factors, with particular attention to legal and official requirements.

**9.2.1 Legal and Official Requirements**

**Introduction to Legal and Official Requirements**

The choice of packaging containers is heavily influenced by legal and regulatory requirements. These requirements ensure that the packaging provides adequate protection for the product, maintains its quality, and is safe for consumers. Compliance with these regulations is mandatory for manufacturers to market their products.

**Key Legal and Official Requirements**

**1. Regulatory Compliance**

- **Purpose**: Ensure the safety, efficacy, and quality of the product.
- **Regulatory Bodies**:

  - **FDA (Food and Drug Administration)**: Oversees pharmaceuticals, food, and cosmetics in the United States.
  - **EMA (European Medicines Agency)**: Regulates pharmaceuticals in the European Union.

  - **MHRA (Medicines and Healthcare products Regulatory Agency)**: Regulates pharmaceuticals in the United Kingdom.
  - **ISO (International Organization for Standardization)**: Sets international standards for packaging materials and processes.

- **Requirements**: Packaging materials must be tested and approved for safety, effectiveness, and quality. This includes compatibility testing, stability studies, and safety evaluations.

**2. Labeling Requirements**

- **Purpose**: Provide essential information to consumers and healthcare providers.
- **Key Elements**:

  - **Product Name**: Clear identification of the product.
  - **Active Ingredients**: Listing of active substances in the product.
  - **Usage Instructions**: Directions for proper use.
  - **Warnings and Precautions**: Information on potential risks and side effects.
  - **Expiration Date**: Indicates the product's shelf life.
  - **Manufacturer Information**: Details about the manufacturer and contact information.

- **Regulatory Bodies**: Similar to those for regulatory compliance, with specific guidelines on labeling content and format.

**3. Child-Resistant and Tamper-Evident Features**

- **Purpose**: Protect children from accidental ingestion and ensure the integrity of the product.
- **Regulatory Bodies**:

  - **CPSC (Consumer Product Safety Commission)**: Regulates child-resistant packaging in the United States.
  - **FDA**: Mandates tamper-evident packaging for certain over-the-counter (OTC) drugs.

- **Requirements**: Containers must have mechanisms that prevent easy access by children and features that indicate if the package has been tampered with.

**4. Environmental Regulations**

- **Purpose**: Reduce environmental impact and promote sustainability.
- **Regulatory Bodies**:
    - **EPA (Environmental Protection Agency)**: Regulates environmental standards in the United States.
    - **EU Directives**: Various directives in the European Union, such as the Packaging and Packaging Waste Directive.
- **Requirements**: Packaging materials must be recyclable, biodegradable, or made from sustainable sources. There are also regulations on the use of certain hazardous substances in packaging.

**5. Good Manufacturing Practices (GMP)**

- **Purpose**: Ensure products are consistently produced and controlled according to quality standards.
- **Regulatory Bodies**:
    - **WHO (World Health Organization)**: Provides international GMP guidelines.
    - **FDA**: Enforces GMP regulations for pharmaceuticals, food, and cosmetics.
- **Requirements**: Packaging processes must follow strict guidelines to prevent contamination, mix-ups, and errors. This includes controls on the packaging environment, equipment, and personnel.

**Examples of Legal and Official Requirements in Packaging**
**1. Pharmaceutical Packaging**

- **Regulatory Compliance**: Containers must be tested for compatibility with the drug formulation and approved by regulatory bodies like the

FDA or EMA.

- **Labeling Requirements**: Must include the drug name, dosage, instructions for use, warnings, expiration date, and manufacturer details.
- **Child-Resistant and Tamper-Evident Features**: Required for prescription drugs and certain OTC medications.
- **Environmental Regulations**: Encouraged to use recyclable or biodegradable materials.
- **GMP Compliance**: Packaging processes must follow GMP guidelines to ensure product safety and quality.

**2. Food Packaging**

- **Regulatory Compliance**: Containers must be safe for contact with food and approved by regulatory bodies like the FDA or EFSA (European Food Safety Authority).
- **Labeling Requirements**: Must include product name, ingredients, nutritional information, expiration date, and manufacturer details.
- **Environmental Regulations**: Packaging should be recyclable, and there are restrictions on certain materials (e.g., BPA).
- **GMP Compliance**: Packaging processes must follow GMP guidelines to prevent contamination and ensure food safety.

**3. Cosmetic Packaging**

- **Regulatory Compliance**: Containers must be tested for compatibility with cosmetic formulations and comply with regulations set by bodies like the FDA or EU Cosmetics Regulation.
- **Labeling Requirements**: Must include product name, ingredients, usage instructions, warnings, and manufacturer details.
- **Environmental Regulations**: Encouraged to use eco-friendly materials and reduce packaging waste.
- **GMP Compliance**: Packaging processes must follow GMP guidelines to ensure product quality and safety.

## 9.2 Factors Influencing Choice of Containers

### Introduction to Factors Influencing Choice of Containers

Selecting the appropriate container for a product is essential to ensure its stability, safety, and efficacy. Various factors influence this choice, including legal requirements, stability aspects, environmental considerations, and cost-effectiveness. This section focuses on the stability aspects that must be considered when selecting containers.

### 9.2.2 Stability Aspects

#### Introduction to Stability Aspects

Stability aspects are critical in choosing the right container for any product, especially for pharmaceuticals, cosmetics, and food items. The container must protect the product from environmental factors that can degrade its quality over time. Stability studies help in determining the optimal packaging that can maintain the product's integrity throughout its shelf life.

#### Key Stability Aspects

#### 1. Chemical Stability

- **Purpose**: Prevent chemical degradation of the product's active ingredients and excipients.
- **Factors to Consider**:
    - **Interaction with Container Materials**: Ensure that the container materials do not react with the product.
    - **Light Sensitivity**: Use opaque or UV-protective containers to shield light-sensitive products.
    - **pH Compatibility**: Ensure the container does not alter the pH of the product.
- **Examples**:
    - **Pharmaceuticals**: Containers for liquid medications should be chemically inert to avoid reactions that could reduce efficacy.
    - **Cosmetics**: Certain active ingredients, like retinoids, require light-protective packaging to maintain their stability.

#### 2. Physical Stability

- **Purpose**: Maintain the physical integrity of the product, such as its appearance, texture, and viscosity.

- **Factors to Consider**:
  - **Moisture Barrier**: Containers must prevent moisture ingress or egress to maintain product consistency.
  - **Gas Barrier**: Containers should provide a barrier to oxygen and other gases that can cause oxidation or spoilage.
  - **Protection from Physical Damage**: Containers must protect against physical stress and damage during handling and transportation.
- **Examples**:
  - **Food**: Packaging for crispy snacks needs to be moisture-resistant to prevent sogginess.
  - **Pharmaceuticals**: Blister packs for tablets provide a barrier to moisture and oxygen, preserving their physical and chemical stability.

**3. Microbial Stability**

- **Purpose**: Prevent microbial contamination and growth within the product.
- **Factors to Consider**:
  - **Sterility**: For sterile products, containers must maintain sterility throughout the product's shelf life.
  - **Preservation**: Containers should support the efficacy of preservatives used in non-sterile products.
  - **Barrier Properties**: Containers should provide a barrier to microorganisms.
- **Examples**:
  - **Pharmaceuticals**: Eye drops require sterile containers to prevent infections.
  - **Cosmetics**: Products like lotions and creams should be packaged in containers that minimize microbial contamination risk.

**4. Environmental Stability**

- **Purpose**: Protect the product from environmental factors such as temperature, humidity, and light.
- **Factors to Consider**:
    - **Temperature Sensitivity**: Containers should protect temperature-sensitive products from extreme temperatures.
    - **Humidity Control**: Containers must maintain the desired humidity levels inside the packaging.
    - **Light Protection**: Containers should protect light-sensitive products from UV and visible light.
- **Examples**:
    - **Pharmaceuticals**: Insulin vials need to be stored in temperature-controlled conditions.
    - **Cosmetics**: Vitamin C serums should be stored in amber bottles to prevent degradation from light exposure.

**5. Mechanical Stability**

- **Purpose**: Ensure the container can withstand mechanical stresses during manufacturing, transportation, and use.
- **Factors to Consider**:
    - **Durability**: Containers should be robust enough to withstand physical impacts.
    - **Flexibility**: For products that require squeezing (e.g., tubes), the container should maintain its integrity under repeated use.
    - **Sealing**: The container should provide a secure seal to prevent leaks and spills.
- **Examples**:
    - **Food**: Canned foods require containers that can withstand the pressure of canning processes.
    - **Pharmaceuticals**: Inhalers need to be durable enough to survive drops and daily handling.

**Stability Testing**

Stability testing is a crucial part of evaluating container suitability. It involves subjecting the product to various conditions and monitoring its stability over time. Key aspects of stability testing include:

- **Accelerated Stability Testing**: Exposing the product to elevated temperatures and humidity to predict its shelf life.
- **Long-Term Stability Testing**: Monitoring the product under normal storage conditions over an extended period.
- **Photostability Testing**: Assessing the product's stability under exposure to light.
- **Freeze-Thaw Testing**: Evaluating the product's stability through cycles of freezing and thawing.

**Example of Stability Considerations for a Pharmaceutical Product (Injectable Solution)**

1. **Chemical Stability**:
    - Use Type I borosilicate glass vials to prevent chemical reactions with the solution.
    - Incorporate an amber coating to protect light-sensitive ingredients.
2. **Physical Stability**:
    - Ensure the vial provides a strong barrier against moisture and oxygen to maintain the solution's efficacy.
    - Use a rubber stopper that does not react with the injectable solution.
3. **Microbial Stability**:
    - Ensure the vial and stopper maintain sterility.
    - Conduct microbial limit tests to confirm no contamination.
4. **Environmental Stability**:
    - Store the vials in temperature-controlled environments to prevent degradation.

- Use packaging that maintains humidity control.

5. **Mechanical Stability**:

   - Use vials that can withstand the pressure during the sterilization process.
   - Ensure the stopper provides a secure seal to prevent leaks.

**9.3 Quality Control Tests**

**Introduction to Quality Control Tests**

Quality control (QC) tests are essential to ensure that packaging materials meet the necessary standards for safety, performance, and regulatory compliance. These tests verify the integrity, compatibility, and durability of the packaging materials, ensuring that they provide adequate protection to the product throughout its shelf life.

**9.3.1 For Packaging Materials**

**Introduction to Quality Control Tests for Packaging Materials**

Quality control tests for packaging materials involve a series of assessments to evaluate their physical, chemical, and mechanical properties. These tests ensure that the materials are suitable for their intended use and that they comply with regulatory requirements.

**Key Quality Control Tests for Packaging Materials**

**1. Mechanical Tests**

- **Purpose**: Assess the strength and durability of the packaging materials.
- **Types of Tests**:
  - **Tensile Strength Test**: Measures the material's resistance to tension.
  - **Compression Test**: Determines the material's ability to withstand compressive forces.
  - **Impact Test**: Evaluates the material's resistance to impact or sudden forces.
  - **Burst Strength Test**: Measures the pressure required to burst the material.
- **Importance**: Ensures that the packaging can withstand mechanical stresses during handling, transportation, and storage.

### 2. Barrier Property Tests

- **Purpose**: Evaluate the packaging material's ability to protect the product from external factors such as moisture, gases, and light.
- **Types of Tests**:
    - **Water Vapor Transmission Rate (WVTR)**: Measures the rate at which moisture passes through the material.
    - **Oxygen Transmission Rate (OTR)**: Determines the rate at which oxygen passes through the material.
    - **Light Transmission Test**: Assesses the material's ability to block or transmit light.
- **Importance**: Ensures that the packaging material provides adequate protection against moisture, oxygen, and light, which can degrade the product.

### 3. Chemical Compatibility Tests

- **Purpose**: Assess the interaction between the packaging material and the product it contains.
- **Types of Tests**:
    - **Migration Test**: Measures the extent to which chemicals from the packaging material leach into the product.
    - **Extraction Test**: Determines the amount of extractable substances in the packaging material.
    - **Sorption Test**: Evaluates the material's tendency to absorb the product's ingredients.
- **Importance**: Ensures that the packaging material does not react with or contaminate the product, maintaining its quality and safety.

### 4. Physical Property Tests

- **Purpose**: Evaluate the physical characteristics of the packaging material.
- **Types of Tests**:

- **Thickness Measurement**: Ensures uniform thickness of the packaging material.
- **Density Test**: Measures the material's density.
- **Flexibility Test**: Assesses the material's flexibility and ability to bend without breaking.

- **Importance**: Ensures consistency in the physical properties of the packaging material, contributing to its overall performance and reliability.

**5. Microbial Testing**

- **Purpose**: Ensure that the packaging material does not harbor harmful microorganisms.
- **Types of Tests**:
  - **Bioburden Test**: Measures the microbial load on the packaging material.
  - **Sterility Test**: Verifies that the packaging material is free from viable microorganisms.
- **Importance**: Ensures that the packaging material does not contaminate the product, maintaining its sterility and safety.

**6. Environmental Stress Testing**

- **Purpose**: Assess the packaging material's stability under various environmental conditions.
- **Types of Tests**:
  - **Accelerated Aging Test**: Simulates long-term storage conditions to evaluate the material's durability.
  - **Thermal Cycling Test**: Exposes the material to cycles of high and low temperatures to assess its stability.
  - **Humidity Test**: Evaluates the material's performance under high humidity conditions.

- **Importance**: Ensures that the packaging material can withstand environmental stresses during storage and transportation.

**Example of Quality Control Tests for a Pharmaceutical Packaging Material (Blister Pack)**

1. **Mechanical Tests**:
    - **Tensile Strength Test**: Ensure the blister pack material can withstand mechanical stress.
    - **Burst Strength Test**: Verify that the blister can withstand pressure without bursting.
2. **Barrier Property Tests**:
    - **WVTR**: Measure the moisture barrier properties to ensure protection against humidity.
    - **OTR**: Evaluate the oxygen barrier properties to prevent oxidation of the medication.
3. **Chemical Compatibility Tests**:
    - **Migration Test**: Assess the potential for chemicals from the blister material to leach into the medication.
    - **Sorption Test**: Ensure that the blister material does not absorb any active ingredients from the medication.
4. **Physical Property Tests**:
    - **Thickness Measurement**: Ensure uniform thickness of the blister material for consistent performance.
    - **Flexibility Test**: Assess the flexibility to ensure easy handling and use.
5. **Microbial Testing**:
    - **Bioburden Test**: Measure the microbial load to ensure cleanliness.
    - **Sterility Test**: Verify that the blister pack is free from viable microorganisms.

6. **Environmental Stress Testing**:

    - **Accelerated Aging Test**: Simulate long-term storage to evaluate durability.
    - **Thermal Cycling Test**: Assess stability under temperature fluctuations.
    - **Humidity Test**: Evaluate performance under high humidity conditions.

www.ingramcontent.com/pod-product-compliance
Lightning Source LLC
LaVergne TN
LVHW021147160826
845679LV00024B/2079

* 9 7 9 8 8 9 4 9 8 5 1 1 4 *